States of Grace

States of Grace

Senegalese in Italy and the
New European Immigration

Donald Martin Carter

University of Minnesota Press

Minneapolis

London

An earlier version of chapter 4 appeared in *Journal of Historical Sociology,* vol. 7, no. 1 (March 1994). Used by permission of Blackwell Publishers.

Published by the University of Minnesota Press
111 Third Avenue South, Suite 290, Minneapolis, MN 55401-2520
Printed in the United States of America on acid-free paper

http://www.upress.umn.edu

Library of Congress Cataloging-in-Publication Data

Carter, Donald Martin, 1955–
    States of grace : Senegalese in Italy and the new European
immigration / Donald Martin Carter.
        p.   cm.
    Based on the author's thesis (Ph. D.—University of Chicago, 1992)
presented under the title: Invisible cities, Touba Turin, Sengalese
transnational migrants in northern Italy.
    Includes bibliographical references and index.
    ISBN 0-8166-2542-5 (hc : alk. paper). — ISBN 0-8166-2543-3
(pbk. : alk. paper)
    1. Senegalese—Italy—Social conditions.   2. Senegalese—Italy—
Cultural assimilation.   3. Muslims—Italy—Social conditions.
    4. Italy—Race relations.   5. Culture conflict—Italy.   6. Italy—
Social conditions—1976–1994.   I. Title.
    DG457.S45C37   1997
    305.896'63045—dc21   97-25951

10 09 08 07 06 05 04 03 02 01 00 99 98   10 9 8 7 6 5 4 3 2 1

To the memory of my father, Charlie E. Carter,
and to my mother, Julia Mae Carter

Workers' Monument

There is something in this hill
where Bufano lives
autumn leaves drenched with
   winter rains
granite cracked and surrendering
as diasporas meet
those passing by
pick up their gait
unaware of the irony existing here
My father
My mother
crafted steel
on ships' bellies
bending beams
like rainbows was their art
working-class artisans
blackened
turning in the welder's arch
Bufano's granite horse is broken now
its ears and mouth have
succumbed
moment to moment Beniamino
   Bufano
inscribed in known works speaks

to the unknown worker's son
and daughter
in some great rolling world of steel
lies the monument to our ancestors
the unspoken arts of labor
the crafting of broken promises
and calloused hands
faces burned and burning stillness
in memory
in the dying of winter's flame
unknown artisans seek their
   monument
and are exalted in the practice of
   care
my parents' ships blaze in the
   loneliness of Bufano's hill
others' lives
States of Grace
Worlds dawning
eyes turn
hearts open
refracting silent places
where working lives join this art
in remembrance.

—Donald Martin Carter

Contents

Preface

This book is a study of the process of reading difference in an Italian social setting in which the arrival of strangers has posed the peculiar problem of the increasing heterogeneity of this society. The distances across
understandings traversed by Italians and Senegalese in the process of
coming to terms with various forms of displacement—from that of
Turin, a post-Fordist city, to that of the declining economic fortunes
of the Senegalese state—are perhaps indicative of the emergent world
of travelers, migrants, and workers over the fragments of industrial societies and the uneasy reformulation of the nation-state. Indeterminacy is
probably the most characteristic feature of this passage between more or
less bounded capsules of knowledge. These new indeterminate spaces
may be the "fluid sociocultural constellations" of a new social order, as
some now suggest, or the tired retracing of routes half-remembered or
untold parts of greater narratives (Olwig 1993, 6). Whether we are wit-
nessing the articulation of a new social dynamics of diaspora, displacement, and dislocation or the continuation of ancient and (to us) unknown migratory dreaming or wanderings just now entering the realm
of social practice, we can no longer assume that migrants arrive in quite
the same type of nation-state they once did—since our notion of the
state in late capitalism has found it to be as multifarious as we once
thought it to be stable.

In 1990 when I set out to conduct research on the new phenomenon of immigration in Italy, I found that explaining the relationship between the arrival of postcolonial Senegalese Muslims in a deindustrializ-
ing European country that was not (for them) the former metropolitan

center required going back to an articulation of Europe and Africa as
conceptual entities and as projects in the process of the emergence of the
nation-state. I found that many Italians spoke of the arrival of Senegalese and other groups as if it were localized in parts of major cities,
around train stations, in airports, and local parks—all sites that had become contested, that people often wish to free of the encounter with the
"Other." As Italo Calvino once wrote, the city "does not tell its past, but
contains it like the lines of a hand, written in the corners of the streets"
(1974). The attempt to recapture the golden age of the absence of the
Other helped me to understand that the "new migrant" was being
thought of within a language of culture similar to that of the southern
Italian migrant of the past. In a complex interplay of notions of nation,
class, race, and gender, the newcomer was being recycled through the
conceptual framework of years of representations that contributed to
the "making of Italians," and the sense of inhabiting particular urban-
scapes out of the backdrop of rural society. Often, thinking through the
newcomer was a way of revisiting old controversies between the North
and the South, and conflicts between the political Left and Right. This
book documents a "crisis" in Italian society in which the arrival of
groups like the Senegalese has played no small part. The designation of
this crisis comes from the way in which these events have been constructed in Italian cultural logic and from the nature of social problems
that have come to national awareness through means of the arrival of
newcomers, such as housing, health care, and abuses of labor practices.
The shifting of political power from traditional postwar parties and the
emergence of right-wing politics occurred largely during the course of
this study. I include the view of these groups that I formulated during
the process of their initial articulation.

My aim is to examine racialist discourse, past and present, as this
relates to conceptions of nation, class, and other distinctions historically
constituted in the convergence of classificatory schemes set to capture
the contemporary context of increasing European social and cultural
heterogeneity. Forms of difference found as representations in the media,
in state discourse, and in popular commonsense ideology provide the
basis for present and future negotiations over the nature of identity,
cultural and political representations, and the contours of an emergent
social world. My purpose in *States of Grace* is to explore the unique circumstance of Italian culture and society in the face of recent events. By
using the term *states of grace*, I mean to draw attention to the encounters

of diverse worlds in moments when this new relationship is being negotiated, creating a brief space between the otherwise well-defined boundaries of sociocultural orders. One of the most common reactions has been
for those in Italy to ask why these migrants are coming "here," not only
meaning to this city and this region but to Italy, when in popular imagination no colonial connection of great importance exists between the
migrants and this country. In short, Italy was often thought of as a kind
of migrant-free zone in spite of the slow acknowledgment in recent
years, albeit hesitant, that Italy is involved in a migratory process that
recognizes no national boundaries, a process that may not only be confined to such notions as Europe.

During my fieldwork many Senegalese arrived in Turin for the first
time—some coming from other Italian cities, some directly from Senegal, and yet others from not-so-distant parts of Europe. Few of these migrants at this time were women; this is changing as many today have
found housing arrangements either outside of Turin or in outlying quarters. Turin was a particularly difficult place for migrant women because
of overcrowding and the scarcity of adequate living conditions. Many
relocated to other cities, often in southern and eastern Italy where the
availability of housing was greater. Some couples lived in the quarter,
and on occasion women would live in the house where I worked most
often, one that contained more than one hundred inhabitants. The
Senegalese were particularly concerned with this situation and were at
the forefront of efforts to acquire proper housing for all migrants and in
the end brought this matter to national attention. I have focused this
discussion on the most pressing problems of this and other communities
of migrants and not on the contours of individual lives.

This book is divided into two parts: the first, "Invisible Cities," begins
with chapter 1 by considering the ideological space across which entities
are produced through the interplay of diaspora and postcolonialism,
that is, a complex set of relationships set across social fields encompassing the processual dimensions of colonialism articulated between Europe
and Africa and other sites (epistemological and social); the desert is used
here as an intermediary tropic terrain over which Europe and Africa
meet (see White 1978, 2–12).[1] Turin, one of the most prominent urban-
scapes of Italian society and home of Fabbrica Italiana di Automobili
Torino (FIAT), the auto company founded in 1899, four years before Henry
Ford set up his company, has also been the heart of contemporary labor

and political activity. Immigration must then be seen through the lens of this historic culture of work and labor struggle. Chapter 2 treats the urban landscape of Turin and the unique work culture into which newcomers are drawn. Chapter 3 sketches the world of Mourid diaspora and the powerful imagery of Mourid religious practice and its presence in many aspects of Senegalese life in Turin. The invisible cities of these chapters are the cities of Touba and Turin: one, the religious center of the Mourid Sufi Order, and the other, not merely a point of arrival in a story of immigration but a site of historical elasticity and conjuncture in which the fortunes of Italian, African, and other residents are worked out in post-Fordist, postindustrial Turin. I wish to point to the lived cities that go far beyond the contours of a built environment, cities that contain the meanings, memories, and struggles in the lives of their inhabitants. This is the terrain over which such issues as racism and immigration are fought and on which nativist ideologies grow.

In part II of the book, "States of Grace," I look at the search for a livable space for Italians and newcomers faced with one another for the foreseeable future. Chapter 4 begins with a discussion of the art of the state that draws heavily on the works of Antonio Gramsci and of Michel Foucault on "governmentality." I examine the role of othering and the state, the media and popular images of newcomers, and some of the emergent anti-immigrant sentiment in Turin and the country as a whole. In chapters 5 and 6, through the analysis of contemporary media and a political cartoon that deals with immigration legislation and the role of the Socialist Party in its formulation, I discuss the manner in which a particular reading of colonial Fascist adventures, contemporary immigration politics, and the caricature of African and other images has introduced the notions of race, nationalism, and gender into Italian political discourse. Chapter 7 examines the Martelli Bill, the first comprehensive immigration legislation since the 1940s in Italy, and its relationship to a conception of the boundaries of social, cultural, and political responsibility of the West for the rest. The concluding chapter, "Closing the Circle: On Sounding Difference," considers the manner in which difference is now inextricably bound to the idea of Europe, or to what Stuart Hall has called the "declining imagined community of the pure" (Hall 1994).

Acknowledgments

Arriving at each new city, the traveler finds again a past of his that he
did not know he had: the foreignness of what you no longer are or no
longer possess lies in wait for you in foreign, unpossessed places.
                                        —Italo Calvino, *Invisible Cities*

This book has been an opportunity to begin a great exploration of what
is happening today in European societies—to and with many of its most
recent residents. Borrowing from the work of Italo Calvino and Antonio
Gramsci, I have made an effort to people an otherwise impersonal landscape across which xenophobia and ignorance have often taken free
reign. As an African American anthropologist, my very presence in the
field is often the pretext for opening up a discourse about racialized subjectivities: from this there is often little escape. And yet it is through this
portal that the invisible cities of Touba Turin began to emerge.

This fieldwork research conducted in Turin, Italy (January 1990 to
August 1991), was assisted by a grant from the Joint Committee on
Western Europe, the Social Science Research Council, and the Ameri-
can Council of Learned Societies, with funds also provided by the Ford
Foundation, the William and Flora Hewlett Foundation, the National
Science Foundation, and a Fulbright-Hays grant. An earlier period of
exploratory research was supported by the Committee for Institutional
Cooperation (summer 1986). A critical period of writing was supported
by a Danforth-Compton Award (University of Chicago) and by the
Chancellor's Ethnic Minority Fellowship at the University of California,
Berkeley.
        During the course of fieldwork I was part of a research project on the

involvement of foreign migrants in the labor market, funded in part by the Istituto Richerche Economico Sociali del Piemonte and directed by Vanessa Maher, Francesco Ciafaloni, and Jean-Marie Tshotsha. My collaboration with and debt to each of the directors and other members of this group go far beyond what space allows me to acknowledge of their collective work experience, political action, and friendship (see Maher et al. 1991). Moreover, this work is an ongoing discussion with Vanessa Maher—an outgrowth of concerns, letters, phone calls, and continuing attempts to grapple with the work of anthropology. Vanessa Maher, Mauro Ambrosoli, Francesco Ciafaloni, and Jean-Marie Tshotsha have contributed greatly to my understanding of Turin and Italian society generally.

This book began as a dissertation submitted in December 1992 to the department of anthropology at the University of Chicago. It is difficult for me to express the depth of my appreciation to Bernard S. Cohn for the intellectual freedom given to me during all stages of research and his continued support over the course of this project. I wish to acknowledge the many insights, discussions, and questions of dissertation committee members Raymond T. Smith and James W. Fernandez.

Over the course of the development of this project I have greatly benefited from the comments and suggestions of many kind readers, and among them I would like to thank Vanessa Maher, for extensive editorial and other insights on the manuscript that have been invaluable; Michael Gilsenan and Donal Cruise O'Brien for careful attention to chapter 2; and Nancy Scheper-Hughes for reading and commenting on early versions of chapters 5 and 6. I would like to thank Laura Nader for her comments and encouragement, and Paul Rabinow for his suggestions and careful reading of chapter 4. And I would especially like to thank Heather Merrill-Carter for readings, discussion, and explorations of this material that have provided much of the intellectual climate in which this work has taken form; I would also like to thank Heather for her contribution to chapter 5. I would like to express my heartfelt gratitude to William Shack for guiding me to Italian colonial materials that formed the basis of my analysis in chapter 5, for his kind encouragement and advice, and for suggesting that I take the steps that have culminated in the realization of this project.

Several Italian institutions and institutional contexts greatly facilitated my work and involvement in research projects in Italy. Carlo Chiarenza and the staff of the Commissione Per Gli Scambi Culturali

Fra L'Italia e Gli Stati Uniti in Rome facilitated my access to documentation and the distribution of portions of my analysis to appropriate agencies and governmental centers that might benefit from such information. In Turin, I was affiliated with the Dipartimento Di Studi Politici of the University of Turin. The Einaudi Foundation provided me with office space, research facilities, and institutional support; I must thank Mario Einaudi and the secretariat and staff of the foundation for graciously taking in an anthropological traveler. I am indebted to Fredo Olivero, former director of the Ufficio Stranieri, for his kind indulgence of my many inquiries and his willingness to seek unique solutions to a wide range of problems facing people during a protracted housing, labor, and social crisis.

During the most recent period of revision of the manuscript I have benefited from the contributions of my colleagues in the department of anthropology at Johns Hopkins University, where through various versions of this work I have entered a most welcoming intellectual community: Eytan Bercovitch, Gillian Feeley-Harnick, Niloofar Haeri, Sidney W. Mintz, Michel-Rolph Trouillot, Katherine Verdery, Brackette F. Williams, and Yun-Xiang Yan. I would also like to acknowledge the contributions of Sara S. Berry and Philip D. Curtin.

My deepest thanks go to the Senegalese community in Turin, and to the many migrants who shared their insights, struggles, and hopes with all of us. And I remain grateful to Maria Viarengo, Roberto Roccia, and family for opening up Turin to us in so many ways.

Of the many contexts in which I have found myself during the course of this project, I have always been sustained emotionally by my wife and fellow traveler, Heather Merrill-Carter. I thank Nicolas for taking us into so many wonderful worlds. I would also like to thank Aurelia and John Worton for providing much-needed weekend breaks that helped to get the work finished. To my brother Charles E. Carter, a thanks for introducing me to the music "live," and helping to keep it tuned in and turned up.

I would like to thank Carrie Mullen, my editor at the University of Minnesota Press, and her assistant, Jeff Moen, for guiding me through this process. I would also like to thank Mary Byers, former managing editor at the University of Minnesota Press, and Louisa Castner, the copy editor for *States of Grace*, for outstanding work on the text and great patience.

I am grateful to Claire Lloyd, publishing administrator, and Blackwell Publishers for permission to reprint chapter 4.

I
Invisible Cities

1

Desert Crossings

Dakar tries to be a small-scale Paris, while Abidjan hovers between Manhattan and Hollywood, only dubbed in French. Africa has lost its bearings here.
　　—René Dumont and Marie-France Mottin, *Stranglehold on Africa*

For this story is also a Desert. You will have to walk barefoot on the hot sand, walk and keep silent, believing in the oasis that shimmers on the horizon and never ceases to move toward the sky, walk and not turn around, lest you be taken with vertigo. Our steps invent the path as we proceed; behind us they leave no trace, only the void. So we shall always look ahead and trust our feet. They will take us as far as our minds will believe this story.
　　—Tahr Ben Jelloun, *The Sand Child*

There is, after Herodotus, little interest by the Western world towards the desert for hundreds of years. From 425 B.C. to the beginning of the twentieth century there is an averting of eyes. Silence.
　　—Michael Ondaatje, *The English Patient*

Crossing the Desert

The Italian poet Giuseppe Ungaretti, who was born and lived a great portion of his life in Egypt, once contrasted in his notebooks the ultimate baroque city of Rome with the wide expanses of the Egyptian

desert: "The desert holds no monument." The great power of the image
of the desert in the West is contained perhaps in its capacity to efface
the traces of time—or so goes the myth of the desert.[1] The city, on the
other hand, monumentalizes its founders and orchestrates the continuity of social, cultural, and political power in its architecture and in the
arrangements of its living accommodations. Yet in spite of the prominence of the city in contemporary folk ideology, it is the state that imposes its authority far beyond the hinterlands of the rural regions surrounding the great cities of the world (Weber 1966; Villalón 1995). Such
tropes as that of the desert, the *caravansérai,* and the city participate in
the arch of the Western imagination, which conjures up an exotic and
dangerous world countered by notions of Western urban civility. This
continuum has run in popular imagination from the primitive quality
of the desert to the sophistication of the city, from the strange world of
the Arabian nights consumed as though it represented some primordial
elsewhere in Victorian Europe, to the contemporary depictions of "famine," fundamentalism, and lack of democratic principles. The European
ideal of the pastoral other world of the countryside finds its ultimate
negation in the desert; of boundaries, it remains the most extreme, the
most remote, the constantly changing, unchanged ideascape (Bunce
1994). Such images are somewhat fixed parts of popular Western imagination and form a part of a daily commonsense world, in which such
images, convictions, and judgments may inform, distinguish, and consolidate one community or another (Nader 1988, 155; Parker 1995, 32–38).

In West Africa the classical imposition of the city in its colonial form
in Dakar by the French has left a legacy of dominance of the rural regions by the urban centers and a pattern of dependence on foreign capital; "Dakar," as René Dumont and Marie-France Mottin once wrote,
"single-handed, keeps Senegal dependent" (1983). Established by the
French as once the capital of French West Africa, Dakar, a bureaucratic
town, has become a classic example of notions of Western development
and planning imposed on a largely agricultural country.[2] Subject to the
consequences of a monocrop agricultural structure centered on the production of groundnuts and the results of soil deterioration, periods of
prolonged drought, and prices of rice that exceed four times that of their
own millet, peasants increasingly find their way to the shantytowns of
the capital city (Dumont and Mottin 1983, 182). Since 1932 with the im-
portation of Indonesian rice to feed Senegalese peasants, there has been
a diminishing need to grow millet and growing encouragement by the

colonial and then the postcolonial state to consume foreign cereals (Dumont and Mottin 1983). The consumption of foreign cereals such as rice and wheat has merely increased over the years to such an extent that the consumption of millet, the only locally produced crop of the three, has fallen far behind the exports, leading Dumont and Mottin to declare in a tragic tone, "Dakar is no longer an African city" (Dumont and Mottin 1983, 197).[3] One of the groups hardest hit by the devastation in certain regions of the country such as Louga is the artisans, who since the 1950s have been seeking their fortunes in Dakar, Paris, and most recently in Turin, Rimini, and other European cities (Findley 1989, 12; Salem 1981; Diouf 1981).

In fact, the Sahara is expanding, moving its boundaries northward and southward; even the winds of northern Senegal aid its march, and sand dunes creep to the outskirts of Dakar—a motion that has gone on unchecked for centuries (Webb 1995). Migrants from many rural regions of Senegal step onto the streets of the capital for the first time in their lives on their way to board a plane and to travel abroad. Some, often speaking no European language and having never seen the interior halls of the elite French schooling system in Senegal, go off to engage in *commerçe*, an activity that has been continuous in some form for centuries. This trading diaspora, often heavily weighted by the former peasant-artisan-worker, is merely an extension of African internal and international migration that now includes the shores of the Mediterranean as points along its pathway of multiple destinations.[4] This research suggests that the new immigration of Third World migrants to "new" receiving countries such as Italy must be seen in the context of African internal and international migration of the past and, in that, of a crisis of West African agriculture, prolonged drought, urbanization, and the fluctuation of international market outlets.[5] The convergence of this phenomenon of the arrival of migrants in Europe with periods of economic crisis in the European social formation has resulted in the imposition of various restrictions by European states on this immigration. It is in fact the European interstate system, the nature and the future of the nation-state, and its relationship with non-European states that are particularly at issue in the contemporary context. Weak European states may provide labor to wealthy states, diminishing the need for non-European migrants and the burden of assistance of the European bloc to the world's poor nations. While previous periods have tolerated or even, as in the case of France and England, encouraged immigration, the immanent closure of

European markets to non-European Community members has led to the imposition of protectionist policies that guard against the access of foreign workers to welfare and other benefits (Wihol de Wenden 1990b). This closure on the national and international levels has often been articulated in both a chauvinist and racialist language and atmosphere in which *migrants* becomes a euphemism for Blacks, Arabs, and Asians. As J. S. Eades has shown in his discussion of the presence of Yoruba migrants in northern Ghana, such tendencies toward national closure are not unique to Europe (Eades 1993). This research will suggest that conceptions of race are pivotal to the understanding of both the classification of a nonnational outsider and an internal Other. Further, in Italy in the absence of an "immigrant construct" that is capable of incorporating the new Third World migrant, the new migrant is appropriated to a model of the historical southern Italian migrant, at once drawing the southern more closely into the national ideology of "citizen" and excluding the racially and culturally distinct "outsider" (Bjorkland 1986).

The ethnographic focus of this book is on the Senegalese migrant community, a community internally distinguished by traces of caste and the patterns of social class formation in contemporary Senegal. The Senegalese who trade in Italy were in their own country primarily artisans, wood-carvers, tailors, welders, and masons with little or no formal education, although with substantial vocational and work experience. Yet the migrant population also contains the traces of a would-be and highly educated middle class, often early school leavers, those who have missed exams or have been unable to proceed in the rigid French educational system for lack of funds or other reasons. Often highly motivated and willing to use training programs that lead to various types of specialization, these migrants who possess a proficiency in European languages and a vast knowledge of Europe act as intermediaries, translators, and guides.

Finally, among the migrant community are the members of the Sufi orders, which Donal Cruise O'Brien suggests were innovators in Senegal in the sense that they essentially granted autonomy from both the world of Islam and the Christian world of the colonial powers. In Senegal there is an association of Sufi orders with anticolonial sentiment (Cruise O'Brien 1981). I suggest that the activities of the migrants of the Mourid order, one of the most powerful and well-organized Sufi confraternities that emerged in Senegal, have allowed the order to shift from its largely agricultural base and employ a kind of flexible accumulation in times of crisis, as peasants of the rural world might have done in the past. The urban Da'ira or Mourid religious center is not only a refuge of the Mourid from the European world but a point of possible conversion to Islam for members of the host society. Through the innovation of urban religious centers throughout the world the Mourid have provided a base also to members in diaspora. The Mourid have then a "mission" to expand the order in Europe and have published journals and created urban centers all over Europe toward this end. This research suggests that an autonomous form of African organization in the Mourid order that once incorporated pre-Moslem religious practices of the Wolof and other peoples has now incorporated the economic crisis and appropriated this change to its traditional practices.

Just a short while ago anthropologists opened their ethnographic studies with apologies for taking the reader to some imperial frontier in an out-of-the-way corner of the globe. The backward and previously unheard-of anthropological locality was part of the image of the "doing of anthropology," at least in the popular imagination (Vincent 1982). Today, what has previously been thought of as the "imperial frontier," that fragmentary and somewhat overwhelming agglomeration of the shards of empires and colonies, seems to be everywhere in diaspora (Mintz 1995). The economic, social, and political problems of "over there"—that is, some imaged space beyond the West—is now "over here," a part of the very rhythm of life in Western democracies. Godfrey Wilson wrote in 1941 of the situation of Third World workers in what was then northern Rhodesia, called an "African territory," that the African workers' "standard of living now depends on economic conditions of Europe, Asia and America to which continents their labor has become essential. . . . They have entered a heterogeneous world stratified into classes and divided into states" (cited in Vincent 1982). This "heterogeneous world" has become increasingly one in which the relationships between states both African and European continue to impinge on the lives of workers and to restrict their movements. The imposition of taxes payable in European currency and various forms of forced labor in the colonial world of West Africa marked some of the most bitterly contested forms of colonial coercion. The railway and labor strikes of 1947 such as that depicted in Ousmane Sembene's *God's Bits of Wood* (1970) denote the contours of categorical shifts from the standpoint of social observers, as former peasants not yet making up a working class engage in forms of conscious protest that is not yet rebellion.

The contemporary context is an unprecedented one in which so-called Third World migrants engage in an uncharted migratory experience, arriving in Italian communities unaccustomed to the very notion of an immigrant in Italy. People from diverse ethnic, cultural, and sociopolitical backgrounds today arrive in increasing numbers in European countries. The reasons and motivations are complex, ranging from those of political and economic crisis to that of the repression of religious and ethnic groups in some home countries. Today, the reality of European society is that of an increasing cultural and ethnic heterogeneity. Italy, which has traditionally been a sender nation, has in recent years become a nation with an immigration crisis. A world in diaspora—from Tunisia, Morocco, Somalia, the Philippines, Zaire, Ethiopia, Brazil, Spain, Portugal, Peru, China, Egypt, the former Yugoslavia, Ghana, Argentina, Jordan, Nigeria, and the Ivory Coast—has converged on this new receiver country as recently as the 1980s (Curtin 1994).

The School of Common Sense

> The sun was behind them, beating ever harder on their backs, but they paid no attention to it: they knew it well. The sun was a native.
> —Ousmane Sembene, *God's Bits of Wood*

The Italian social philosopher Antonio Gramsci once noted in his *Prison Notebooks* that society could be looked at as a vast school: "Every relationship of hegemony is necessarily an educational relationship" (cited in Adamson, 1980, 142–43). Gramsci's conception of bourgeois society as a vast school placed both the intellectual cadre of bourgeois society and the "organic" intellectuals of the subaltern classes in similar relations to the formation and articulation of the "ordering ideas" of society. These ordering notions were inculcated into the subject in every context, from those of institutional settings to those of daily life at work and at leisure, and in virtually every social context. Every interchange therefore stands in some relationship to the hegemonic ideology of a given society, age, or social order. The school is undoubtedly one of the most complex social sites in contemporary capitalist societies. The convergence on the school of the processes of class formation and the inculcation of the student into the world of the nation make the school a key site of ideological and social conflict. For Gramsci the school "as a positive educative function" was one of the most important activities of the state. The achievement of the hegemony of the dominant classes for Gramsci was always a contested process, one that was accomplished through the formation of both consent and coercion. The school can then be seen as a social site in which the dialectic between consent and coercion is crucial. According to Gramsci, one of the critical functions of the educative system was to place each citizen in the "general" condition to govern. It was not enough merely to give the unskilled worker the opportunity to become skilled; something more was required. And thus we may say in a Gramscian fashion that the school in the society at large is the social context of everyday life in which the social and political contours of the life of each member of the community are negotiated, transformed, and lived. In light of various systems of difference, including that of social class, the school may be seen as the large context in which the educative form is inscribed in social practice. In this way we may see the introduction of the concept of race with the arrival of Third World peoples to Italy as part of a broader ethnotaxonomy of difference. Race simply provides another "objectified system of classification" that is part of the day-to-day practice of social life in the contemporary urban context (Bourdieu 1984). Its incorporation and appropriation into structures of difference in Italian society are already predicated on the articulation of internal racial taxonomies that relegate the South to a separate and other reality, compared in commonsense ideology with the more prestigious and wealthy North.

In the quotation at the opening of this section from Sembene's *God's Bits of Wood*, a procession of women marching from Thies to Dakar feels the warmth of the sun and, feeling this warmth to be familiar, consider it "native" as opposed to the colonialist residents of the European sections of the country. Even the sun is encompassed in this arch of ideological reading of the world, in a manner that vividly demonstrates the power of ideology to transform the world into a school in which the cosmological, the natural, and the social gain significance in the taxonomy of "all there is," the commonsense contours of a world that seems to be, and in a very compelling manner is, "the only possible world." It is precisely when different orders of common sense collide that a world of common sense no longer appears to hold the same refractory quality, that the sun becomes no longer familiar. The entire world is inextricably shaded with the multiple meanings that actors cast on it or have cast in the past. Every relation has some aspect of this larger ideological hegemony.

Since capitalism transformed the Western world, there has been a preoccupation with the characterization of modern capitalist society. The term *capitalism* itself is a historical product of the early nineteenth century (Smith 1984; Williams 1976). The stuff of social reality has been increasingly segmented into such terms as *working class, the capitalist,* and, in the political sphere, *bureaucracy* and *citizenry* (Nisbet 1966). It is difficult to remain ever attentive to the various contours of thought and displacements of location that have transformed these categories, designed initially to explain broad and previously unknown social processes in Western Europe, and that then spread to much of the world throughout the nineteenth and twentieth centuries with the expansion of the West.

The category of the working class is particularly important in the context of this study, set in Turin, Italy, the classical workers' city where Antonio Gramsci organized his most intensive labor and political activities. Turin was one of the most clearly Fordist centers in all of Italy. The social and political life of the city harmonized for decades with the rhythms of the factory, primarily Fabbrica Italiana di Automobili Torino, or FIAT, whose plants center on the production of the automobile.

Recent transformations of the labor process in Western capitalist democratic societies, which became particularly acute with the economic crisis of the 1970s, have been translated into present-day conditions of economic insecurity. Turin in the post-Fordist era, while still dominated by industry, is beginning to take on the contours of an emergent "technocity"; the urban center of the future will be focused on a core of high-tech production units. Today, with the shifts away from mass production toward small firms and automation, Turin has become a center of industrial-automation and robotics firms (Piore 1984). Global trends have accentuated regional disparities, which have been a recurring feature of Italian post-World War II industrial expansion (Barbano 1987). The structure of the Italian economy characterized in the postwar period by persistent yet uneven economic development between the southern and northern regions of the country continues to define separate Italies, whose territorial boundaries are drawn by both the demographic drain on the South and the industrial concentration in the northern and central regions of the country (Bagnasco 1977). In spite of attempts at bringing about parity in the urban and industrial arrangements of the two regions by the 1970s, northern and central Italy contained 90 percent of all firms employing more than fifty workers (Douglas 1983). Massive internal migrations toward the expansive engineering, textile, metallurgical, and chemical production centers of the North have dramatically affected the composition and texture of urban social life in these areas. In this process more than half a million southern immigrants have found their way to Turin alone. During the postwar period Turin continued to contain the highest percentage of southern Italian migrants of any Italian city north of Naples.

In Turin, the massive migrations of the past were related to the expansion of the automotive and related industries grouped around FIAT. But the new demands of the labor process and the actions of those who direct and shape its course have resulted in the displacement of many workers into the realms of irregular and unstable forms of employment (Sabel 1985). Plant closures and labor force reductions shift to increasingly global economic and political rhythms. The unregulated and irregular work of the Italian *economia sommersa,* or the underground economy, is of particular importance to the structure of the Italian economy (Chiarello 1983; Barbano 1985). This off-the-books world of work allows small firms that are the core of the current innovative industrial expansion to relax safety standards, avoid taxation, and cut labor costs. The exclusion of new immigrants from some legal, political, and other social provisions only accentuates the marginal position these groups hold in relation to the entire workforce (Barkan 1984; Piore 1984; Minigione 1986). It is in the world of *lavoro nero,* or precarious labor, that the migrant often finds initial employment, yet many including Senegalese soon find employment within the official market.

Turin is unusual among Italian cities because of the particularly rigid segregation of its residential communities along class and regional lines. This peculiar arrangement stems largely from the experience of massive migrations toward automotive and related industrial labor opportunities, which the region offered in the postwar years with the growth of FIAT (Negri 1982). The southern migrants from Abruzzi-Molise, Campania, Basilicata, Puglia, Calabria, Sicily, Sardinia, and other southern regions to the northern industrial triangle of Turin, Genoa, and Milan in the postwar period were confronted with an antisoutherner bias. The migrants were said to be volatile, prone to various forms of criminality, largely illiterate, unable to speak the Italian language properly, and wanting in the exercise of proper personal hygiene (Douglas 1983; Fofi 1964; Kertzer 1977; Pellicciari 1970). Stereotypes drawn from commonsense folk ideologies ensured that the world that was to take shape in the wake of the migrants' arrival would contain some of the most exploitative systems of social and class exclusion in contemporary Italian history (Negri 1982; Barkan 1984).

The differences of the southern Italians are regarded as innate and fundamental. In the postwar experience southern Italians in the North are and have been seen as social inferiors; there is a marked social separation between migrants and northerners in areas of social life, leisure activities, and residential life. The word used by Italians to describe the nature of the responses to migrant communities in cities like Turin is *racism*. This is the same term often used to describe the response of some to the new Third World immigrants in contemporary Italy (Chiaramonte 1987; LaPalombra 1987).

I argue that there are many forms of racism in contemporary Italian society and that present forms of difference incorporate structures of difference that have been developed in Italian society since its foundation and consolidation under Vittorio Emanuele II in the 1860s. Many of the forms of northern racism were developed in relation to the southern territories of Italy, which were seen as a distinct and other world quite different from the North. The nineteenth-century social theorist Cesare Lombroso, from his first major inquiry in the South, *In Calabria (1862–1897)*, through subsequent works, began to lay out the scientific foundations of an ideology that distinguished the "atavistic" and backward regions of the emergent nation from those of the more civilized and advanced regions. According to his theories, one could draw a map of the arch of civilization in Italy that would show the distribution of backward and less civilized traits and customs throughout the peninsula. What began as scientific theory soon combined with the preferences of the everyday lives and attitudes of the ruling elite, who withheld no amount of contempt for those unlike themselves. From the very court of the king a regional and social preference for the North was expressed; Vittorio Emanuele II preferred to remain silent at state functions since he chose to speak either his native Piedmontese or French rather than Italian. What some have called *campanilismo*—literally, a preference for those within the sound of the local bell tower and a disdain for those who originate beyond it—is part of a very complex structure of difference that operates particularly in Italy along regional, sectional, and linguistic lines. Families that arrived in Turin decades ago are still not considered by some to be Turinese, to say nothing of the southern internal Italian migrants who arrived in the fifties.

This brings us to one of the more troublesome additions to this construction of difference: social class. Class formation in Italy is a rather recent phenomenon. Although today about 8 percent of the population still clings to the agricultural world, less than fifty years ago Italy was largely an agricultural society. The character of Italian class structure derives much of its texture from this agricultural base, which was affected at the turn of the century by a gradual rural exodus and later by the abandonment of the most unstable part of the agricultural world, the *braccianti,* or day laborers. The workshop artisan tradition owes much to this vast agricultural world that transformed in a short period of time into the urban world of work. In Italy there is an extensive stratum of artisans and small family-owned firms and an unusual profusion of small factories and cooperatives, the large-scale plants FIAT, Pirelli, and Michelin being the exception.

The social life of interclass relations, however, still has much of its nineteenth-century quality when the social divisions between *signori* and others were very pronounced. Education is a clear indication of status and social class in Italy. But one must enter into the shops and hallways in order to appreciate the nature of Italian classism. Italian dialects, wrongly labeled, are not derivatives of one standard language but often languages in their own right.[6] The ability to speak standard Italian, then, for many has been acquired through a process of schooling. The inability to master the language is a sure sign of lower social standing, but many well-educated people use dialect in certain contexts. This is difficult to explain, given popular images of Italy, largely because standard Italian has only been widely diffused in Italy since the postwar period and only began to be taught in schools nationally during the Fascist period beginning in the twenties. A former president of the republic, Giovanni Leone, was often ridiculed because of his strong Neapolitan, hence, southern accent; I was often told that, although he spoke with this accent, "he is a legal and constitutional scholar." The former president no doubt deliberately maintained this Neapolitan flavor, which enhanced his regional appeal. Regionalism and localism have become fashionable again in recent years, as the local dialects of the North are being hailed as monuments to northern culture and society, which are quite distinct from the rest of the country; some right-wing groups even advocate making some local northern dialects municipal languages.

It is interesting that when Turin is mentioned the reaction is often, "Oh, yes, the city of FIAT" or, rather, "the city of Agnelli." But it is never called the city of Vittorio Emanuele II, who at the age of forty-one be-

came king of a united Italy. The industrial city has eclipsed the city of
the House of Savoy, the monarchy that was dispatched by referendum at
the end of the Second World War and whose male descendants to this
day cannot set foot on Italian soil.[7] Between the monarch and the industrial leader lies Italy's history since unification, one that has in a relatively short time undergone tremendous transformation. The industrialists such as the Agnellis a generation ago took over the residences of the
former House of Savoy and consolidated their industrial wealth with
marriages into the most ancient noble families. Today, while the interest
of multinational firms like FIAT set up offices in the former Soviet Union
and in Douala and Dakar, a new group of workers comes to Turin, foreign born and trained.

Some of the most characteristic images of the pathways and streets
in many Italian cities like Turin are those of foreign-born migrants on
their way to work during commuting hours and the polyrhythms of languages on the trams and buses. A young Senegalese-born worker operates a painting device in one of the sections of the Turin FIAT plant and
speaks an Italian slang composed of standard Italian with many words
from Italian dialects and some fragments of Wolof. In the evening this
same worker meets other Senegalese on the way home; they greet one
another in Wolof and from time to time slip into French or Italian. The
tram may then stop near what was formerly a southern quarter at a
house of other Senegalese workers, just above an Italian bar where retired Italian workers are playing cards in the summer heat and young
boys ride their mopeds in circles on the otherwise deserted street. The
young man greets his housemates, who take his hand in turn and press it
to their foreheads in a manner characteristic of the Mourid. In this context the gesture often emphasizes a kind of making fun of those who
might think themselves better than others. Other distinctions fade away
as forms of vanity and attempts at the imposition of power along the
lines of old pathways to power. The joking helps to reinforce a notion of
solidarity: "Here we are all the same—only God is superior," one migrant explains. This marking of the daily commute draws the arch across
a world that reveals in a glimpse the texture of a new Europe, of the fu-
sion of the local with the distant reaches of a once-colonial world. From
the dawn of the day, as African and Moroccan workers sweep the streets
of Turin, help to build or restore its buildings, or enter one of the FIAT
plants as the first African cohort of engineers, to the end of the day,
when the world of work draws to a close and the quarters come alive

with returning schoolchildren, the last dash of evening shoppers, and the last of the after-work commuting trams and buses, we may sense the new face and rhythm of Europe.

The Phoenix and Its Song

Former Senegalese president and founder of the nation Léopold Sédar Senghor once wrote in one of his poems: "The Phoenix rises, he sings with wings extended." The phoenix was one of his favorite images of transformation for Africa and for Senegal. The poetic voyage of the phoenix—the creature who lived for five hundred years, consumed itself in a fire, and then rose purified from its own ashes to live for another five hundred years—was the metaphor most common in Senghor's poetry. Senghor was a proponent of a vision of Euro-Africa: of an Africa inextricably tied to the fate of the West and by a West whose fate could not be separated from that of its proximate southern counterpart. The struggle with the past, the effort to create a new and renewed identity in the future, and a sense of the search for a more encompassing notion of "community" are all themes prefigured in his poetry. The contradictions of the relationship between African states and the West are ironically present in the figure of Senghor, who during his tenure as president of Senegal spent half of the year in France, was holder of one of the highest French academic honors, and was the non-Moslem president of a predominately Moslem country.

These contradictions are no less significant in the lives of the migrants who find their way to Europe. Senegal has been plagued by a series of crises brought on by economic changes, urban overcrowding and lack of resources, rural isolation and drought, and a growing threat to the state represented by a rival Moslem coalition. Demographically, the growth of the Senegalese population was evident in the 1920s and then increased significantly after the Second World War. In spite of the common belief that rural families involved in cash cropping were large, these families actually tended to be smaller than those on the periphery of cash cropping in Senegal (Colvin et al. 1981).

The agricultural world has drifted between cash cropping and the seasonal migration of cultivators; migration has been essential to agriculture in Senegal, Gambia, and western Mali as well as parts of Mauritania for some time (Colvin et al. 1981, 6; Baker 1995, 80–81). Drought in this region has often been related to increasing urbanization. Kathleen M. Baker notes that Gambian youth often sought the life of the city for adventure and as part of "a survival strategy rather than for capital accumulation" (Baker 1995; Gardner 1995). Drought contributes to out-migration and in turn to the problems of rural farming, labor shortages, and in the event of falling yields to the need to buy greater quantities of food through outwork (Baker 1995; Copans 1975, 1978). Rural exodus has not been offset by the countervailing augmentation of productivity in urban areas, so that largely Sahelian cities, for the most part colonial cities, are centered on administration, transport, and commercial activities rather than production (Colvin et al. 1981). With the increasing effects of drought in the rural regions, urban migration has become permanent for many. The inequalities between rural and urban regions have only increased with the urban, educated elite draining more and more resources toward urban centers. Even the clearing of urban shantytowns, a policy of the Senegalese government, only points to the widening disparity between the educated elite and the growing subproletariat of the urban world. The frontier cultivation of the Mourid in Senegal and the clearing and settlement of new areas will soon come to a close as available fertile land is exhausted (Colvin et al. 1981). For some migrants now, arrival in such city centers as Dakar occurs only as they pass through to board the plane for international African and European centers.

The effects of migration to European destinations have been felt particularly in areas of Senegal such as the Senegal River basin, which sent a significant number of soldiers to fight in the Second World War for France. The soldiers in the 1950s constituted the first wave of migrants to France after the war. In 1981 Lucie Gallistel Colvin and colleagues wrote that "only a tiny but rapidly growing population of migrants to Europe taps into the wage structure of the developed world and repatriates some of that wealth" (Colvin et al. 1981). This situation has been significantly changed since the 1960s, when (particularly around 1966) a rapidly emergent community of Senegalese was evident in France, many of whom were artisans, wood-carvers, and tailors, groups hit particularly hard by the lack of cash-cropping income in the rural areas. Much of this vanguard of migrants to France was Soninke, and, according to François Manchuelle, after 1979 only a small portion of those said to be Senegalese in France were actually Wolof (Manchuelle 1994). This migration, as Fernand Braudel suggests, must be seen as one of the new exports destined for the European social context: labor (Braudel 1992).[8]

The appearance of Wolof in Italy opens yet a new dimension in the relationships among agriculture, migration, and postcolonial economic relations. The backdrop of this period lies in the struggle of rural Senegalese to survive the fluctuations of a depressed economy and the imposition of government pricing controls. Peasant disaffection and resistance to this imposition of the Senegalese state and its management of the monocrop economy have been particularly pronounced in recent years. Increasingly, peasants have chosen to plant their own millet and beans and to reduce spontaneously the productivity in peanut cash cropping. Greater amounts of the cash crop find their way outside of the state-dominated marketing system into the informal markets of Gambia or, rather, are converted into items for the peasants' consumption. Touba has a parallel market, which Donal Cruise O'Brien and Christian Coulon have called a "veritable clandestine Harrods, Senegalese style," that the state cannot control without angering the leaders of the Mourid (Cruise O'Brien and Coulon 1989, 160). And many of the younger generation seek to help build homes for their parents, support relatives, or just experience a different life through travel to Paris or Rome or Turin, where others have traveled and established bases before them. Many migrants from Senegal, however, speak of political rather than economic troubles. The state led by the technocrats of the new president, Abdou Diouf, has attempted to curtail the authority of the traditional power structure of the Maraboutic leaders and the politicians—the "barons" or clans, as they are referred to in Senegalese politics. The great agricultural base of the economy is seriously in danger. As Cruise O'Brien and Coulon point out, the production of the groundnut can no longer sustain either the peasant or the massive state apparatus:

> Senegalese agriculture is in a state of near collapse. Groundnuts, which remain the basic product of the agricultural sector and which are crucial to budgetary and external revenue, no longer "nourish" either the peasant or the state. Due to drought and/or farmer disaffection, production is chronically irregular. (Cruise O'Brien and Coulon 1989)

Peasant strategies of evasion along with natural conditions have cut into state revenues. While peasants continue to evade state marketing boards, urban unrest has become a new concern of the state. Rice, which must be imported, has become almost a staple in the cities; in twenty years the rice consumption has doubled, and partly because the government discourages the peasants' millet and bean production, more and more rice is imported each year (Cruise O'Brien and Coulon 1989).

The efforts of the new government under Diouf to create a greater dependence of both rural and urban populations on the state has as yet failed to bring about a coherent hegemonic state policy capable of casting a wide enough circle to enclose all of the many components of the country. The state policy of capitalist modernization and its so-called civilizing mission has merely shown the persistence of problems that the state has greater and greater difficulty solving. The problem of human congestion in the urban areas is one example of this; the government policy of leveling the dwellings of this congestion—that is, of street sellers, the disabled, and other subjects too weak to protect themselves from the imposition—has merely postponed the question of state responsibility and policy toward the "marginal." The imposition of control has not eliminated the problem. Instead, the Senegalese government has resorted to the turn-of-the-century colonial practice of "slum clearance"—the removal of urban shantytowns from time to time—dramatizing the widening disparity between an educated elite and the growing subproletariat of an all-but-abandoned urban world. In 1914 the establishment of a separate African quarter by the French colonial administration formalized the notion of a divided city in the rationale of colonial urban planning. The state's prevention of urban disorder and its interventions in the lives of its urban populations for the purposes of sanitation and public health are merely part of the routine of the colonial legacy (Goldberg 1992, 48–49). This disparity between diverse urban worlds is most dramatically demonstrated in such areas as health care and access to a host of other services.

The Senegalese economic crisis has become more acute since 1965 along with the growth of the national debt, which picked up sharply after 1970, reaching in 1984 a level more than fifteen times that of 1970. Although the economic crisis has allowed government intervention in many areas and thus extended the powers of the state, the ruling elite has a very unstable social base. The greatest threat remains the possibility of a coherent Moslem alternative to the democratic multiparty system. As Jean Copans has suggested, a lucid, multiethnic ideology is already offered in the beliefs of the Mourid Brotherhood, which could be easily adapted to the purposes of a national ideology (Copans 1981). The Brotherhood already has a heroic figure in Cheikh Amadou Bamba, who is associated with the emergence of an anticolonialist stance, an aspect of the life of the Marabout that the young Mourid emphasize in their formulation of Mourid ideology. Should efforts to develop the state through the projects of multinationals and the government fail, the ability of the Mourid structure to extend its sphere of influence, through the classical combination of agriculture and remittances from petty trade and other activities, may play an even greater role at the national level in the coming years.

Simmel's Stranger

> This is what I wanted to hear from you: confess what you are smuggling moods, states of grace, elegies!
> —Italo Calvino, *Invisible Cities*

The stranger in Georg Simmel's words is the "person who comes today and stays tomorrow," and in the classical image of the stranger the trader embodied those qualities of ambiguity that characterize the near, yet far, newcomer.[9] Simmel goes on to say that the stranger is in fact the potential wanderer who, "although he has not moved on . . . has not quite overcome the Freedom of coming and going." This freedom that the Other has "not quite overcome" is a kind of inability "to be free from" the intervention of the state. The coercive powers of the state may intercede through an endless intervention of documents that inhibit the comings and goings of people throughout the world. It is only through the reification of the state as the legitimate arbiter of movements of migrations and populations and of the creation of "boundaries," "frontiers," and "citizens"—through what one might call the *politics of location*—that the itinerant becomes a problem, an object of state intervention (Federici 1983). Any discourse on immigration is one in which the encounter with the Other is prescribed and delineated, in which the appropriate distribution of persons can be definitively highlighted in the light and shadow of legislation and governmental practice. Thus immigration is a discourse of enclosure of the "specification of a protected place" in space and time; this protected place is the nation or, rather, the particularly inscribed "community" in which some persons cannot overcome the freedom of coming and going or the imposition of the boundaries of the nation-state (Foucault 1979a). Ruth Schachter Morgenthau (1979) once wrote of "strangeness":

> Where many become viewed as strangers, there is a loss of equilibrium
> between power, production, and distribution. . . . Harassment of the
> weakest strangers shows that there is a crisis, but it is not necessarily
> its cause; the weak strangers may be scapegoats, who suffer in place of
> richer and more powerful objects of resentment.

The presence of these "scapegoats" opens up a horizon in which class
ideology is deflected through the use of race and other categories such as
ethnicity. In the European resurgence of xenophobia, a process of scape-
goating seems to have recovered the once-fringe neofascist elements
from near obscurity (European Parliament 1986). Racism and xenophobia have converged with a growing anxiety of middle classes about their
position in a period of rapid change and economic crisis. In Florence
and Turin, for example, Italian commercial and business groups have
called for measures to remove immigrants from tourist centers and local
quarters.

A silence pervades the Italian discourse on immigration, a discourse
peopled by the immigrants themselves, by the men and women for whom
endless comings and goings are a part of the meanings and significations
of their daily lives. Thus this discourse cannot be exhausted by the official pronouncements of Italian media or government or by what is said
of it here. This desert crossing must provide the hope of future refuge
in which such a silence may be broken and is thus an exploration for
that more complete understanding, which may converge in other states
of grace.

2

Turin: Work and Its Shadow in a Post-Fordist City

They are fully aware of the insecurity of their tenure in Rooiyard and have not come to regard the place as their "home." It is merely, owing to the force of circumstances, their temporary refuge.
>—Ellen Hellmann, "Rooiyard"

And Polo said: "Every time I describe a city I am saying something about Venice.

"When I ask you about other cities, I want to hear about them. And about Venice, when I ask you about Venice.

"To distinguish the other cities' qualities, I must speak of a first city that remains implicit. For me it is Venice."
>—Italo Calvino, *Invisible Cities*

Invisible Cities: Turin Touba

The city is a historical figure that embodies various changes and conflicts entailed in particular historical and social struggles recorded not only in architecture, but in memory. On the local level cities such as Turin are marked into the micropractices of its inhabitants, not only in the movement of the traffic and the rising and falling of its environmental rhythms but in social memory of the classes and social orders that comprise the city. Whole areas of the city become reminders of the social and political struggles that various communities have leveled on them. The centrality of work to the many memories of Turin and the formation of the context in which Senegalese migrants encounter these "cities of memory" are our concerns here (see fig. 1). Invisible cities, those cities constructed in ideology, in memory, and in the instances of reference and urban identity of particular communities are also our concern here. The term *cities of memory* is used by architects to refer to the projected city of architectural imagination not yet realized, which constitutes a kind of potential city in the minds of both specialists and nonspecialists apprised of the possibility. I employ a notion here of *invisible cities* to define a complex of ideology or discourse about possible cities, cities of memory, and imagined cities that become the focal points of certain communities in a particular location (Calvino 1974).

Turin was the site of the dream of continuous industrial expansion, a dream that a whole society participated in, in various ways. Today, the global recession has stilled this dream and the internationalization of production has left industry intact, with a greatly reduced workforce. It is the Turin of the past that is often referred to in passing in the shops and stores of the city. We turn briefly to the contours of this Turin below in order to give some indication of the world between Turin and Touba, the invisible cities of Italians and Senegalese that form the basis of daily significations and social practice (Fernandez 1988).

While throughout Italian history Turin has been one of the core cityscapes in the construction of the powerful locomotive of Italian industrial change focused around the automobile industry, the holy city of Touba has been the spiritual center of the Sufi Order and one of the central reference points of religious practice for all Mourid. There is a Turin that is populated with work and memories of work and by the traces of the labor movement, which in Italy was born and put to rest in Turin. From the vacant factory corridor to the gatherings and demonstrations in Piazza Statuto, where the labor movement finally came to rest, Turin has been a key protagonist in the cosmos of the Italian economy and in the memories of Italian workers, industrialists, and union officials (Goddard 1996, 26). The great mosque at Touba was built in large part through the participation of the government of Léopold Senghor, the Christian Senegalese president who in a predominantly Moslem country negotiated the fine balance of power between competing factions of

Fig. 1. Senegalese in such northern cities as Turin, Milan, and Florence have launched well-publicized campaigns against discrimination in housing and health care provisions, while less well-known groups of Senegalese are found also in the South, throughout many agricultural and industrial areas of the Italian mainland and the islands. (Washington, D.C.: U.S. Government Printing Office, 1996. Base 802448 [A04844] 3-96)

many religious orders, which although powerful were never able to join forces against the government.

The many factories of the Turin landscape were run and disappeared in the shadow of state participation and collaboration somewhat unparalleled in Western Europe. The layoffs from FIAT in the 1980s were the sign of an industrial city that now moves toward various forms of flexible accumulation, including small electronics plants, robotics, and a proposed technocity in which the industrial proletariat will be greatly reduced among the ranks of middle-sector workers, managers, and entrepreneurs. The Turinese working class was expected to become entrepreneurs overnight when the great industries failed and restructured. The loss of the centrality of the worker in the economy of northern Italy has meant a further loss of prestige for the city. As with the loss of the capital to Florence, the industrial worker is left with memories of the greatness of the labor movement and the time when the union leaders were called the uncrowned kings of Italy. The many advances of the labor movement have not compensated for the new kinds of difficulties facing the region—chronic unemployment and a massive housing shortage—difficulties that attest to northern Italy's place among wealthy nations (Jullien 1992; Lerner 1990). This image is rather new, however, and many Turinese do not see themselves as living in a wealthy nation but, instead, see Turin as a small city with big problems and a large industrial base. Despite its large tertiary-sector growth in recent years, Turin remains a working-class city, with the tone and pastimes of a working-class city. This has led some to say that while Turin is postindustrial to some degree, it is premodern in its social world. The median level of literacy of its inhabitants does not accord with its size as one of the largest Italian cities. The world of leisure provides only the sleepy diversion of the weekend soccer match and the *passagiata;* in the evening the city closes up like a small provincial town. Yet Turin is the site of Italian unification under an Italian king, the worker schools of Antonio Gramsci, and its streets flowed with the largest worker demonstrations in all of Europe. In short, there are many cities in the mist of the Po on a Turinese morning, and these form parts of the lives of the inhabitants and the stories told or imagined about them. Among these cities of the memory or the imagination are the emergent cities, the cities made from the interplay of all possible cities and from the unique circumstance of the meeting of old and new.

Turin: From Worker City to Technocity

The construction of large housing projects in Turin for southern immigrants in the late 1950s and early 1960s created a protracted discourse about the nature of housing and social integration of the southern immigrant in northern Italian society. Much Italian sociological work of the 1970s and 1980s attempted to get at the contours of the problems of social exclusion and segregation of the southern immigrant in northern Italian metropolitan areas (Re and Sistri 1988). It is clear that there is a pronounced ceiling on the possibilities of mobility for the southern migrant and a prominence in certain categories of work of the initial migration to the North (Negri 1982). The class structure of the early years of the internal migration was marked in Turin by a polarization between the large proletariat, the most numerous in any European city, and a bourgeoisie with a small middle stratum. The dimensions of this pattern have changed little over the years. Although there is a growing tertiary sector largely related to industry, this stratum has failed to impose its mark on the city. The city remains largely working class with the cultural pastimes of an Italian elite still in place (Goddard 1996, 52–56). Turin has the peculiar distinction of being the home of the former monarchy of Italy; thus the city was once an international center of a certain court society. Even with the placement of the capital of Italy at Florence and then at Rome, the private clubs of the aristocracy, some of which still exist, made Turin a special site that presented two quite distinct worlds: one elite, a center of music and art, and another restricted in its arch to the world of work (Smith 1989; Castronovo 1987; Cardoza 1991).

During Fascism, leisure was organized into a sector of state intervention, and the centers of *dopolavoro* and sports stadiums provided some of the forms of mass entertainment (de Grazia 1981). After the war many of the large industrial firms operated recreation centers in Turin, along the banks of the Po River; many of these facilities operated for a short time, more recently directed by the "red" local government authorities, which eventually gave many of the facilities to local quarters (Maher 1991; personal communication). The quarters, having no funds to operate the centers, often closed them, and many today remain closed. Many Turin residents attended the weekly films projected at the former *dopolavoro* centers and remember the largess of the great industrial giants like Pirelli that ran these centers. The polarity between the forms of elite entertainment, such as musical performances attended by the president of the republic and a very affluent group of residents, and the relative scarcity of mass forms of entertainment remains a feature of the city. This polarity and the absence of a developed middle range of activities, given the growing middle strata of the city, make Turin a peculiar Italian city.

It was once said of Turin that it was a factory town and that when people came home from work, the doors closed and the residents remained within this other world, the world of families, friendships, and domestic obligations. This feature led Arnaldo Bagnasco in his sociological profile of Turin to define all sectors of the Turinese as *domestico-centrica,* or centered on the domestic world (1986). There is, according to Bagnasco, a marked preference for activities of low cost and those that require little specialization, such as visiting and television viewing. During the 1980s the Turinese showed no great interest in more expensive activities such as attending plays and skiing, which also required specialized equipment. Generally, much of the social activity of Turin was focused around this domestic center and visiting, which Bagnasco links to both the cultural patterns of internal southern immigrants and to a quality of the preindustrial world that seems present in many dimensions of Turinese life and is in turn related to the dominance of work and its requirements in the day-to-day lives of Turin's inhabitants.

Bagnasco also characterizes Turin as a metropolitan center too small for the great processes that have occurred within its confines, the concentration of industrial structures, and a massive proletariat. In short, in Bagnasco's view, Turin has redefined itself continually in terms of the events that have structured its contours, particularly the impact of the loss of the capital in 1864, early industrialization, and the massive immigration of southern workers to the automotive and related industries of the region. From the unification of Italy to the current traces of the unfolding of a postindustrial context, Turin has been in the center of both national and international processes. The city's concentration of a single grouping of industrial components focused around the auto industry has rendered it less able to confront the massive changes of its position in the world and national markets. Severe cyclical recessions and expansions of its economic realms have characterized its postwar history. Today, although the great working class of the past still exists in Turin, it is no longer working. Work has disappeared; only the shadow of work remains—that is, the large number of jobs for workers with little specialization has vanished. A new technocity is projected that will have no place for the worker of the past; anticipating this change, observers speak of the loss of social identity related to the loss of work (Michelsons 1986). These various worlds, so significant and central in the lives of the largely working-class population, are integral to an understanding of the context of the new immigration of Third World migrants into Turin. The context of work is, in a place like Turin, written into the cornerstone of every factory or construction site and embedded in the work practices and memories of its workers. The culture of work in Turin is like no other in Italy, and it has been partly responsible for Senegalese migrants' respect and honor in the work process.

Notwithstanding the complications of the "invidious distinctions" of race and national origin (Berreman 1976), the Senegalese worker enters a world of hard-won rights and privileges that are fundamental to the Italian labor context and highly important to a vast number of Turinese working-class people (*Rinascita* 1986). The hidden world of work has overwhelmingly defined the lives of Turinese, both new and recent arrivals, and the centrality of the worker in this process has given him or her a sense of pride and social prestige highly valued in a culture of work and a tradition of both Communist and Catholic trade unionism.

The importance of Turin in Italian society comes not only from its central role in the creation of the nation, as both the home of the influential aristocratic architects of the state and of the House of Savoy, but also from its postwar role in the industrial complex, which set Italy among the leading industrial powers in the world. This centrality has given rise to an important elaboration of a "working-class ideology" from the turn of the century, which has rendered Turin the quintessential worker's city (Adamson 1980). The great concentration of workers in Turin in the first decade after 1900 led Italian theorist Antonio Gramsci to think of the northern working class as a kind of "school of culture and socialist Propaganda." Gramsci promoted the idea of "worker councils" and "labor schools" to educate the workers on the "true" significance of being a "producer," laying the groundwork for an "emerging proletarian state which might replace the 'bourgeois' order" (Adamson 1980).

Home of one of the most powerful family-owned businesses in the country, the FIAT car-making firm, Turin became the heart of the continual exchange of political parties, trade unions, and the largest industrial proletariat in Europe. The Turinese working class represented the "capitalist dream" of the effective and obedient worker; its culture of work developed as did its attendant spur to the development of an arena of contestation, monitored by such organizations as the trade unions, the Communist Party, and the many Catholic worker organizations, which cast every aspect of FIAT under scrutiny. The centrality of the worker for the nation and the development of the workers' movement placed workers in a crucial position. Much of Italian sociology in the 1960s, when the discipline got its start in Italy, was industrial sociology, and much of this focused on FIAT; several leftist journals developed that were concerned with worker issues, notably, *Quaderni Rossi* and *Quaderni Piacentini* (Bagnasco et al. 1985). In short, work became the focus of projects for the reform of society, education, health, and urban social life—that is, "socialism with a human face" (Birnbaum 1986, 98). The massive migration of southern workers to the industrial North created a rift in the social landscape of the northern cities, which was deeply felt in the absence of infrastructural accommodation for the changes brought about in such a short time; housing shortages and the inadequacy of leisure facilities, educational centers, and health care provisions have plagued large Italian cities since the 1950s.

In the 1980s the threat of Japanese expansion into the automobile market called into question the recovery of this industry, and for the first time since the turn of the century a whole class was threatened with its disappearance. Turin's monoindustrial development placed the city in a precarious situation: if the locomotive of economic growth, FIAT, was in trouble, then the almost 90 percent of related industries were also in trouble. The movement toward a postindustrial world and robotics, the diminution of the working class through layoffs, and the loss of jobs through the internationalization of production were to leave a devastating impact on Turin and its environs.

Italy has, in the span of some thirty years, as Paolo Ceccarelli points out, undergone an extraordinary transformation from a largely poor agricultural country at the end of World War II to a postindustrial country (Ceccarelli, personal communication). While the infrastructure of its major cities were drawn into the rationalist patterns of a modernist industrial project, the most intimate centers of its urban worlds held closely to patterns of premodern sociality, friendship, and familial life. In many ways the large expansion of urban centers like Turin presented, from the perspective of certain sectors of the country, a bridge between rural poverty and relative urban prosperity. There are many small towns not only in the south of Italy, but in the surrounding territories of the large industrial centers where almost entire populations were transposed by the life of the factory. Francesco Rosi's film *Three Brothers* (1981) is a compelling dramatization of the death of an older classical vision of Italy in the rural world of the parents of three brothers, who embody the diverse and dynamic patterns of economic, political, and cultural dimensions tearing at the fabric of Italian society during the years of transition. One son is a factory worker in Turin taken up in the labor movement of the city and at once caught in a spiral of alienation from a rural past and an industrial future that seems both uncertain and wrought with conflicts; the second is a priest preoccupied with the vast sectors of impoverishment in southern Italy and the world and the progressive disenfranchisement of the world's poor; and, finally, the third brother is a judge involved in the trials of allegedly leftist terrorists in Rome and the uneasy relationship to order that the Italian republic has carried with it in postwar years. The visionary work of Rosi has posed the central problems of Italy's position in a postindustrial or postmodern world, or, rather, to use a different language, the film places four quite distinct problems before the viewer: (1) the death of a vision of a classical, idyllically rural world and its seemingly timeless values of continuity and stability; (2) the relationship of the Left to the process of capital accumulation and the various forms it takes (the labor movement in Italy became a platform for representing such issues as health, the disparity between the *Mezzogiorno* and the North, and basic work legislation and protections; the working class became a special-subject *portatore,* a carrier of other issues, including social alienation and environmental issues); (3) the restructuring of critical institutions, including the judiciary and the parliament, the massive state apparatus in banking, education, and state enterprise—in short, a definitive break both with "fascist legislative" remnants and with the structure of Christian Democratic politics that has controlled Italy since the end of the Second World War; and (4) an accounting of the responsibility of Italy in a new image, as a country that figures among the wealthy nations of the world (this also entails the question of the relationship of the Catholic world to the state and to the emergence of a consumer society with values competing with those promulgated in Catholic ideology).

The Social Economy of a Worker's City:
The School of the Working Class

The only way to save Turin, according to Arnaldo Bagnasco, is to liberate it: "One must not burn oneself with the game of the *La Longue Durée*."[1] It is no doubt necessary to change the extreme reliance on the monoindustrial base. The centrality of the worker to Turin and in fact to the self-conception of Italy is something that demands some comment. Workers, now mostly retired from the great factories of Pirelli and FIAT, give rise to a similarly imagined city of the past. The working-class employee of the great firms was crucial to a complex of social, economic, and political processes, and the worker was often conscious of this fact. Through the peculiar prominence of the Fordist firm in Turin and the historical development in factory centers of worker representation, initially through factory councils and later by means of external organizations, working-class members were often made aware of the highly politicized context in which work took place and its central role in the economic fortunes of the nation. This kind of worker centrality was underscored during Fascism (Passerini 1984).

The labor movement of Italy was in great measure centered on the large factories, particularly FIAT, and on the contracts for categories of workers that were fought out in these contexts. "If you wanted in those days to become a union leader or organizer you went to Turin. Turin became the school of the working class," according to Italian architect Paolo Ceccarelli (personal communication). Turin became in many ways a school for all Italian labor contracts of the large firms, setting precedents that affected workers all over the country for generations. From the *scala mobile* to the concessions of 150 hours of instruction for every worker in the area of his or her choice, the large firms set the tone of labor conflict from the 1960s through the 1980s. Of the many unskilled workers who came to Turin in the 1950s and 1960s, many came from artisanal workshop and peasant backgrounds. In their first encounter with the metropolis and its work regimes, these workers who had seen Turin as their "temporary refuge" in the industrial North were put off by the apparent exclusiveness of the trade unions, which held their meetings in the local Piedmontese dialect, often unintelligible to the newcomers. Soon, however, as hopes of returning home faded, the elements of the new work regime became all too obvious to the southern Italian migrants, and as Charles Sabel points out, their attention turned more toward changing the conditions of this temporary refuge:

> Peering as it were around the edges of their preconceptions, they slowly realized that economic circumstance was trapping them in the industrial cities. As their confidence in a speedy return home diminished, they started to ask pointed questions about the industrial society they had entered and its relationship to the more rural society they had abandoned. Unable to answer these questions themselves, they turned to ideologically sophisticated, left-wing Northern craftsmen for help. (Sabel 1985:17)

Death of a Fordist City

The echo of Sabel's analysis of the division of labor in Western industry now rings through the Turinese streets like a ghost; the Fordist city has now turned on its side and emptied out all the interchangeable workers it once needed. They form the lists of the unemployed or, worse, the world of the *economia sommersa*. Stable demand for large numbers of standard products is the cornerstone of Fordism (Sabel 1985, 195). Sabel recalls: "Many signs suggest that the Fordist model of organization is being challenged by new forms of the division of labor" (1985, 194). The international economic crisis between 1973 and 1983 marked the death knell for the Fordist industrial organization as it was constituted in the beginning of the postwar era (Balliano 1986). Although the process of restructuring the large firm carried its own costs and marked a decided investment in labor-saving technologies, transport, storage, and a renewed exposure to international market fluctuations, the brunt of the cost of the internationalization of production was paid for by the displacement of workers once central to the process of industrialization in Western democratic countries (Balliano 1986). The early strategies of design and the placement of plants in France, which was followed by Renault, resulted in a dispersed impact on local communities, while Turin with a monoindustrial base was placed in an inferior position socially and economically. In spite of massive layoffs of Turin workers placed in *casa integrazione* (a wage-supplement fund maintained by the government and the employer to pay a percentage of workers' wages during layoffs), plants did not for the most part close, and today Turin remains a center of industry complemented by the introduction of a rapidly growing sector of small soft-technology firms (Barkan 1984).

The close organization of postwar production was largely confined within national boundaries. In Italy, this process was hurt by the lack of innovation in the productive centers and little diversification of the product. While the saturation of domestic markets was continuing apace already in the 1960s, little had been done to transform the project as labor costs and loss of productive periods began to increase over the next years due to labor struggles, strikes, and contract negotiations. The periods between 1971 and 1975 and between 1976 and 1980 saw increases in investment of up to 70 percent in large European firms partly because of new technologies, new systems of production, and global restructuring of the industry. The impact of Japanese products led many European and American firms to search for greater flexibility. In 1970 the Japanese auto industry produced some 14 percent of the world share of the industry; by 1984 the figure was closer to 23 percent. The same products entered both European and American markets still geared to either domestic or export production with very different types of products (Balliano 1986).

In the 1970s the introduction of automation into large firms of the European auto industry had already begun in an effort to calm the "hot spot" of labor conflict and to "recover productivity"; the microprocessor and the low cost of automation along with interindustry international cooperative strategies began to displace more and more workers (Bianco 1986; Sabel 1985; Balliano 1986; Viano 1986). The relationship between nationalism, industry, and the identification of the worker with the labor process changed radically and definitively. Workers displaced from the great firms as in Turin felt themselves thrown off the great locomotive of the historic "economic miracle," the auto industry.

There are still *paesi* FIAT in southern Italy, small towns whose entire population either took the train north for Turin or were related to someone who had and remained home to participate on the other end of the industrial world through remittances or myths of its founder. Many workers returned to these small towns after the decline of industrial production; Turin no longer required armies of unskilled labor at the beginning of the 1980s (Lerner 1988). Some were able to build houses in the South from their earnings from both FIAT and second jobs of double work in the North; some were not so fortunate and retained the benefits of one primary income from the factory, which now is of little solace in retirement (Viano 1986). In the 1980s about two-thirds of Italian workers were members of trade unions and about half were already the second generation of working-class laborers (Viano 1986; Bonazzi 1990).

Work and Its Double

In many of Turin's quarters the rhythm of daily life still bends to the chime of the working world of FIAT or one of its related industrial centers. In the wake of the restructuring many feel they are survivors of the tumultuous years, keeping their politics out of the factory. As one worker at FIAT put it, "It's not good for them to know you are a Communist inside here." Yet in spite of the centrality of the worker in this industry and the at times pivotal role of the shop floor in national politics, it was never easy to just make a living at FIAT. Work at FIAT, in short, was never enough to get by in the consumer centers of the North. For this reason, many resorted to double work, or *doppio lavoro.* Workers could not live on the thousand one hundred lira or more they received per month, an income far more modest than that of office workers and others. After their turns at FIAT or other large firms, workers would shuttle to other jobs as masons or even to the fields of nearby towns to help in the harvest of tomatoes. The double job was often *in nero,* and this income, along with that of others in the same household, helped many workers realize the modest dreams of owning their own homes and gardens in retirement. In the Turinese labor market there has been little mobility. In Turin the categories of work for those who left their small towns, often recruited by local officials and agents of the large firms in the South, remained the same categories of work that they maintained years later. This rigidity of the labor market was in some sense compensated for through the practice of double work, according to the classic study of Luciano Gallino, *Il Lavoro e Il Suo Doppio* (Gallino 1982; 1985). This practice is widespread in large urban centers in Italy including Bari, Catania, Pisa, and Ancona. The participation in this system of largely industrial categories at Turin is, however, more pronounced (Scamuzzi 1985). Many of these second work contexts are now filled with foreign workers. The marginal and often off-the-books nature of this work has remained a part of the structure of labor in the Turin area for almost forty years.

The problem of double work, a national concern, is particularly important to the context of the foreign worker, the temporary worker, and the once-central industrial worker, whose work history spans the expansion of northern industry. I argue that the double work phenomenon not only applies to official and nonofficial work contexts but also the European national work context and the insertion of a multinational regime that incorporates nonnational employees into the margins of a work world. Although nonofficial, this type of work is a crucial part of the capitalist process in Western democratic societies today, as it has been during the whole of the postwar period. In this light we may see the European social formation as a system that developed in the broadest sense as an interlocking international system of commerce and trade, in which the exchange of various raw materials, labor, and other commodities has progressed for centuries. Thus, the relationships of European colonialism must be seen as part of a long-term connection between African and European contexts, one outcome of which in recent years has been the availability of African labor to European society.

The labor regimes, time schedules, and European consumer patterns that are residuals of colonial and neocolonial relations have been a part of the lives of many migrants long before they set foot on French, German, or Italian soil. Many Senegalese see themselves as French—not as French citizens but as part of a community whose cultural and social heritage is linked to that of the European context in France (Fanon 1963, 218). At the same time, many see Europeans as very similar in their relationship to Africa. It is often asked why Senegalese have come to Italy since it is not a former colonial power directly related to Senegal. Yet Italian design, construction, and other enterprises are third following only the business dealings of the United States and France throughout the African continent. And the separability of one European state system from the fortunes of others has been only a convenient device of historical analysis seen from the perspective of Europe. In short, West Africa has provided various forms of the commerce of goods, persons, and things—from slaves to peanut cash crops to, most recently, labor. While Europe, in myriad forms imagined and material, from the colonial arch to the paving of roads and laying of pipelines, in tonalities of world leadership and intervention, has attempted to dictate the character and trajectory of this relationship with an elusive continent, it has rarely known the singularly evocative Africa.

Although the migrant is often thought of as a transitory figure in the host country, a figure that had almost disappeared in contemporary Europe for a time (Castles 1986), he or she is in fact a participant in the social life and class structure of that host country (Castles and Kosack 1985). John Rex argues that the migrants from the Punjab or Jamaica in England are to be considered part of what he calls an "imperial system of class relations," which encompasses both the metropolitan and old colonial worlds. Workers are seen in his view to be moving within this total imperial system to a relatively privileged position in relation to the whole system of recent migrations to England (Rex 1986). In fact, the worker who arrived in Paris several years ago and worked for some time in France and who subsequently transferred to Italy, currently working in construction or another industry, is a participant in a total social formation whose boundaries are not easily defined by any particular national borders. The system must at least take in Europe as a social formation in its relationship with postcolonial Africa. The migrant participates in an international labor market and, what is equally important, in an international cultural interchange that is continuous—although much less tangible than the labor market—and ideologically very effective.

Proficiency in European languages and educational background have provided an introduction to the so-called West for some, while the practical observances of agricultural developments and economic crisis have merely expanded the notion of what work is. Migrations also occur across varying notions of time; the period of stay that seems excessive to a stable, urban sensibility is in fact not so for the migrant, who for a relatively short period helps to build a house in his town or contribute to the education of brothers or sisters. As is the case with migrants in other historical situations, many migrants think of Senegal or their country of origin as their primary residence and point of reference. What is not often considered is that the absence from Senegal may last for periods of up to two years without a return trip in the interim. Moreover, although the possibility of bringing family members to reside in Italy exists, it is a process that entails at best a year's wait for the arrival of the visa for those family members and a staggering quantity of paperwork. Many Senegalese migrants are married and have families in Senegal, and many have young children.[2]

The Fetishism of Working-Class Skill

The unskilled worker has often been viewed as just that, unskilled. From some perspectives the downgrading of the manual worker may be seen to be an integral part of the Fordist work regime, which has dominated Turinese work practices (Braverman 1974; Harvey 1990, 134). In Italy there is a pronounced stratum of artisans, many of whom participate in the context of industrial employment and the world of craft production simultaneously. Most workers considered in Fordist terms to be un-skilled are in fact only unskilled in one work context in which their par-ticular skill or trade has no outlet. There are many manners in which this dual skill capability has been utilized, and perhaps its best represen-tative was the Piedmontese peasant worker, whom southern immigrants called the *barotto* or in dialect *barot,* named after a brand of wood. This image of the Piedmontese peasant who mounted a bicycle in the early morning mist to ride several miles to the gates of the Fordist factory with the rigid mentality of the closed rural world and a disposition to hard work was typical of the early days of the factory city. Generally, the notion of the closed or reserved northerner and the open and warm-hearted southerner remains a part of contemporary folk ideology, and countless stories and jokes emphasize this point. The southerners were in turn called *napuli* and were seen as unruly foreign guests by their northern counterparts, although many came from a similar agricultural base and set foot in the city factory for the first time with an employ-ment slip for one of the FIAT factories or many of the feeder industries related to it. The trajectory of peasant cultivator to factory worker to tem-porary worker has been the work career shared by many; women often following a similar trajectory as peasant, factory worker, and domestic or other service worker. The contextual nature of skill is often not taken into consideration and is of great importance in the case of such foreign workers as the Senegalese, who indeed have work backgrounds similar to those of the FIAT workers of the 1950s and 1960s, the cultivator-trader-industrial worker of recent times.

Until quite recently Italy was largely an agricultural society. Even workers in industries such as FIAT maintain rural connections that have been a continuous part of the work experience in Italy. Senegalese work-ers have close relationships to the rural world in Senegal, and this has been modified to some extent by participation in trade and petty trade. For many of the Senegalese in Turin, mostly Mourid, the most signi-ficant category of work is that of trader or *commerçant;* although the workers may be involved in a host of other occupations, the central fea-ture of self-identification remains, for many, trade. The passage from the agricultural world of peanut production occurred recently through involvement in trade, which remains a pivotal skill enabling workers to move from poverty into more intermediate strata in Senegal. Many of the Senegalese in Turin come from a rural background and will cite their initial work as that of cultivator or peasant, although this often masks other skills such as welding, carpentry, and masonry, which they have often acquired either in Senegalese rural contexts or in urban settings through their travels. Where factory work has been the school of the Turinese working class, one might say that trade and travel have been the schools of the Senegalese. Senegalese attach a great deal of importance to the experience of travel and of work in a variety of work contexts. Many Senegalese enter the work world in Italy with years of work experience in Africa, Saudi Arabia, and other European countries; few are simply common laborers when they begin work in Europe, but like southern workers and northern peasants before them they are categorized as common laborers and relegated to this *masione* (job, task). There are, however, many Senegalese who have come to Italy for their first foreign experience outside of Senegal. These persons tend to be part of a network of kin already in Europe and may be helped into the labor market by those already present.[3]

The Senegalese have been integrated into many of the medium and small firms that in Turin offer the most stable employment in industry as welders, masons, and manual labor. These along with a few positions in large firms such as *verniciatura* (painting) at FIAT or jobs at small chemical plants represent the official world of Senegalese employment. The small firms and those large firms involved in hazardous employment have offered the most stable, long-term positions in the labor market for Senegalese: construction, transport, and light industry. Here the workers enter into the system of Italian labor legislation, benefits, and health care.

Claude Meillassoux has noted in the notion of a double labor market the subtle processes of discrimination that exclude the migrant from central or core work contexts; the worker is, according to Meillassoux, divided into two categories: the integrated worker migrant who is entitled to all benefits in the national context of work, and the worker who is seen partly to reproduce himself outside of the capitalist economy:

> The first major discrimination relies on the distinction between direct and indirect wages. Family allowances, unemployment benefits, costs resulting from illness or accidents at work, pensions are allocated in a

discriminatory way; various pretexts are given to refuse all or some of
them to those workers expected to maintain and reproduce themselves
wholly or in part outside the capitalist sector. (Meillassoux 1981, 120)

The reproduction of Senegalese workers is seen to exist in the form of
their return to Senegal and in their precarious identity, which relegates
to "nationality" the cost of reproduction while exploiting the labor
power of the migrants. In Italy such benefits as health care were system-
atically denied to those who were in fact eligible for them. In some cases
migrants were told that hospitals did not know how to treat blacks:
"What can we do for you here?" some were asked. Thus many rights
were in practice negated, creating a work context that was mediated by
race and by a preference for the national rather than the foreign worker
(Layton-Henry 1990). The whole notion of skill in this context is suspect and subject to the interpretations of various ideologies that transform its very significance:

> Various procedures are employed to reinforce, guide and facilitate the
> operation of the double labor market. In particular there is the culti-
> vation of racist and xenophobic prejudices among the population of
> the host countries. These prejudices class foreign workers as being a
> priori unskilled and result in their being arbitrarily directed into the
> most badly paid and least stable employment. Racism, xenophobia
> and other ideologies of discrimination are indeed vital to the opera-
> tion of the double labor market. (Meillassoux 1981, 121)[4]

Short-term contracts, such as those at FIAT for four months, were offered to many workers during 1990 and 1991. With the recession of these
years, however, large firms were forced to cut back on production, and
four-month contracts were not renewed. Yet this experience gave these
workers decided advantages in future labor contexts and access to benefits denied to many other workers. This also provided an opportunity, as
in many other official contexts, to join unions and participate in the culture of work that this membership provides.

The limited permission of stay in Italy, the *permesso di soggiorno*
granted under the Martelli Bill, was supposed to give the worker the
right of stay for two years. This period in many cases was really only one
year on the initial *permesso,* to be renewed often on the criteria of employment in the official sector. Thus for those workers in the shadow
economy, the *permesso* assured a limited stay and/or a clandestine existence—in any case, at no cost to the state. Meillassoux notes the similar-

ity of the work permit and its regulation of the labor market in South
Africa (with its now dismantled pass system) and France:

> Work-permits are granted only for limited periods and renewed only
> on specific conditions. The "pass" system once operating in South
> Africa, by which African workers are moved about as it suits their racist
> employers, is matched in France by the various permits (residence-
> permit, work-permit) which leave the immigrant worker vulnerable
> to the hazards of police, administrative and employer control and
> make it easier to fix their length of stay in accordance with the needs
> of economy. (Meillassoux 1981, 122)

Although Meillassoux tends to cast capitalist ideology in altogether too
classically nineteenth-century tones, noting the "barbarism of absolute
'profitability'" as the "last stages of the metamorphosis of human beings
into capital," his analysis of the creation of the marginal world of work
(which encircles the migrant placed in a contemporary context where
the "domestic" becomes a transnational issue, not a relic of "tradition")
seems to highlight some useful conceptions.

In spite of the heterogeneity of skill among the Senegalese community, as for the peasant Piedmontese and the southern Italian before it,
many have been categorized in official documents as unskilled or generic
workers. Changing this classification is simple enough. In Italy one may
go to the proper office and perform the task—let us say, welding—and
the official will list on the worker's *libretto di lavoro* the proper grade of
work of which the worker is capable. This is true for masonry and some
other skills; others must be learned in the process of a *formazione,* a
training and apprenticeship program that may occur either on the job
or in the firm. Some Senegalese have enlisted in this type of program,
usually designed in Italy for young people entering the labor market and
financed with special funds set aside for youth. Some of the legislation governing immigration allowed immigrants access to many training courses. One Senegalese mason named Amadou complained to me
one day:

> Do you see any Africans on the lists of tradesmen? No, they are tied
> to this *commercio.* They don't understand—the young people—that
> here you are nothing without a trade. I have worked in Germany, in
> Libya, and all over. I went to the union. . . . I had been working as
> a *lavoratore commune.* I am a mason of the third grade, and my boss
> was forced to pay me back pay up to my grade. Look at the Africans

here: they are all listed as "common workers." That's all they do. I went
to the *collocamento* and asked them to change my *libretto* because it
said "common worker." I had to get upset up there at the window,
and others came over to find out what the problem was. . . . I said, "I
am a mason of the third level. Do you think that because I'm African
I can't have this changed? . . ." And afterward all the other Africans in
line wanted their *libretto* changed as well.

The lack of knowledge of work practices and labor laws often keeps
many migrants from challenging unfair labor practices, yet the wide
experience of some workers like Amadou seems to drive them to utilize
worker organizations to their own benefit. At large firms such as FIAT
unskilled workers still make up about 60 percent of the workforce.
Second- and third-level workers, usually the young and those coming
directly out of the various government-financed training programs,
constitute the next largest portion of the workforce. The actual skilled
worker of the fifth degree is part of a relatively small portion, or 20 to 30
percent of the work population. The manual or first-level worker is said
to be able to learn his or her task in a week, while the periods of preparation for other levels run from weeks to years.

This fetishism of the skill level has, however, masked the great disparity between workers' levels of income and social and cultural integration. The work of trade unions, which tended to treat workers of the
same category as equal, never touched this significant region of utter inequality. While the established worker in industry is able to exploit double work, much of this world rests on introductions and recommendations for entrance. Often, the second job context has been familial or
recruited along familial lines. Small family business and illegal work
done for family members are some of the most common forms of second work. The closure of this world of work to those outside of familial
networks is relative to the social and cultural life of the urban environment, from which many Italian internal migrants of the past were excluded. This makes the entrance into this world of work even more difficult for many Third World migrants.

For some workers the factory stipend has never been enough, and
those who have few other resources have increased the numbers of the
urban poor. Many Italian working people receive some sort of government subsidy, either for housing, travel, or other services. It is a small
wonder that, as Ceccarelli puts it, "Italy's self-conception hasn't changed[:]
many people think of Italy as still a poor country. . . . This makes it dif-

ficult for many to see the responsibility of Italy towards the immigrants as that of one of the wealthy nations toward those less wealthy" (Ceccarelli 1978). For the less stable sectors of the working class, the southern migrant working class that moved more slowly to the privilege of skill than local counterparts and had no firm base in the region, the process of proletarianization has left no clear future. Some could not become entrepreneurs overnight, as the demise of Fordism seems to demand. Today, in the shadow of work those without the skills for the new technocity, with its promise of economic flexibility rising up in the place of the old industrial world, have their gaze fixed on, and are still attached to, a now invisible world of production that exists largely in collective memory and in the urban voids left by the closure of large plants like FIAT Lingotto, monuments to its passage.

The Question of Modernity

> Italy's main cultural export . . . is itself.
> —Geoffrey Nowell-Smith,
> "Italy: Tradition, Backwardness
> and Modernity"

> Use never does anything but shelter meaning.
> —Roland Barthes,
> *The Eiffel Tower and Other Mythologies*

One of the questions that sociologists like Bagnasco address about the urban structure of Turin is the presence of premodern elements linked to an Italian background of agricultural production and family structures (Bagnasco 1988). In the distance from its present-day prosperity to the postwar years, Italy has become one the world's leading economies. Inside the homes and lives of the residents of Turin, however, commentators are often perplexed to find that in spite of a marked commercialization of the social world, inhabitants stay within a fairly clearly demarcated "domestic-centered" world (Bagnasco 1988). In spite of the presence of exclusive shops and aristocratic clubs, Turin has remained a quiet Italian company town, which does not display the sophistication of Rome or the dominance of a middle stratum as in the social and cultural world of Milan. Perhaps the routinization of the factory life and the monuments built to emphasize its prominence in the city such as the Lingotto factory (which now stands as an urban void largely unused and which the Piedmontese partisan Piero Gobetti once called the "temple of a new religion") have not stilled, in the lives of the residents, the pulse of patterns that do not follow the expectations of economic rationality. Notions of Italy's tradition, backwardness, and modernity—to borrow from the title of a work by Geoffrey Nowell-Smith—are entangled in the many Italies that offer themselves to the imagination. There are, of course, many Italies in the sociological literature, most notably the three—North, Central, and South—that Bagnasco and other sociologists take for granted (Bagnasco 1977). There is the classical image of northern and southern Italy noted in terms of cuisine, linguistic differences, and historical divergence. The Italy of Italian cinema balanced between the neorealism of the postwar years (Grundle 1990), in which the working classes were cast in a bitter struggle with the many problems of reconstruction, poverty, and the legacy of fascism, and the seemingly changeless world of one of the great comic actors of film, Totò (Nowell-Smith 1990). Catholics strongly opposed the neorealist portrayal of Italy's harsh side in such films as *Roma città aperta* (Rome open city), *Ladri di biciclette* (Bicycle thieves), and *Sciuscià* (Shoeshine). These films gave a "newsreel flavor" to representation meant to counter the "escapism of fascist cinema" and were banned from local parishes (Grundle 1990; Dalle Vacche 1992, 136–37). Yet whether they are found in the data of the world of social science or the darkened hall of the cinema, portrayals of a world of backwardness, poverty, and neglect have been a continuous theme in representations of Italy throughout the postwar years. As Nowell-Smith points out, the image of cultural backwardness has its origin in romanticism:

> The northern view of Italy has its roots in English and German romanticism and sees it as a country of deep and continuous cultural traditions, cultivated (cultivated people, cultivated landscape), slightly corrupt (sexually, politically); also as in some respects primitive, innocent, picturesque in its poverty. Within this view, or views, there are already contradictions, but what is consistent is the representation of Italy as non-modern, or pre-modern, a condition alleviated only by the existence of a few modern emblems such as Ferraris and Benetton. (Nowell-Smith 1990, 50)

While premodern Italy is one of Italy's greatest exports along with its jewelry and the vast world of tourism (which brings countless visitors each year to immerse themselves in Quattrocento painting or the tombs of Santa Croce in Florence), there is indeed another world, a high-tech world of robotics and software companies and the family-owned multi-national world of industry. The world of cultural heritage is the world many think of in relation to Italy, however, as they make the summer pilgrimage to the site of tourist consumption in search of the treasures of medieval Europe, the home of Western humanist traditions. Yet this world of tourism at times clashes with the world of immigrant labor. For example, one of the great battles with Senegalese and other migrants was waged in an attempt to clear the historic center of Florence of the Sene-galese traders, who, it was feared, might offend visitors to the city—those who came, like Stendhal, to view the "Home of Dante" and Santa Croce, the emblem of "national" Italian figures:

> "Behold the home of Dante, of Michelangelo, of Leonardo da Vinci," I mused within my heart. "Behold then this noble city, the Queen of medieval Europe! Here within these walls, the civilization of mankind was born anew; here it was that Lorenzo de' Medici so brilliantly sus-tained the part of Kingship, and established a Court at which, for the first time since the reign of Augustus, military prowess was reduced to a secondary role."

> Within, upon the right of the doorway, rises the tomb of Michelan-gelo; beyond lo! there stands Canova's effigy of Alfieri; I needed no *cicerone* to recognize the features of the great Italian writer. Further still, I discovered the tomb of Machiavelli; while facing Machiavelli lies Galileo. What a race of men! The tide of emotion which over-whelmed me flowed so deep that it scarce was to be distinguished from religious awe. The mystic dimness which filled the church, its plain, timbered roof, its unfinished facade—all these things spoke volumes to my soul. (Stendhal [1826] 1959)[5]

The world of Stendhal's utopian Italy and the religious awe inspired by the cultural ruins of past centuries are what the new traveler-consumer arrives on Italian soil each year to find. The trouble in Florence with the Senegalese migrants and the war in the Persian Gulf, however, hurt the tourist trade badly in the initial periods of that particular season.

The recent labor process in capitalist democratic societies has been transformed by present-day conditions of economic instability. The re-gional North-South disparity has been a persistent feature of Italian post-World War II industrial expansion through continued development of the industrial North and uneven, slow, and often nonexistent growth in southern regions. Massive internal migrations from the South have dramatically affected the composition and texture of northern Italian social life. In this process more than half a million migrants found their way to Turin alone, which now contains one of the largest southern populations of any Italian city north of Naples and Palermo.

The unfortunate convergence of Third World migrants such as the Senegalese in times of economic insecurity has only served to augment tensions in metropolitan, urban Italian centers like Rome, Milan, and Turin, which are plagued by high rates of unemployment, especially among young people seeking to enter the job market for the first time. It must be noted that incidents of intolerance toward Third World migrants are also reported in rural areas, particularly around Naples. However severe the instability of central capitalist economies such as those of the seven major industrial powers of Europe and the United States, this instability pales in comparison to other state systems of the world market, which are relegated to positions far less advantageous than those held by the great economic powers. Keith Hart has referred to this as the main "class opposition" in the contemporary world, that between rich and poor nations. Writing in 1982, Hart noted that the widening "productivity gap" between the northern and southern nations was placing West African nations in a situation of perpetual disadvantage: "Fundamental change in this global class structure can take place only through a combination of rapid increases in Third World productivity and massive transfers from the rich countries" (1982). The question of equity between rich and poor nations is fundamental to the understanding of the current transfer of labor in the form of the many diaspora populations, who, voting with their feet, move within a global system that has been in place since the first European incursions in African trade markets. As Hart notes, the growing economic inequality is the core of global interstate system patterns:

> Global industrialization has generated both a widening productivity gap between north and south and a net transfer of resources in the former's favor. The result is that differences between these groups of nations are overwhelmingly more significant than inequalities within any one state. (Hart 1982, 137)

More than a decade after Hart made this observation the prolonged impact of drought and depressed world-market pricing in core agricultural and other products has even further accentuated this distance between rich and poor nations. Moreover, the breakup of the former Soviet bloc nations has created the unsettling possibility of the massive transfer of Eastern European populations and/or the massive investment into Eastern economies of many nations, as in the case of Albania. The situation in West Africa is such that the overexploitation of the labor power of countless migrants takes place in the context of an international labor market in which the reconstitution of this labor power is absorbed completely by poor nations such as Senegal and in which the inequality of pension programs, health care costs, training, and low wages represents net savings to the international employer.

In Italy, the major portion of the immigrant workforce was assumed under special contracts in the official labor market, which in effect limit the nature of the migrants' possibility of becoming in any sense the charge of the employer. The special contract in Italy favors the Italian national who may have rights to health care, pension, and other privileges that derive from work contexts. The migrant, restricted to the special contract, works for periods stipulated by the terms of the contract and does not usually attain the privileges accorded national workers of the same category. When the contract expires, the migrant is eligible for no unemployment benefits and may be further subject to expulsion from the national territory, for employment is a criterion for the migrant's presence. The situation of the labor reserve, which Claude Meillassoux described for "thousands of workers" who moved "permanently between the reserves and the mining and industrial areas," in fact occurs across ever-widening areas because no area remains untouched by capitalist accumulation or by the extension of a global economic context. A growing number have, in short, "nothing else to sell but their labor-power" (Meillassoux 1981). And yet their situation is due not only to the inequitable economic balance but also to the fact that after having been drawn into global and neocolonial relations, inhabitants have been infused with significant cultural influences and international styles. It is not only the creeping poverty of rural life that drives peasants out of the village, as Meillassoux maintains, but also the fact that the "natural reserve" of labor power is also a reserve of consumers. Through the constant "advertising" of capitalist society one may buy Italian shoes in Dakar (at five times the original cost in Italy) or any of a host of consumer goods from European countries (Meillassoux 1981).

The proletarianization of West African migrants like the Senegalese must be seen in the context of a vast transnational system and in the conditions of the diaspora of these workers, which has created in many contexts a natural reserve of labor that remains subordinated to national working classes, and which, through the complication of other distinctions such as race, carries an additional stigma. The absence in many contexts of antiracist tenets in legislation further impedes the incorporation of workers into the European social formation.

There is in fact in West Africa a marked rural exodus, once formerly linked to "periodic or circulatory migrations" to cities, constituting a kind of "floating population," as Michael Watts has called it within these urban centers (in Pred and Watts 1992, 40–41). The 1960s and 1970s marked the emergence of long-term emigration characterized by a great flexibility across and between diverse localities and labor contexts, as with the Mourid trading diaspora. The workers are not moving into a dynamic capitalist sector in Europe but, rather, to one that is shifting into a mode of flexible accumulation and downsizing its concentration of Fordist methods of labor organization. Thus workers are flowing toward diminishing, not expanding, labor markets, as in the case of Turin and northern Italy. The natural reserve of labor may in fact only be maintained if the migrant worker does not achieve full parity with national workers, and this is largely an issue of the access of the first generation to the benefits of the welfare provisions of the host society inasmuch as these provisions figure in the reproduction of the labor force in second and subsequent generations. I would argue that the reserve is a juridical closure of the migrant in a grid of cultural, legal, and social encumbrances that inhibit the migrants' negotiation of temporary migrant status into a long-term legal status, ensuring that the migrant does not become a subproletariat—that is, someone excluded from the national market and forced to work in the shadow world of "submerged economies" (Meillassoux 1981, 110–35).

Senegalese migrants, largely Mourid, belong to an Islamic Brotherhood that was taking shape even before the French embarked on their first colonial expeditions. The contours of the Senegalese world of agricultural production are most similar to the large estates of the South of Italy, the *latifundia,* remnants of Roman land disposition and sites of the impoverishment of a peasantry that saw its heroes in the brigands who defied an emergent state. In Senegal, the Senegalese Brotherhoods (the Mourid of Cheikh Amadu Bamba, in particular) became rallying points for the opposition to French incursion. To the West the practices of such groups as the Mourid have for centuries seemed mysterious and pre-modern; the brotherhoods have presented themselves as one of the fea-tures of a postmodern world in the streets of New York, Paris, Rome, and Tokyo as traders and in the small businesses of these and other cen-ters as workers and tradespersons. Like the Sanusi of the Cyrenaica whom E. E. Evans-Pritchard wrote of in 1949, the Mourid have shown themselves to be resilient and innovative in the context of a new inter-national market trend (Evans-Pritchard 1949). The Sanusi, who adapted their own structure interstitially to that of the surrounding tribal groups and established their Sufi lodges along major trade routes or *caravansérai*, in places outside of the structure of power, gave themselves a privileged position from which to build their own power base.

The Mourid in the early nineteenth century existed on the borders of the Wolof states, teaching the Koran to the royals and acting as their intermediaries with certain unseen forces through the making of gris-gris. The Mourid managed a position between the traditional power of the Wolof state and the emergent colonial power of the French, eventu-ally incorporating the lower orders of Wolof society and its rigid hierar-chy and adopting groundnut production from the French. Although the Mourid are still the most powerful political *tariqa* (the way or path, in Islam) or Sufi order in Senegal, the economic fortunes of the slump of the peanut market have shown up all the disadvantages of a one-crop economy. Like the auto industry in Europe and America, the produc-tion of the groundnut has been devastated by world market competition and by unfavorable innovation and diversification in the national econ-omy. The Mourid confraternity, however, is not a business but a mis-sion, and its move to a flexible form of accumulation is signaled by the migration of many would-be cultivators to Europe as masons and weld-ers. Their primary self-identification, however, remains with the order and with a community of faith that expanded rapidly in Senegal toward the end of the nineteenth century.

While the economy has been apparently detached from the concep-tions of progress in Western Democratic countries with the pronounce-ment of such words as *postindustrial* and *postmodern*, to the Mourid, whose founder's most characteristic statement of the early order was "go and work," this new restructuring of Western economies has merely brought about a change in locality and gravity of national economic cir-cumstances. While Italians often see the arrival of African migrants as a disjunction with the past, from the migrants' perspective their experience is a continuation of relations of colonialism and neocolonial situations. As one migrant put it, "There has been a lot of talk of the colonialization of Africa. . . . now we have come to colonize it over here, and they don't like that." The Mourid, armed with the photograph of Cheikh Amadu Bamba and riding on the tram toward a small industrial job on the outskirts of Turin, is the most recent manifestation of a transnational world that can no longer be conceived of merely in terms of "national" boundaries and the movement of raw materials toward industrial Europe (*Time* 1990).

The Hidden World of Work: Work and Lavoro Nero

In Italy by the end of the nineteenth century, the largest category of workers was the *braccianti,* the day agricultural laborers, *disobbligati* or *avventizi,* who were under no direct or regular relationship to an employer (Kertzer 1984). They were forced to take whatever type of employment presented itself, agricultural or other. Wages for the *braccianti* were very low; employment from day to day was erratic and unpredictable. The Senegalese and other migrants appear somewhat analogous to the *braccianti.* Today, that most precarious worker in Italy is the foreign worker, and although residents of Turin will say that the market of day labor is gone (*il mercato delle braccie,* a market that once existed for southern Italian migrants on the corners of the *Piazza della Repubblica* in the *Porta Palazzo* area of the city), it still exists for those without steady employment. During the first few months of 1990 the employment possibilities of foreign workers in Turin were particularly serious; it was during this period that the market of day labor was most pronounced, and this meant nonofficial, off-the-books work.

Before we proceed, it will be necessary to give a brief outline of the Turin labor market, the structure of which is largely determined by the dominance of large firms. There is, however, a marginal world of *lavoro nero,* an off-the-books shadow work world, in which a substantial portion of the population is employed in construction, transport, and some services. Much of the double work is done in this sector of the economy by workers who either work at *official* industrial jobs or by those retired workers who can earn, in this way, an additional unregistered income. It is important to note that in Italy health benefits and insurance once derived from the work context. A worker who has worked for one day or even one hour and who has been assumed in the manner stipulated by Italian work legislation is entitled to health benefits, accident insurance, and pension benefits should this work result in the permanent disability of the worker. The official worker also contributes through payments taken directly from his or her stipend to housing benefits subsidized by the government. The foreign worker is entitled by law to the same benefits as the Italian worker in the official context; in practice, however, this is not always the case. The worker *in nero* is entitled to no benefit package.

During the late 1980s in the early morning hours before the mist of the Po and Dora had cleared from the streets in Turin and when the road to Milan was immersed in a thick fog bank, potential employers could be seen making the rounds to houses of Senegalese and other migrants. Sometimes as early as four or five in the morning the cars pulled up and loaded the Senegalese day workers, who, unable to find other employment and frustrated with the slowness of the municipal employment office, went off to the nonofficial work world. This situation did not last long, however, and Senegalese soon preferred to wait for the official list of job offerings. The jobs offered on the *lavoro nero* market for many of the workers are often construction in private residences in which Senegalese work with their *padrone* and one other worker in a small job that requires several days to complete. Other offerings include construction work for masons and skilled jobs carried out by manual labor workers without the proper compensation of the correlating work classification or specialization in the official work world. Senegalese, often unfamiliar with work legislation, would perform such work as welding while their work classification and pay scale matched those of the generic manual laborer; this situation might persist until the worker had an accident that had to be reported immediately to the proper authorities. Then the worker would have to claim that he was in fact not welding but performing some other task when injured. This, although a very serious case for the worker and an incident of fiscal and legal transgression, is not a case of *lavoro nero* proper, in that the worker is official and therefore entitled to certain benefits. Yet in the complex structure of the labor market in Turin, a place where in medium and small industry historically there has been very little *lavoro nero* practiced, it represents a dangerous slippage into a less formal and more marginal realm of labor exploitation.

Senegalese were often confined to their homes as they waited for the call of the employer in the morning until they had obtained the *permesso di soggiorno,* which would allow them to receive the *libretto di lavoro* and to apply for a job on the official work market. From the houses of the Senegalese in the mornings, the first waves of workers would leave as day laborers, while others prepared to set up in the streets of Turin to sell *roba Africana,* African stuff. In the face of pressure from authorities to get the sellers off the streets, more and more Senegalese were entering the world of *lavoro nero* and leaving the streets where they had set up stalls on small pieces of carpet. A considerable reaction against the street sellers was complicated by their presence for some time and by their great diversity.

The Senegalese traders or sellers are divided into many categories. There are those who define themselves as *commerçant* and who enter this occupation as their line of work on all official documents, and then there are a number of young people who sell as a transitional activity until something else comes along. There are artisans such as the Laube woodworkers who sell their own wares; the Laube sell small articles of African art that they prepare for sale in their rooms and houses. The categories of articles sold are also very diverse: the more traditional articles, *roba Africana;* African jewelry in leather and other materials; the articles of wooden sculpture of the Laube woodworker; small elephants and other animals; ships and statuettes of Peul women; and other articles. Many also sell African clothing, leather bags, masks, and often families of wooden animals. Master woodworkers often finish the materials they receive from Senegal via Rome or Marseilles and sell them to younger traders who do the actual selling in the street. The activity of finishing and preparing the articles for sale gives some woodworkers little time to sell as much as others. They often sell late into the night near the Porta Nuova train station on the last bit of the promenade of the Via Roma.

Work and Language Mastery

The world of *lavoro nero* is where the Senegalese and other foreign workers converge with former central Italian workers who have retired from large firms or are taking on a second job. The social life of the firm *in nero* has its own quality. Often, the Italian workers speak their own dialects, and formal Italian is only spoken by those in the offices; the heterogeneity of language usage is nothing new and did not begin with the arrival of the Third World worker but has been a continuous feature of the Italian workplace. One Senegalese mason complained about the difficulty of learning Italian on the job.

The problem of the heterogeneity of language practice is of course nothing new to the Senegalese, who have, since the end of the eighteenth and beginning of the nineteenth century, experienced a pronounced cultural and linguistic "Wolofization." The cultural influence of the Wolof is widely diffused through Senegal, and Wolof has become the mass language of two-thirds of the country (Diarra and Fougeyrollas 1974). The Wolof, according to Agnes Fatoumata Diarra and Pierre Fougeyrollas, tend to conflate nationality with Wolof ethnicity and thus "think themselves more fundamentally Senegalese" than others:

> Wolof, like other ethnic groups, generally have a high opinion of themselves. They consider that they are intelligent and have a great talent for social adjustment, and above all that modern Senegal is mainly of their making. They further claim to be good Moslems.
> (1974, 17)

In Turin the work context is one of the points of major association with Italians. For many migrants it is the main situation in which language skills and information about the host society are transmitted. One of the difficulties for many migrants is the use of dialect in many of the work situations. Migrants find themselves faced with the great variety of nonstandard Italian dialects of, among others, Calabria, Sicily, and Piedmont. In short, the language that many migrants learn at work is not easily translated into a standard Italian that might be used in offices or to communicate with great facility in other contexts. The migrant worker is often restricted in his or her ability to attend language instruction by the rhythm of the workday. For many migrants in Turin, for instance, the lack of housing forces many to live a great distance from the workplace. The workday then begins very early in the morning and ends quite late at night, effectively prohibiting such activities as language classes. Since the linguistic distinction is such an important indicator in Italy of status and social class, in popular ideology the migrant takes on this extra stigma in addition to those already present merely because of the fact that the migrant is foreign. The subtle forms of discrimination that the southern Italian migrants and those associated with them underwent are an important part of local folk tradition and history. Children of migrants often consider themselves "southern," although born and educated in Turin. For instance, many speak local dialects of their home-towns or families but do not teach these dialects to their children, in-stead placing a great stress on speaking proper Italian. The contempo-rary migrant, however, is faced with yet another difficulty—that of the conception of race, an "invidious distinction" assumed in commonsense notions to be fundamental and innate (Berreman 1976). Although much of the social separation and exclusion of the foreigner seems to derive from a certain process of closure in Italian society to the foreigner or even the *forestiero* (an Italian from another town), the addition of a racial di-mension complicates the issue of exclusion even further (Portelli 1989).[6]

It is often in the workplace that the migrant encounters for the first time the many commonsense and taken-for-granted conceptions of Italian society, conceptions that indicate the natural way to be and do things (Gramsci 1971). One of the significant signs of Italian society along with those of dress and manners is language use and mastery; sig-nificant Italian regional linguistic distinctions make the judgment and classification of language mastery particularly important. The distinc-tions are marked in that some accents and dialects are more prestigious than others, and the mastery of standard Italian is preferred over the use of dialect in many social contexts. Although dialect may be used to as-sert adherence to a certain group or region, the use of Italian in formal situations is preferred. The dialects are not derivatives of standard Italian but are really separate languages, such as Piedmontese, with their own histories and integrity. Thus, the dialect speaker is not speaking Italian poorly but, rather, not at all. Of course, there have been many words and expressions imported into dialect and dialectical components im-ported into Italian, yet this has little changed the difficulty.

There is another feature of the problem: many Italians normally speak dialect, and the relatively low rate of literacy among an older gen-eration in Italy has confined many aged Italians to an arch of dialect speakers. In 1860 between 2.5 to 10 percent of the Italian population were capable of using the national language. There has been a great deal of controversy about the impact of television on the language, the lan-guage of television personalities being defined as a poor, "medium Ital-ian." Giulio Lepschy has argued that rather than look at the loss of lan-guage through television, dailies, and weeklies, we may consider this the growth of Italian (Lepschy 1990). It is interesting that in many contexts television is considered a primary vehicle for the acquisition of language, and although Italy has a multichannel television system unparalleled in

Europe, the language of the television is still considered poor and unsophisticated (Nowell-Smith 1990). Lepschy comments on this loss that has become a popular ideology about the language:

> There seems to be a widely shared opinion which is vocally aired in dailies, weeklies, and inspires countless volumes, large and small, devoted to castigating the decay of the language. People don't know Italian any more [*sic*], is the general complaint. This is interesting, if we consider that . . . exactly the opposite is true: that is, people are in fact just beginning to know Italian a little more than in the past. (Lepschy 1990, 67)

There is, in fact, a wide range of varieties of Italian. The concept of popular Italian has been used to designate an Italian created by the masses in the years of the First World War. This concept was introduced by the Italian linguist T. De Mauro in the 1970s to account for the social, economic, and cultural achievements of the Italian working class (Lepschy 1990). Regional and national languages provide other levels of diversity resting on the base of "local" dialect. These features comprise the basic elements that are augmented by the relative education and social background of the speaker. The distance between the formal written and the informal colloquial in Italian remains rather great; the notion of "medium-usage Italian" is somewhat related to this distance. The formal written-based spoken language is what we might call standard Italian, and yet there is another ordinary everyday Italian that is an "educated" Italian, although much less formal than the standard. This whole range seems to me to incorporate a great deal of the ideology about the respective levels of the cultivated and the masses with a very unsatisfactory language mastery. Some of the features used to distinguish this middle level are often merely regional and class-based biases of the linguist (Lepschy 1990). In the commonsense world of the middle strata in Turin, many of the features of language are used to distinguish the middle strata's own world from that of the vast working-class world around them. Their children are carefully taught to speak a proper Italian, and a great deal of emphasis is placed on the "proper" execution of grammatical forms, the minimization of slang, and the acquisition of a second language, often now English.

In this manner migrants who approach the preferred mastery of Italian are classified in a way that is different from that used to classify those with a poor command of the language. A familiarization with lit-

erate practices considerably enhances the prestige of the migrant and increases his or her social possibilities within Italian society (Bourdieu and
Passerson 1977). The migrant with greater language mastery has greater
access to all dimensions of Italian society, and the interlocutors of the
migrant with a high language proficiency tend to be those Italians with a
high mastery of their own language and culture. For those newcomers to
Italy who perform labor requiring little conformity to verbal standards
that range beyond the most practical language mastery, the social world
appears very different. The search for the proper interlocutor becomes
much more difficult for those with limited skills and knowledge (Bourdieu and Passerson 1977). The migrant may be classified according to
the subtle criteria of grammar, tone, accent, and delivery, which are the
established order in Italian society (Bourdieu and Passerson 1977). The
newcomers are then forced into the channels of gestural dispositions
and traditions that lack the social prestige of verbal mastery.[7]

3
Mouridism Touba Turin

When you die you are reborn in Touba.
—Senegalese migrant

Invisible Cities: Touba Turin

Just as the images and memories of Turin pervade the daily experience of its inhabitants, so the contours of the holy city of Touba figure prominently in the lives of Senegalese migrants (see fig. 2). Touba (finest or sweetest) is re-created in the routine activities of the migrants and through recurrent parallels of the migrants' lives with that of the founder of the order, Cheikh Amadu Bamba (Ebin 1996, 99). The vacant factories and railroad yards of Turin stand as monuments to a now distant rhythm of work and society, while the suitcases of the migrant are monuments to the world of agriculture and groundnut production, from which diverse Senegalese derive a certain self-definition and experience. Many call themselves *commerçants;* prior to this, many said, "I was a cultivator." Yet the identification with Touba goes even further, and for its importance we must look at the bridge between the contemporary order, its formation, and expansion in the face of a mediating of colonial and precolonial power relations. The black nylon bags of the Senegalese street seller in Turin, New York, or Paris, however, link the migrant in a complex Mourid cosmology in which travel, work, and the extension of a

community of faith encompass the daily activities of the migrant in an
arch that collapses all spaces into Touba, the heart of the order.

Senegalese Islamization, Mouridization, and Wolofization

In Senegal 90 percent of the population is Muslim, many belonging to
one of the Sufi orders. The major Senegalese Muslim Brotherhoods, the
Mourid, Tidjan,[1] and Quadriyya were introduced into Senegal from the
powerful North African confraternities of the late eighteenth and early
nineteenth centuries. Some of the characteristic features of these mystical orders were already prefigured in the brotherhoods of the Maghreb.
Such notions as a hereditary succession to the leadership of the order,
the head of the order being a Khalifa, and the hierarchical structure that
allowed the leaders of the brotherhood to act as intermediaries between
man and God for the great masses of the followers were already well
developed in the North African brotherhoods.[2]

It is not altogether clear just when the Wolof first came under the
influence of Muslim ideology, yet as early as 1455, the Alvise de Ca' da
Mosta observed Walo Muslim priests called Marabouts both at the court
of the Wolof king and in the countryside (Behrman 1969). The Islamization of Wolof society in the late eighteenth and nineteenth centuries
was to have a profound impact on the development of contemporary
Senegal. This Islamization was to a large extent the conversion of much
of Wolof society to Mouridism, the order founded by Cheikh Amadou
Bamba (1850–1927).[3] The Cheikh was exiled by the French, first to Gabon
(1895–1902), and then to Mauritania (1903–1912). The French feared his
alliances with resistance leaders. The popularity of the brotherhood
increased greatly after Cheikh Amadou Bamba's exile by the French, and
the Mourid became a kind of symbol of colonial resistance. The French
were later to favor the brotherhood.

The Mourid organized their followers into tight-knit production
units that worked the lands of the order under the direction of the
Marabout; the workers then gave a portion of the product of their labor
to the brotherhood (Behrman 1970). The organization of this type of
work group predates the foundation of the order. Communities of
Marabout who lived in the Wolof kingdoms prior to Islamization were
supported in part by the work of their talibés, or followers. This organization became for the Mourid, however, a crucial part of the structure of

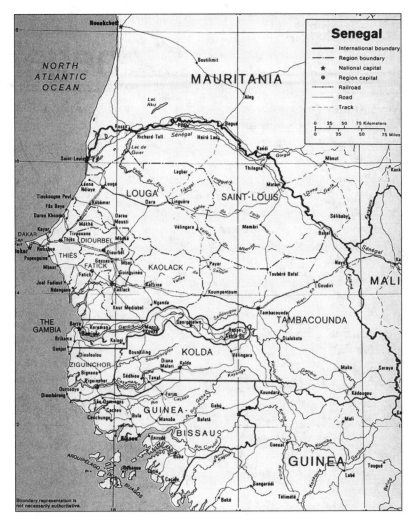

Fig. 2. Touba is located slightly to the northeast of Mbacké. (Washington, D.C.: U.S. Department of State Publication 7820, 1991)

the order by which they were able to incorporate lower strata of Wolof society into the relative democracy of the order (Cruise O'Brien 1975). This helped to develop a system of production that came to dominate the commercial production of groundnuts in Senegal (Hart 1982).

The production of the groundnut, which had been introduced by the French in the nineteenth century, in fact came to dominate the Senegalese economy. The considerable representation of the Mourid among the cash-crop producers of the country, including both rural Serer and Wolof, gives the order a great deal of influence in dealings with the state. The Khalifate, or head of the brotherhood, in effect can act as the intermediary between the government and these many producers. However, the lack of crop diversification coupled with crop failures and prolonged drought in much of the Sahel region may have encouraged both some migrations from the agricultural world toward the large cities as well as some attempts by producers to shift to the production of other crops in some areas (Cruise O'Brien 1979).

This concentration on groundnut production, however, rendered the entire national economy into "one compartment of the world economy," as Keith Hart notes in his analysis of West African agriculture (Hart 1982). With the French withdrawal of the preferred trading status from Senegal in the 1960s, the national economy was thrown into a downward spiral from which it has never really recovered. The difficulties of the Senegalese national economy, as Hart points out, can only partly be attributed to metropolitan capitalism; much of the difficulty must be found in patterns of an absence of soil conservation, "a reliance on an indebted peasantry in a depressed export industry," little diversification in the economic structure, and little recourse to appropriate technical innovations (Hart 1982; Pélissier 1966; Dumont 1974). Senegal is in many ways the classic colony. The French had little interest in the colonization of Senegal until the groundnut as a source of vegetable oils became an important commercial issue well before the twentieth century (Hart 1982). Hart notes that Senegal is a country made "homogeneous by its incorporation into the global economy as a supplier of raw materials." The French, previously confined to their trading posts in Gorée and Saint-Louis before 1854, by 1890 had expanded and secured much of the area of the former Wolof states (Cruise O'Brien 1971; Hart 1982).[4] The Maraboutic leaders created a hierarchy that distinguished itself from the traditional elite of the Wolof states:

> The Moslem community created a political hierarchy which could
> compete with the traditional elites. Islam was not the religion of
> the chiefs. If anything, it was the religion of the free peasantry, and
> when it emerged as a military force, it was with the egalitarian and
> puritanical ideology of a group that felt itself oppressed by this traditional elite. An egalitarian ideology did not lead to an egalitarian
> society, and Senegalese society maintained its traditional hierarchies.
> (Klein 1969, 93)

Slaves and low castes of the former Wolof states quickly found their way, along with poor peasants, to the patronage of the Maraboutic leaders (Klein 1969).[5] The encouragement of cash cropping groundnuts by the French and the Maraboutic organization of agricultural production units soon covered the whole of the Wolof zone with the cultivation of the groundnut (Cruise O'Brien 1971).

The Wolofization of Senegal was a complementary process. Along with the drawing of the national economy into the domain of the world market, Wolof became the language of about two-thirds of the country, and many Wolof cultural practices became a part of an emergent national society. Historically, the Wolof have had the "most contacts with foreigners and have become the most intensely involved in the urban life of centers such as Saint-Louis and Dakar" (Diarra and Fougeyrollas 1974). Today, the vanguard of the diaspora is Wolof (Diarra and Fougeyrollas 1974). Wolofization provides a means of communication and solidarity between migrants of various ethnic groups, although some bitter tensions exist between Wolof and these groups, especially those of the southern regions where separatist feelings are common and where Wolof are often identified with the notion of a repressive central state apparatus. Many migrants from the Casamance area of Senegal were essentially escaping social and political repression as well as the economic impoverishment of one of Senegal's most prized regions.

Mouridism and Islam

The Sufi Brotherhoods or *tariqas* are largely responsible for the spread and conversion of great numbers of people to Islam from Central Asia to Indonesia including much of Northern and West Africa. Muslim mysticism has often been opposed for its relaxation of orthodox Islamic practices. And yet it has often been one of the most dynamic and accessible varieties of Islamic practice and has been especially popular with an impoverished urban proletariat (Crapanzano 1973). The Mourid of Senegal have been criticized by the International Muslim League for the order's popularized Islamic practices, which incorporate pre-Islamic traditions and in some cases reject orthodox practices altogether. The league does not in fact recognize the Mourid. The Baye Fall, a subgroup of the Mourid, does not perform the five required daily prayers of orthodox Islam and prays, rather, twice a year. The Baye Fall do not observe

Ramadan. The group has an emphasis on intensive work following the example of Cheikh Ibra Fall, the first Mourid disciple. Other than the Baye Fall, however, the membership tends to observe Ramadan and the prayers. In fact, the recent revival of orthodox Islamic practices seems to have had a considerable effect on the youth of the founding families of, for example, the Baye Fall. There is, in any case, a great emphasis on the mystic teaching of the order within this elite (Fall 1984). At the same time, much of the following of the order has remained less informed and receives instruction through the Marabout.

The Mourid do not place great emphasis on the pilgrimage to Mecca. There are pilgrimages, however, to the tombs of the founding Marabout of the order that follow the practices of the *talibés* to honor the Marabout. Travel to the holy city of Touba is very important to the follower, and in fact now that many followers find themselves in Europe, Asia, and North America, some of the Marabouts now travel, giving benedictions and prayer services for those unable to attend the celebrations of the holy city. The financial contribution of the Mourid disciple is said to be given each month rather than each year, usually being about 10 percent of one's income. As Donal Cruise O'Brien has pointed out, this is more of a target than an actual amount of the offering (Cruise O'Brien, personal communication).

The Sacred City of Touba

> At the end of the end of the world, the last piece of earth left will be a piece of Touba.   —Senegalese Migrant

Touba, the sacred city of the Mourid order, is another invisible city. There are many Toubas much like the many Turins of memory and experience; each year the sacred center is enveloped by the pilgrimage to the tomb of Cheikh Amadou Bamba. Stretching out for miles the roads come to a standstill; crowds fill every empty space. The camera crews of Mourid register the event for those abroad who cannot attend the *Magal.* The Touba most vividly present to the migrants is that which is closely associated with founder Cheikh Amadu Bamba, popularly referred to as *Serin Touba.*[6] "The Saint," Michael Gilsenan once wrote, "serves as a kind of lens through which members see" (Gilsenan 1982). In his later years of life, Amadu Bamba lived in Diourbel and from this center undertook the project that was to distinguish Mouridism from other Sufi orders. This was the construction of a mosque in the village of Touba, the site of one of Amadu Bamba's revelations, a mosque of monumental proportions.[7] The mosque is an important center of both political and religious ceremony, as the *Magal* is attended each year by officials of the state and by religious leaders of various orders as well as international religious figures.

The project began in 1924 and was followed by Amadu Bamba until his death, with the appointment of his son Mamadu Mustapha Mbacké as his successor, or Khalifa, by a family council a week after his death. The construction passed to the Khalifate, and Touba became the site of the tomb of Amadu Bamba and one of the most sacred sites in all of Mourid ideology. The first anniversary of the founder's death marked the consolidation of many dissident Marabout under the new Khalifa, Mamadu Mustapha Mbacké. In 1928 a reunion of all Mourid was organized at Touba. This pilgrimage was made an annual event. The *Magal* is now one of the most significant symbolic events of Mourid practice. During the *Magal,* the vast international diaspora converge on the sacred city from all corners of the world; for those who cannot attend, the event is often videotaped and viewed by other Mourid when those who have made the pilgrimage return. This practice was initiated by the Paris Da'ira fairly early on in its foundation. For those who cannot travel to Touba for a blessing, there are a number of Marabout, often the sons of key branches of the Mbacké or Fall, who travel and give the blessing to those members abroad. The Marabouts often travel with several younger members of their families and other members of an entourage. The structure of Touba, however, is not only a part of Mourid tradition on high ceremonial occasions; it is a part of the structure of everyday life.[8] Touba is reconstructed in the diaspora communities of Mourid all over the world, in the living spaces and through the Da'ira (see fig. 3).

The expansion of the Mourid "sacred geography" has resulted in the eclipse of Mecca and Medina as sites of pilgrimage. Travel to the *Magal* is an obligation of a Mourid if he or she is able to perform this pilgrimage. Many Mourid in Europe travel back to Senegal each year for the *Magal;* travel agencies handle the travel plans of the Mourid in France, often organized by minor Marabout who specialize in this type of service. Ruth Mandel has shown how travel back to Turkey for migrant Turkish workers in Europe has often proved to be more compelling than the pilgrimage to Mecca and Medina (Mandel 1990; Gardner 1995, 126).

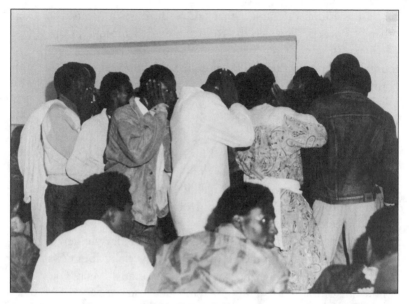

Fig. 3. Prayer circle or singing circle of Mourid in a theater attached to the grounds of San Giaocchino. (Photograph by Heather Merrill-Carter, 1990)

Although the movement toward purification of practice has been initiated in Senegal, especially by orders that see themselves in competition with the Mourid politically and socially, the pilgrimage of the Mourid to Touba remains paramount. What has proved perhaps more significant in the interchange of the various "idiom[s] of the cosmopolitan community of believers" (*umma*) has been the meeting of various traditions in Europe (Eickelman and Piscatori 1990c). In Turin many of the ceremonial practices of the Senegalese were attended by especially Moroccan migrants, and there was some attempt to set up an informal relationship with the two mosque centers in Turin that have been established for some time. Locality and difference play no greater role than in the lives of the Senegalese migrant who has traveled, lived, and worked in a variety of Moslem societies. The knowledge that derives from travel, *xam-xam,* is prized and considered a part of the knowledge essential to young migrants in contemporary contexts (Ebin 1990).[9]

Travel is an important conception in both Mourid ideology and in Moslem ideology generally. Muhammad Khalid Masud has argued that a new dimension of the notion of *hijira* (emigration) has emerged since the nineteenth century, which encompasses such notions as reasons of

travel for education, training, and employment (Masud 1990).[10] The freedom to travel within the Moslem world has been increasingly limited by
the development of the nation-state where the citizen has privileged
rights in the national community. In recent years conditions have become better for the propagation of Islam in the United States and Europe
than in many Moslem countries, as Masud has noted (1990). Travel and
the hardships associated with it have become a core of the Mourid imagination and a justification for the political importance of the Mourid.
The period of exile by the French of Amadu Bamba has become the key
constitution of travel as knowledge and sacred activity. The exile gave an
added prestige to the religious leader, and Mourid proclaim him today
as a national anticolonial figure:

> The exile in Gabon, which was to last seven years (1895–1902), gave
> a new dimension to Amadu Bamba's prestige. During the first four
> years the followers had no contact with him, and in this time they be-
> lieved the founder to have endured extraordinary trials at the hands
> of the French, from which he only emerged by miraculous means. He
> was said to have been imprisoned in a cell with a hungry lion, cast into
> a fiery furnace, buried for seven days in a deep well, kept on islands
> inhabited by snakes and devils. All of this, and more, he survived.
> One of the most popular legends concerns the voyage to Gabon, when
> the ship's captain is said to have refused him permission to pray; the
> founder jumped overboard and laid his mat upon the ocean to pray
> in peace before the astonished French crew. (Cruise O'Brien 1971, 43)

The young Mourids especially emphasize the steadfastness of the
founder in his faith in opposition to the colonial powers.[11] When called
to the office of the French governor before his exile in 1895, Amadu
Bamba stopped to pray before hearing the reasons for which he had
been requested to appear. The account of the founder in fact casts the
incident in a mystic light; Amadu Bamba explained that he did not go
into exile as the prisoner of the French but, rather, was accompanied by
the immortals, the companions of the Prophet at the battle of Badr: "I
left with the pious (the immortals) when I had to leave for exile. The
enemies thought that I was going as a prisoner. Thanks to the immortals
of Badr I gained a military victory, and separation from the enemies of
God" (cited in Cruise O'Brien and Coulon 1988, 150).[12]

The hardships and travels of the founder have become part of an
exemplary life for the Mourid followers. The solidarity of the Mourid
community of faith abroad gives the Mourid a particular connection to

both the travel of the founder and the growth and expansion of the community of Mourid in diaspora.[13] In every way the *talibé* is drawn into a sacred circle of the order through work, travel, exchange, and the miraculous occurrences of the founder's life. The life of the *talibé* is encompassed by that of the founder, and the spaces of Touba are re-created in the Da'ira, which are held in the rooms of the Senegalese in Turin: through the placement of photographs of the *Serin* in the houses and on pins that are worn daily (an innovation resembling the pins of Italian political parties); in the drinking of the tea and the turning of the tea cup three times before handing it to the consumer of the tea; in eating Senegalese foods ("We eat in the African way altogether from the same pan"); and extending hospitality to others.

"There is constantly someone coming into the house—I never know who will be sleeping next to me," one migrant said to me. The house contained about 120 persons in six rooms. Because of discrimination in housing in Italy, it was difficult for migrants to find housing, and Senegalese extended hospitality to other Senegalese arriving from other cities and to other Africans who had trouble finding housing. Selling in the streets, the traders often came into contact with new arrivals to the city and thus opened their homes to them until they found other accommodations. All of these manifestations of solidarity are activities that manifest the *Baraka* (blessing) of the order and of the founder. They place the receiver and giver in the arch of the community of faith of the Mourid:

> Touba is much on the giving. . . . You must give particularly to those who don't have anything. This makes you equal to the other. Only God is superior. Giving and respect are always for God. . . . The moment that a person does something for Cheikh Amadu Bamba he already knows, and Cheikh Amadu Bamba will be in their heart until they finish that task. (Senegalese migrant)

The attention to service of the saint, then, is part of an ongoing practice in the lives of Mourid and enters into everyday practices. In the migrant's, we see the substitution of *Touba* for *Serin Touba* or Cheikh Amadu Bamba in the explanation of a precept of Mouridism.

As mentioned above, travel has become a sacred activity for the Mourid. Even the suitcases of the founder have been preserved along with his books and writings (Ebin 1990). Moreover, there is said to be a set of suitcases of the Khalifa that are somehow in the arch of secrets given by the Jinns:

My grandfather had disciples that were Jinns, and there is a suitcase
in the chambers of Khalifa. . . . Only the Khalifa can open it, and he
can take out money as he wants. . . . Whatever he wants, he can take
it out of the suitcase. The case came from the Jinns. . . . When the
Khalifa comes into the palace, there are many people who come and
give money for this case. . . . It is a secret. . . . I cannot go into the
chambers where the Khalifa sleeps, but there is a room for visiting
there, now only when you are very young. Now that I am an adult,
I can't go there. . . . My Father [the present Khalifa] has transferred to
the residence of the Khalifa and in there is a visiting room. . . . I have
asked the guards of the Khalifa many questions about the suitcase,
and they said that there was once someone who came there like me
who was trying to open the suitcase, and it was too heavy for them
and that it is light to the Khalifa. . . . The Khalifa is the only one who
can move it. . . . This is a miracle. (Senegalese migrant)

The suitcases that only the Khalifa can move accord the Khalifa
an extraordinary power derived from the *Baraka* of Cheikh Amadu
Bamba—suitcases filled with money, with wealth at the disposal of the
Khalifa alone. This source of wealth comes from the ingenuity of the
Jinns, who, devoted to Amadu Bamba, gave him the suitcases, and thus
the cash economy is subordinated to a mystical or spiritual economy of
the proper devotion of *talibé* to *Serin* or Marabout.[14] The secret is the
passage of this unparalleled sign of ritual authority and "otherworldly
knowledge," in Max Weber's words (1966). This is, of course, a miraculous occurrence. "A miracle," writes Michael Gilsenan, is "performed
each time it is retold" (1982), and in the ideology of the Sufi order the
retelling of miracles is important to the very construction of the order's
cosmology. Miracles both demonstrate the "truth of the holy man's mission" and place the *talibé* in a world revealed only through the particular
lens of mystical knowledge and practice that constitutes the day-to-day
existence of religious practice. Since the 1970s, with the movement of
the "young Mourid," which began with the first high school groups
and then with Mourid prayer groups of a circle of students and others
around the University of Dakar, there has been a challenge to what
Gilsenan has called the premodern and uncontrolled quality of the conception of miraculous occurrences in Mouridism. This "problematic nature of the miraculous" since the 1960s, in the wider context of a kind of
"purification of practice," has been a concern of reform currents within
the Moslem community. Concerns with "orthodoxy" and "superstitions"

have led many to criticize the practices of the popular Sufism. In Mouridism, the young Mourid began to understate the importance of these miraculous occurrences, emphasizing, rather, the "anti-Western" activities
of Cheikh Amadu Bamba and appealing to the more literary projects of
the religious scholar.

Yet the vision of the saint (Wali) who is revealed through a series of
miraculous events is crucial to many of the practitioners of Mouridism
as for other Sufi Orders (Gilsenan 1982). Everyday life holds the possibility of miracles, and the connection of members to the world of the
miraculous is very important in the lives of Mourid in Turin. Mentioning miraculous events of the founder is part of everyday conversation:
"Cheikh Amadu Bamba was so great that he pulled himself up on his
own power and went to Jerusalem and back." Such statements both
reconfirm the efficacy of the saintliness of the founder and places the
talibé in a matter-of-fact context of miraculous happenings. Nothing is
accidental: the hardships of the founder are directly related to the hardships encountered by the members. In many ways the life of the saint
becomes for the Mourid a "scheme of interpretation" and a bridge across
which the Mourid has access to the miraculous, to the "purposes of Divinity." The saint, Edward Westermarck once wrote, "can see the whole
world as though it were exposed on the palm of his hand, he can see the
seven heavens, the seven earths and the seven seas. He knows what is
happening in distant places and foresees the future. He works miracles"
(Westermarck 1968).

"My Marabout told me I was going on a long journey, and at that
time I didn't even know I was coming here. He told me they know
things," one migrant once told me. The saint reveals through the miracle the contours of a cosmology not always visible.[15] Unlike the belief
and practice of other Sufi organizations, particularly the Hamadsha described by Vincent Crapanzano in Morocco (1973) and the Sufi mystical
brotherhoods studied by Gilsenan in Egypt, the notion of Baraka and
its manifestation through miracles in the Mourid system are linked to a
highly structured ideological base of religious, political, and economic
power, constituting what Gilsenan has called a kind of "religious technology" that accords a high degree of personal and institutional legitimacy to the "guardians of the Order" (Gilsenan 1982). Baraka to the
Mourid system, Gilsenan has argued, is the "key ideological transformer"
in the entire structure of the Sufi order. I agree with this statement and
would like to further argue that the core of this tariqa (way or path, to

Islam) lies in the ability of the order to transform patterns of exchange into mystical and religious capital.

The Suitcases of the Khalifa: Jinns and Flexible Accumulation

The suitcases of the Khalifate indicate a problematic in the structure of the order, which is pervasive in the minutiae of the life of every Mourid and yet encompasses the entire order. The suitcases are the symbolic pivot of a system of mystical flexible accumulation, which draws the "work" of the *talibé* toward the mystical center of the *Baraka* of the founder and his guardian, the Khalifa in Touba, the holy city and heart of the order, which in turn manifest the great power and endowment of the *Baraka* of the founder. I call this "mystical flexible accumulation" since the activities of the followers are widely dispersed through trading and various working-class occupations such as those involved in Italy in construction and other trades or as common laborers. This group, due to the irregular nature of the work and the reliance of the transitional periods of trading articulated with wage work, may be said to be a kind of occasional proletariat or subproletariat (Marcus and Fisher 1986; Crapanzano 1973; Gilsenan 1982). Further, the "accumulation" is in fact a part of the collection of "offering" of the followers from the many urban associations of Da'ira dispersed throughout the world and the income generated by the involvement of the Mourid in peanut farming (Cruise O'Brien 1975). The great mosque at Touba is often considered a sign of the disciples' economic devotion, yet the mosque was actually financed to a great degree by the union Progressiste Sénégalaise of Léopold Senghor,[16] which took up this financial support from at least 1960, and the former colonial administration (Cruise O'Brien 1975). The followers view *Baraka*, Cruise O'Brien has argued, largely in financial or material terms. This is, however, only part of the picture. The material is a manifestation of grace that transforms the material into the spiritual and results in the blessing of all members of the order (Cruise O'Brien 1975). The Jinn or Junn[17] of Islam in Mourid ideology have been appropriated and combined with notions of spirits and divinities from pre-Islamic ideology.[18]

The Marabouts have become important figures in Senegalese political life for the production of gris-gris, which is called *maraboutage*. The interference of the Marabout in the political life is achieved through the making of powerful amulets that give undue influence to the politicians for which they are made. The practice of making the gris-gris or amulet is widespread in Senegal and has been associated with the Marabout for some time. Le Maire writes in 1682 that nobles carried so many amulets that they were often forced to ride on horseback: "Nobles, above all, have their shirts and caps covered with them, and they cover themselves with them to such a degree, that they are often obliged to be placed on horseback" (quoted in Gamble 1967). David P. Gamble, in his study of the Wolof of Senegambia, notes the use of the amulets:

> In spite of the impact of Islam, there is still a much deeper layer of pagan belief and observance among Wolof than among the Mandinka or Torobe. Wolof men and women are loaded with amulets, round the waist, neck, arms, legs, both for protection against all sorts of evils, and to help them achieve certain desires. Most frequently these contain a paper on which a religious teacher has written a passage from the Koran, or a diagram from a book on Arabic mysticism, which is then enveloped in paper, glued down, and covered with leather, but sometimes they enclose a piece of bone or wood, a powder, or an animal claw. (Gamble 1967)

Many of the early references to the Marabout among the Wolof are associated with these "magicians" and their making of amulets. Cruise O'Brien points out that the use of the gris-gris in Wolof society seems to have been universal, as it seems today.[19] The gris-gris of the shells and teeth that Gamble mentions were replaced to some degree by the gris-gris with written verses of the Koran or cabalistic signs and were directed to specific purposes, including making one invisible or promoting trade or protection against mystical or natural powers (Cruise O'Brien 1971). G. T. Mollien in *L'Afrique Occidentale en 1818* notes that "not an individual is without the papers . . . which they call gri-gri" (quoted in Cruise O'Brien 1971, 24). In Turin, the Laube were the only Senegalese who wore the amulets on the arms, neck, and waist, while the waist belts were the most common among most Senegalese. The Jinn are often supernatural beings from which one needs protection; the guardian spirit of the village in Senegambia and the spirit of the village well were often associated, according to David Ames, with the "jinni of Islam" (quoted in Cruise O'Brien 1971, 22).[20] The vulnerability of the follower to forces against which only the Marabout can offer protection has made the gris-gris an important link in the relationship of the follower to the Marabout and through this relationship to forms of divinity. The lack of formal education and rudimentary religious training of the traders places the *talibé* in a postion of inferiority to the religious leader in this world and the next. And yet such practices as the wearing and the obtaining of the gris-gris and the "singing" of the name of god during the Sufi prayer ceremony mark the encompassment of the *talibé* in the cosmology of the order. And it is in this realm that the *talibé* seem to seek above all else a union with *Serin Touba*. The gris-gris is a little bit of *Baraka* that transforms the body of the follower into a channel of this transformative power and subordinates other forces to its logic. One migrant told me that when he was in Senegal he could not leave his compound without his gris-gris waist belt: "My mother would stop me at the door and ask if I had it on . . . and if I didn't I would have to turn around and put it on. . . . But here I do as I please and no one tells me what to do; sometimes I leave it at home." The gris-gris cannot be worn by another and are often sent to migrants from Senegal; when a powerful gris-gris maker is found, people will travel great distances and have another belt made to protect their children abroad. Many Senegalese have gris-gris made for them specifically for going to Europe so that they might not be harmed by police or other forces. The gris-gris in fact encircles the wearer in a world of the community of faith and protects and promotes free movement in dangerous or potentially dangerous situations. The gris-gris is a device that collapses all time into sacred time and into the circle of the Marabout, and in the case of the Mourid into the *Baraka* of the founder, *Serin Touba*.

The Jinn, then, populate a world of the unseen; their service to the Marabout is another manifestation of the *Baraka* of the founder. The "technology" and special information of the Jinns have been in the narrative of the suitcases of the Khalifa placed in the service of the entire order and its ability to persist through time and continue its mission. Although some features of the Jinns resemble other discussions of the Jinn, the Mourid ideology seems to gloss particular qualities of the Jinns, which seem to embody at once fixity and innovation. The Jinn are said in Mourid ideology to hold the knowledge of many inventions and technological advances: "All inventions come from the Jinns." Although wealth has often been associated with them, this relationship between innovation and fixity seems peculiar to the Mourid gloss of the Jinns.

W. Robertson Smith argues in the *Religion of the Semites* (1894) that
the Jinn had many of the qualities of "totemism" and that the "communities of jinn [are] precisely identical with the savage conception of the
animal creation."[21] He further argues that the sanctuaries of the Semitic
world were in many ways similar to those of the "haunts" of the Jinns
and so may be viewed as replacing the early conceptions of "plant and
animal demons" (Smith 1894, 119, 120, 138, 139). The association of the
Jinn with place, however, is one of the features that seems important in
the Mourid ideology. The locality of the artifact of the Jinn, the suitcases, gives them a kind of fixity in the cosmology of the order and places
their capacity to reveal innovations both to the founder and to the
guardians of the founder, the Khalifate, in the forefront of the Mourid
structure, which may allow change in the form of mystical innovation.
The trading diaspora now offers such an innovation by providing a new
source of remittances from Europe.

The suitcases in effect contain monies given to the Khalifa. The
Khalifa is the only one who can accept monies from the remittances of
the urban religious associations of the Da'ira. These urban associations
are under the direct control of the Khalifa, who must sanction their
establishment. By locating this new source of money in the suitcases,
the story implies that the work of the follower condensed in the form
of money or wages becomes a blessing and approaches the purposes of
divinity of the founder. Every activity in service of the saint is said to
carry a blessing with it and to be guided by the founder: "Cheikh
Amadou Bamba is with you while you are doing this thing; he is with
you." The role of the *zakat* (Arabic) or *Assaka* (Wolof), an annual fee
given to the Marabout by the peasant farmer for the use of the lands in
the system of land allocation is replaced by the offerings of the urban
brothers in the form of monies that become manifestations of the
power of the Khalifate.

The Da'ira in Turin has printed stationery that reads "Touba Torino,
the road to paradise." The urban centers of religious activity that span a
transnational world have become an integral part of the legitimacy and
power of the contemporary order. The *Magal* completes the cycle of
travel that brings the follower once again to the center of the holy city of
Touba or, rather, is brought to the Mourid follower through the many
videotapes that are made by members of Da'ira in Europe or the United
States and then circulated to those Mourid who are unable to attend.
The mobility of the order and its new form of mystical flexible accumu-

lation is opposed to the fixity of the center and the source of power of the Khalifate. Travel reduces distance rather than accentuating it since the Mourid trading diaspora is drawn closely into the dynamic of the order through its travel, work, and worship. Thus, grace through work is closely tied to knowledge through travel, as both become sacred activities in the service of the saint.

The narrative of the suitcases of the Khalifa is also a kind of trope for conversion to Islam. The Jinn, who gave the suitcases to Cheikh Amadu Bamba, are in fact converts to Islam. They are among the Jinns who converted to Islam, and so innovation comes from the power of conversion and the gifts of these converts (Westermarck 1968; Smith 1894). The Jinn, associated as they often are with the tomb of the saints and other holy places, in many ways signal the presence of various kinds of divinity, blessing, or holiness. The extraordinary psychic state of the popular orders may denote either the presence of demons or Jinns or the union of the practitioner with God.[22] Vincent Crapanzano has extensively described the attack of the Jinn in Moroccan Hamadsha ideology and the manner in which Jinn participate in illness. There seems to be a great emphasis in Mourid ideology on the "therapeutic gifts" of some Marabout who may frighten the "devils" out through the power of their endowment of *Baraka* (Crapanzano 1973).[23]

The suitcases, moreover, provide a very powerful trope of the lives of the Mourid in diaspora. The most prevalent image of the Mourid is the trader carrying the black bag of goods through the street, or the arrival of the Mourid at the train station with suitcases overloaded with clothing, articles for sale, and religious texts and tapes of the singing of the Koran. One afternoon while at the Senegalese house in Turin I saw one of the migrants preparing to leave for Senegal. For days a battle had been going on between various persons over the number of gifts for children and parents that the travelers would be able to carry; the suitcases, large, black, and plastic, were filled to capacity. I attempted to lift one and was unable to do so. "I can't lift it," I said, and the Marabout turned to me somewhat angrily and said, "You must understand how hard this life is for us. This is the life. . . . We must carry this." As Amadu Bamba said, "Le Corps humain, depuis sa création existe pour accomplir le travail ordonné par dieu" (Since its creation, the human body has existed to carry out God's work). Each of the items in the suitcases required a visit to the various relatives of the migrants to place the gift in the hands of the person in Senegal to whom it was destined.

Work in the service of the Marabout has been an important part of the Mourid ideology of the rural world, particularly as this conception has figured in the production units of Senegalese agriculture.[24] The work ideology accords the *talibé*, in the re-creation of patterns of the order's formation and expansion and draws much of its economic activity into the mystical realm of the Marabout. The successful businessperson is assumed to have a powerful gris-gris offered by the Marabout and to have great privilege and access to the Marabout.[25] No greater contrast can be made between the rural cultivator and the urban trader than the innovation of the technology that enables the trader's movement in the form of the suitcase, which, like that of the Jinns, indicates a flexible form of accumulation and yet also the singularity of purpose of divinity through its sanctification in the hands of the guardian of the order, the Khalifa. Through each act of labor that culminates in offerings to the Khalifate, various forms of knowledge, technology, and wealth and knowledge through travel or travel as a sacred activity reverse all activities toward a sacred center.

The Great Marabout and His First Disciple

A. Bamba est bien l'homme saint, le mystique, le symbole de la pureté, le détenteur d'un pouvoir charismatique. Cheikh Ibra est en quelque sorte le contraire d'Amadu Bamba. C'est lui qui met en avant les idées d'activité et de travail. Il est considéré comme l'inventeur du daara et favorise le développement de la production agricole (Bamba is the saint, the mystic, the symbol of purity, he who possesses charismatic power. Cheikh Ibra is in a sense the opposite of Amadu Bamba. It is he who puts forward the ideas about activities and work. He is considered the inventor of the daara agricultural development).

—Jean Copans, *Les Marabouts de l'Arachide*

The first disciple of Cheikh Amadou Bamba, Cheikh Ibra Fall, organized the early Mourid followers into tight-knit production groups that farmed under his direction. Cheikh Ibra Fall at the same time rejected the religious practices of Amadou Bamba and refused to fast, pray, or pursue the study of the Muslim teachings. The study of such practices were not what Ibra Fall sought; rather, he spent his time working and producing benefits for the Marabout. This relationship is emblematic of the relationship of the Mourid to Islam. The emphasis on work and the rejection of some of what others consider the basic practices of Islam have created an ambiguity in the relationship of the order to Islam, at least ideologically. The devotion to the Marabout of Cheikh Ibra Fall is one of the important aspects of contemporary Mouridism; the discipline and organization of the order and adherence of the followers make the Mourid one of the most significant political, economic, and religious powers of the Senegalese Muslim Brotherhoods.

The absolute devotion of the *talibé* and the commercial activities that support the structure of the order have become essential components of the order's expansion into a dynamic system that maintains a vast international network of followers and economic relations. The work ideology, which by some Mourid Marabout is said to be crucial to both the power of the central organization of the Khalifate and to the individual support of the Marabout themselves, has been an important part of this dynamism. The work in the service of the Marabout is the same as the life of prayer to some Mourid, and some Marabout argue that Ibra Fall was so powerful a figure that he could confer a certain spirituality to followers who had "only worked" and not participated in the more traditional life of prayer.

Peasants, Artisans, and Intellectuals: Mouridism in Immigration

The world of Mouridism in immigration is vast and extends from the holy city of Touba in Senegal to the major cities of Africa, Europe, the United States, Italy, Spain, France, Germany, Japan, Canada, and Australia: New York, Atlanta, Los Angeles, Turin, Livorno, Milan, Rome, Paris, Toulon, Lyon, Hong Kong, Berlin, London, Yaounde, and Madrid.[26] Many of the Mourid, for at least the past fifteen to twenty years, have traveled to Belgium and France. More recently, the patterns of trade and travel have reached England, Spain, Portugal, Germany, the Netherlands, and Australia. Long-standing migrations of the Mourid *talibés* have occurred in such countries as Mauritania, Mali, the Ivory Coast, Algeria, Guinea, Benin, Morocco, Niger, Nigeria, Tunisia, Saudi Arabia, Guinea-Bissau, Cameron, Gabon, Madagascar, and Libya. The travels of the followers are similar to many of the other Senegalese, many of whom left Senegal to travel and work in much of Africa before coming to Europe.

Many of these African countries constitute the first areas of effective migration. This migration has gone on for generations, not simply years. The families of some of the Senegalese in Turin have been involved in the trade of cloth, food, and other items throughout Africa for some time. Many Senegalese have spent as much as five to eight years in African and other countries working and trading. The migrants travel to Europe and have a great deal of collective knowledge about the European context. Some of the younger members of the community for their first experience of travel to Europe have arrived directly from Dakar via some of the agricultural regions of Senegal such as Louga. Many travel with skills already learned in Senegal or on the long voyage to other countries; many were already bakers, tailors, carpenters, masons, electricians, welders, drivers, painters, and mechanics when they arrived in Italy. Although these skills are often not recognized and the migrants are often not compensated for the level of skill they actually perform, the migrants nonetheless enter a market that utilizes a relatively cheap form of labor compared to the cost of providing welfare and other benefits to national workers.

There is a great diversity among migrants, some of which derives from the timing of the particular trajectory of the migration (Maher et al. 1991). Among the Senegalese there are several groups that may be distinguished broadly as artisans, peasants-traders, traders or *commerçants,* intellectuals, and Marabouts. Many of the Senegalese in Turin considered themselves traders and engaged in petty trade or street selling at least initially upon their arrival in the city. Although the dominant vision of the Senegalese is that they are for the most part petty traders with no other skills, this judgment is quite mistaken. The way that migrants define work contrasts markedly with the official designation of the *vu' comprà,* which is actually a kind of slur describing the immigrant as being unfamiliar with Italian and saying, "You buy" or "Vuoi comprare?" Do (you want to buy?) to the potential customer. The expression *vu' comprà,* which Italians variously gloss as Calabrian or "some southern dialect," denotes an assumed lack of education and command of the Italian language meant to demean the migrant. "They call me the leader of the *vu' comprà,*" a young Senegalese Marabout once explained. "That is what they [the Italians] call me." Senegalese refute the classifications of Italians and often comment on their arrogance in defining them. The son of the youngest son of the founder of the Mourid order, Modu Mustapha Mbacké, during a visit to Italy told me, "We are well known in France, and in America they are beginning to know us. Soon here they will know who we are. Now they do not know, but soon they will know who we are." The Mourid have established more than twenty urban religious centers of the Moslem order throughout France, and more are being founded each year.

Many migrants define their activity as *commercio* or themselves as *commerçant* or *marchand,* using the French term for Wolof traders since the eighteen hundreds (Boilat 1853 [1984]). The petty traders are the most visible part of the diaspora, lining the streets of towns such as Turin, especially in the winter months and selling in the seaside towns during the summer. The traders are distinguished both by the articles they sell and the manner in which their trade is practiced. Those that trade in articles of European manufacture are often the most peripheral to the "African market," as the petty trade is called by its practitioners; many, selling such articles as sunglasses, cassette tapes, and watches buy these articles in Italian discount stores and sell them on the street in order to make a quite modest living while attempting to find other work. These traders are only transitory and would prefer other forms of work, while some traders selling more expensive watches and jewelry are really traders proper and often have a background in Senegal or elsewhere involving a similar trade.

The way of life of the traders is very modest. Many of them live just beyond the historic center of the city, in neighborhoods that once housed internal Italian migrants from the South and that have had no signs of renewal or restoration in recent memory. Senegalese in Turin belong primarily to the Mourid Muslim Brotherhood. The community of Senegalese in Turin is not restricted to the Wolof, who are most often associated with the Mourid but is, rather, a very diverse community that represents many of the major ethnic groups in Senegal such as the Wolof, Serer, Peul, Toucouleur, Laube, Lebou, Mandinka, and Diola and contains migrants from all over Senegal including Dakar and the regions around Dakar, the rural areas, and Casamance.

Artisans, especially wood-carvers, are descendants from an artisan caste of Wolof and other societies with distinctive traditions of carving and work only in wood. One master wood-carver explained that "My father did this work and his father and his father's father. . . . We have always done this work." These artisans were among the first migrants to France in the 1950s and have extensive networks throughout Europe and the United States and are now even found in parts of Asia. In Turin one family of wood-carvers is several generations deep and has extended-kin networks in other Italian cities. The younger generations are the most widely divergent, with some members having attended French schools and leaving the practice of wood-carving in order to extend markets to Los Angeles and New York. The wood-carvers in their forties to sixties who are mostly Laube, an artisan subcaste of the Wolof, have no Western education, never having attended the French schools. Many of the older carvers are literate in no language although verbally proficient in many; they know more Italian than French. The fact that French is a colonial language has had a great deal to do with the preference for Wolof as a common language among Senegalese from various backgrounds and traditions.

The raw materials for the carvers come from Senegal and are first roughly hewn from the wood in so-called factories, under the direction of a master carver or sculptor in Senegal. The unfinished pieces are then transported to Rome, Marseilles, or Paris where one may go and purchase them or pick them up. For about $500 (U.S.) a master craftsman may obtain enough elephants, boats, musical instruments, or masks to finish and sell to others and also to sell on his own account for several months. Some of the younger carvers even worked at FIAT for a time but prefer the work of woodworking to the factory life. If a trader did well over a season or longer, he would return home, returning to Europe the following season. In Turin most wood-carvers are Mourid and often ask for the blessing of the Marabout: "Bless us for we are Laube," they say. Blessings are also given to the goods of the trader. In Senegal some of the powerful Marabouts and other ritual specialists also make amulets to help the trader. Along the arcades of Via Roma in Turin from time to time a small group of Senegalese traders may be seen gathered around one of the collections of articles for sale, as some of the young men raise their hands for the blessing of the Marabout, washing themselves in the blessing, passing their hands briefly over their faces as they return to their business.

Many Senegalese in Turin were from cultivator or peasant backgrounds; they were from the peanut regions, especially Louga, Thies, and Sagatta. The sons of peasants, some leaving the rural areas for the first time, were encouraged by a brother or cousin to join them in this new destination, Italy. For those of cultivator backgrounds the transition to jobs in small industry was not difficult. Many had vocational training where schooling in the French system was absent and had skills as welders, carpenters, and masons. There were also a number of French-school-educated and thus French-speaking sons of factory and other professional workers. These Senegalese tended to seek trade qualifications and to enlist in training programs whenever possible in order to "get something that I can carry home to Africa." Italian local authorities run training programs open to foreigners to fill jobs for which there are few trained applicants (for example, welding, masonry, and the building trades).

The work careers of the Senegalese migrants in Turin reveal a rich diversity of experience and work histories. Some of the migrants have worked in their own businesses, opening auto mechanic shops and even small construction or artisan enterprises, while others came essentially from agriculture or the world of commerce. There are extensive networks of commerce and trade that extend between major European cities, linking the Senegalese community both with Senegal and with the communities of cities like Milan, Rome, Paris, Marseilles, Turin, and Brescia. There is also an extensive network of trade, visiting, and commerce in Italy that connects such cities as Genoa, Lecce, Pisa, Rimini, Ancona, Messina, Cagliari, Nuoro, Agrigento, Catania, and Asti. Much of this trade is conducted within the Senegalese communities in these cities and does not extend to members of the host society. Many of the articles that these networks provide are important to the life of the community itself (Carter 1991a).

There are many school dropouts, unemployed schoolteachers, and former university students among the migrants. This group is often referred to as the "intellectuals" by other migrants. These highly educated migrants often act as interpreters and assistants to those with less skills. Many were involved in student protests against the government and are very critical of the policies of Abdou Diouf; others sympathize with the Communist Party of Abdoulaye Wade. Many of the *intellectuals,* a term often used by the Marabout who believe that education leads to a challenge of religious authority, are not Wolof or Mourid. Many are Tukulor, Serer, or come from various groups of the highly educated South in the Casamance who trained in Catholic schools and have a closer relationship to Italian Catholic circles. Many, though by no means all, of the intellectuals are also nobles or descendants of nobles who see themselves as having certain responsibilities toward other members of their community. While the nobles are most often from urban centers like Dakar and are French educated, many having gone to university, including some schoolteachers who found themselves out of work during the recent economic crisis in Senegal. The intellectuals differ greatly in diaspora from Maraboutic travelers from founding families of the Mourid order. There are few choices for those who wish to follow the path of spiritual authority, and incorporation in Western education must be tempered within the framework allowed by the heads of the order. Western education may prove a barrier to becoming Khalifa of a lineage or maxilineage.

Trade and the Urban Da'ira

The commercial activities of the brotherhood and its members' involvement in petty trade date back to the earliest formation of urban satellite communities in Saint-Louis from about 1892 (Cruise O'Brien and Coulon 1988). This marks what Cruise O'Brien and Coulon have designated the first phase of Mourid economic and commercial activity and migration toward urban centers. The spreading out from the base of the religious center of the brotherhood established at Touba has continued straight through the end of the nineteenth century to the expansion of the orders abroad. During the 1940s the settlement patterns in a second phase reached the confines of Dakar, which soon became, especially with independence in 1960, the focus of Mourid commercial activities. The consolidation of a firm urban base in the capital was demonstrated in the Mourid control of the *sandaga,* the principal open market of the city toward the end of the decade. What Cruise O'Brien and Coulon call the third phase occurred when the Mourid street trader began to appear in France after about 1966, and then in other areas in Europe including Germany, Spain, and most recently Italy (Cruise O'Brien and Coulon 1988). This periodization of Mourid urbanization is somewhat flexible and the phases overlap often, yet the basic trajectory gives some idea of the process of the Mourid expansion into larger circles of trade. Much of this expansion has centered on the organization of the urban Da'ira and the religious order of the Mourid.

The Da'ira is an urban organization of the members of the order that apparently became an effective type of association in the 1940s in Senegal and then spread also to the villages (Cruise O'Brien 1975). More recently, the Da'ira in urban centers in Senegal have made an effort to recruit urban youth to the order. Often the Da'ira takes on the role of the *darra* or religious school in the urban world, training and organizing religious ceremonies (Carter 1991b). The context of the Da'ira provides the followers a chance to study the texts and chants of the founder. The Da'ira may collect funds for various purposes and may even act to organize members for job recruitment. The Da'ira may also place the members of the community into closer contact with the central organization of the Khalifate in Senegal or for those urban Da'ira with the rural center of the order.

The Da'ira in Senegal is the structure that the order takes in the urban environment. The Da'ira may be organized by followers who take it on themselves to create the informal Da'ira, or by a Marabout. Should the Da'ira be organized by the Marabout according to the nature of the Marabout's relationship with the order and the powers that the followers attribute to the religious leader, the character of the Da'ira may change considerably. The Marabout provides a reference point for the community around which it may gain a great coherence; the obedience to the religious leader may be emphasized by the Marabout in the urban environment, with the Marabout acting as an intermediary in formal relationships with employers, public offices, and other officials. In short, the Da'ira organized by the Marabout essentially provides them with a group of adherents who are affiliated through the Marabout to the central authority of the order (Diop 1982).

Another aspect of the Da'ira in the urban context in Senegal is the fact that many of the rural youth have very low levels of education. Many of the migrants in Turin, in fact, have only attended the *darra* schools of the local Marabout and not the state-run schools. The level of preparation in French is often restricted to those who have attended these schools or those who have come from the cities and not just arrived there recently from the rural areas (Cruise O'Brien 1975). There is a great tendency to use Wolof when Senegalese speak among themselves. "French is not our language," someone may say in the midst of conversation, and the conversation will then slip into Wolof. Many of the young people who come from the cities and who have had training in French are at somewhat of a disadvantage in conversation compared to the Wolof speakers and feel that they best express themselves in French. Many of those who have chosen jobs that do not require literacy only speak Wolof or Arabic and often do not speak French. This places many of the members of the urban Da'ira at a decided disadvantage in the urban world in which the language of the state bureaucracy is dominant. In the urban Da'ira of Senegal, then, often the Marabout or some other member of the group educated in French will act as translator and advocate for those with language difficulties.

There is a sharp distinction made between the religious and non-religious organizations, and this is especially the case in the association structure in Italy. For foreign groups to have a voice in the local structure, if they do have the backing of one of the major parties, they must construct some sort of association. The association is based on the model of Italian voluntary associations and clubs. These juridical entities enjoy certain privileges in the Italian administrative structure: the groups may be eligible for the use of local facilities and funds, for example. There are in Turin a number of groups or associations of foreign communities. These groups, often dominated by intellectuals and students, represent the foreign community to some degree. These groups formed an informal coalition on certain issues during 1990–1991, although conflicts between and within these organizations have often divided them and hampered their ability to act as a cohesive political force. These divisions have often occurred loosely, although not exclusively, across racial and ideological lines. For some years there was a rift between black organizations and communist-based factions, for example.

The Marabout in Turin pointed out that there was an association in Milan and that it was not based on religion, as the Turin group was, and that this was a mistake of Pap Khouma, the Senegalese leader of Milan and the Milanese Senegalese association.[27] Because the group is an association, there is the possibility of the "thing going astray and being used for other purposes." This possibility does not exist in the Da'ira, which is linked to the wider organization of the brotherhood and controlled only by Mourid. "With the Da'ira the faith remains in the Da'ira; the confidence rests there. Rigazzi non si fidono in nell'associazione Loro insultano L'Associazione" (The boys don't trust the association, they insult it), the Marabout explains. There is considerable distrust of "intellectuals," in essence anyone who has attended French schools for an extended period of time or is influenced by the secular more than by the spiritual. For the maxilineages that may attain the Khalifate-General of the Mourid order, there are two primary schools "within the family" for the children of Marabout; it is only recently that a younger generation has been allowed to attend Western-influenced schools and even more recently that students attend schools abroad.

Some of the young sons of the heads of some of the lineages prefer to go to Europe. Many are often sent to Saudi Arabia or North African countries for a proper Moslem education in Arabic. Some of these students have in fact left school and transferred, initially without the knowledge of their parents, to Europe, where their cousins had set up Da'ira that offered the possibility of attending European schools. "We are making a revolution here in Europe," some of the Maraboutic family will say. "What my brother and I are doing is new. Many people still do not trust Europe, and they feel that you can't do this kind of work here and still do spiritual work. So we have to make some kind of revolution." The whole process of this revolution of the young Mourid really began in Dakar around the Dakar University circle and the urban Da'ira, which began to appeal to the students there. Many of the intellectual Mourid students began to reinterpret Mourid ideology and use the works of Amadu Bamba as an introduction to the order for those not familiar with Mouridism. In Paris among the student Mourid community, Cheikh Amadu Bamba Cultural Weeks were soon organized, and Mouridism, often without Marabouts, was firmly in place by the 1980s. The young Mourid claimed that one did not have to be a Mbacké in order to be a "spiritual guide" or have the more traditional title of Cheikh (Cruise O'Brien and Coulon 1988). This tendency to diminish the hierarchical quality of the order is very interesting and accords with the intellectuals' appropriation of Amadu Bamba, emphasizing the writing of the mystic and opening up the works to modern interpretation. This lends a kind of democratic quality to the young Mourid along with an anti-Western stance that was popular in the 1970s when the official youth organizations were sanctioned by the Khalifate-General in Senegal. This anti-Western stance went hand in hand with a somewhat strained relationship with other major religious orders in Senegal including the Tidjanis and Quadriyyas. The enthusiasm for the expansion of Mouridism that has accompanied the youth movement has led some young Marabout to attempt to undermine the other orders while maintaining a stance of universalism. Many of the followers will say, "We are all Moslem," while Marabout are quick to point out the losses of the other orders, especially the Tidjanis, in comparison to the dynamism of Mouridism:

> The Tidjanis don't have anything anymore; they have only their city. We have taken everything away from them. There are some Guel, some former slaves that have risen very high; now they are rich. And there are even some rich Tidjanis who convert to Mouridism now because they want to be with the Mourid; the Tidjanis don't have anything.

The founder is said to have initially democratized the organization by making low-caste people leaders of certain sections of the order. In the course of the long-term agricultural expansion, the order has through its land-use policy given landless cultivators access to and ownership of land once blocked to them (Cruise O'Brien and Coulon 1988). The ideology of caste is still very much alive, however, at some levels and is contradictory to this democratization. While some young Mourid from the Maraboutic families prefer to be called "spiritual guides" rather than Cheikh, the possibility of marriage remains a matter of the maintenance of Mourid lineage ideology:

> There are some in the family who are old-fashioned, and if they heard of these things outside of the family they would get really angry and say the Marabout said this and said that. . . . But, for instance, my mother doesn't want me to marry the sister of _____. He is a noble from the mother's side, but the father was a ___, and they were former slaves. There are names like Gueye in which about 80 percent of the people are not noble and _____ is like this 80 percent. . . . You can tell from the name. . . . Oh, I don't know. You have to call down there in Senegal and the old people of the family. They know these things; they know who is or isn't noble. But Cheikh Amadu Bamba fought against this. He took the Guel and made him leader of the Jola and the Guerre. And he took the Serer and made him head of the Wolof. They said that the Wolof were a little dominant there, and there is a little war. . . . There couldn't be a war now between the Wolof and the Jola. *They have one voice.*

Mourids in Turin

There were at least two major poles of Mourid migration in Europe and other areas during the 1980s. The first was the creation and expansion of commercial networks and activities by the Senegalese traders and the propagation of Mouridism through the centers largely of the established Da'ira organization. The second was the increase of the following of Mouridism and its teachings (Ebin 1990; Diop 1990). This economic pattern reflects the theme of the *hijira* or exile of Amadu Bamba by the French in the nineteenth century, followed by the celebration of his return to Senegal in the *Magal*, which is commemorated each year with the return of hundreds of thousands of persons from all parts of the world to Touba, the sacred city of the order (Diop 1990). The Senegalese in all areas of emigration are accustomed to many hardships and often set up their settlements in the most run-down and peripheral areas of the cities to which they migrate (Ebin 1990).

After saturating the market in African art in France in the 1980s, Senegalese began to move into Italy. In Turin, many of the Senegalese set up make-shift shops to sell trinkets, leather goods, and objects of African art, *roba Africana*. Italians believe that these articles are made by Italians in Naples, not understanding that the Peul figures, for example, are made by the hands of Senegalese—and are not the cottage industries of Neapolitan workers.

All this street selling occurs across from the gates of Pelagio Palaggi, one of the great masterpieces of neoclassical Italian architecture, gates that once led to the former seat of the House of Savoy in the Palazzo Reale, and the small piazzetta to which the gates open, now diminished greatly by its use as a parking lot. The Senegalese street sellers line up along the streets that intersect the long baroque arch of Via Po and that of Via Roma, where the most exclusive shops in Turin line the way to Porta Nuova, the train station conceived in the event of the unification of Italy and responsible for making Via Roma the main artery of Turinese social life.

The street seller is one of the most despised social categories of immigrants in popular Italian imagination, a subject of both pity and disdain, and the sellers are constantly approached by the police: "I move over here and they come, so I move down Via Po and later they come." The sellers have no license to sell and do not think of themselves as needing one. Before the passage of the Martelli Bill, which regularized the status of migrants, the sellers could have been given a *foglia di via,* an order to leave Italy. Now their wares are seized and they are told to stop selling in the street. Few of the sellers know of the forms that would require the police to return their materials. The local commercial people complain that the street sellers frighten their clientele away and that they are in competition with Italian commercial activities. Yet the seller with a plywood rack full of watches lined in consecutive rows or the small wooden forms of Peul women, elephants, and sometimes small jewelry boxes seem hardly in competition with Fendi or Cartier.

The sellers organize their day around the Italian *passeggiata,* when Italians come out to walk, talk, and window-shop and may thus buy from them. In the evening the Senegalese pack up their large black nylon bags and return to their homes across town, and the trains and the

streets are aware of this passage, as friends stop to accompany one another and chat at the tram and bus stops. There are different rhythms of
the selling: some take the late-night shifts near the Porta Nuova train
station—often the wood-workers, since their days are spent working the
wood and preparing pieces to go out or to sell to other sellers. "Bless us,
we are only Laube," a wood-worker once said to the Marabout after a
prayer circle, their hands outstretched as if to take a drink of water, and
then taking in the blessing they washed themselves in the blessing as if
it were water. The Mourid practice cannot be separated from work or
work from religious practice; the traders frequently ask for the blessing
of their goods, and the passage of the Marabout for blessings is a regular
occurrence in the streets of Turin.

The traders wear pins or buttons with the photograph of their
Cheikhs or Marabouts from Senegal. A few traders, mostly the Laube
wood-workers, have pendants of Cheikh Ibra Fall.[28] Devotion to the
Marabout is often hereditary, and the son will follow the Marabout of
the father. The first disciple of the Marabout's son has a special relationship to the son of the Marabout. Soon after their arrival, the Senegalese
in Turin displayed large photographs of the Marabout in their cars, and
as they sped down the motorway, the photograph of Cheikh Assane Fall
or another Marabout could be distinguished in the rear windows and
the sounds of reggae music could be heard.[29] The Senegalese who meet
one another take the hands of their friends and press them to their foreheads in greeting or hold one arm at the elbow as a sign of deference.
This handshake is part of the young Mourid culture, as is the habit of
wearing African clothing. Many other African migrants say they respect
the Senegalese for remaining "African" and maintaining African culture
in the face of the many hardships in Europe. One Mourid migrant told
anthropologist Victoria Ebin, "We know misery so well that we have
come to love it so much that now we conjugate it as a verb: Moi, je
misere à New York; toi, tu misere à Paris." "Hardship," Ebin writes, "is a
part of their religious heritage," referring to the hardships experienced
by the founder Cheikh Amadu Bamba during his exile (Ebin n.d.). This
African cultural pride is a very attractive quality that the Mourid present
to many young people along with the Pan-African ideology expounded
by many of the spiritual guides. In New York there are informal relationships with many of the followers of American Moslem traditions (Ebin
1990).

Mouridism in Europe: "La Vulgarisation du Mouridisme à L'Etranger"

One of the important features of the development of Mouridism in Europe is its relationship with European people. Beyond the difficulties with the host countries, there are a whole series of problems that reflect the "mission" of the order in Europe. Many of the activities of some of the intellectuals of the order in Europe concern the translation of the thought of the founder into a version of his philosophy and theology that is accessible to the West. As El Hadj Fallou N'Diaye (son of Serin N'Diaye Guèdè) writes in *Ndigël,* one of the difficulties in presenting the ideas of the founder is what he calls the "de-Senegalization" of the thought:

> The fundamental problem of the popularization of Mouridism is intrinsically the de-Senegalization of the thought of Cheikh Amadu Bamba, who with brilliant foresight took from the Koran and the Sunnah of the Prophet. From this moment Mouridism would have the right to worldwide recognition (N'Diaye 1990).[30]

The conquest of new frontiers is an essential part of the order. In the founding of the order the conquest of new lands for the followers led the *talibé* into conflicts with peoples residing in uncultivated lands that encircled the far reaches of peanut cultivation. The passage of lands into the hands of followers was an important feature of the expansion of the order. What Cruise O'Brien has called the agrarian colonization of the Mourid was particularly evident among the lower classes of Wolof society, who participated in the formation of pioneer settlements founded by the Marabout in which they had rights to use the land. In many areas this meant the displacement of some of the Fulani (Cruise O'Brien 1975). (The Fulani are a pastoral group living on the fringe of Senegal's central desert [the Ferlo].) The need to essentially give the use of land to a labor force that receives no wages to some extent has resulted in the transient basis of the "pioneer zones." The estate is broken up after a brief period and has to be reformulated elsewhere (Cruise O'Brien 1975). The scarce resources of land and the fluctuations in agricultural prices have marked the beginning of a rural exodus of the cultivators toward urban centers.

From Agricultural Production to Urban Labor

In the urban context the relationship to the Marabout has changed. Although the founding of a town and the agricultural cultivation that accompanies it still give a great deal of prestige to some Marabout, for many the followers will become more and more committed to the international labor market. The conquest must move from the rural lands to the urban labor market and from the organization of production units for cultivation to concerns for particular categories of workers and relations with foreign governments. The emphasis of a mission in Europe for Mouridism is very much circumscribed by the urban context both in Senegal and in Europe, and the need to diversify economically and culturally in this new context—a process that has been occurring for some time. In 1973 there were already about one hundred thousand urban Mourids, according to Cruise O'Brien (1975), in towns such as Dakar, Koalack, and Thies. It must also be noted that in Senegal the Mourid tend to be relegated largely to the lower levels of urban employment, in some degree because of the low levels of instruction in the French educational system (Cruise O'Brien 1975). These towns were the formative ground of the migrations of Mourid and other Senegalese to international cities like Paris, New York, and Turin. And through these migrations the religious order has had the opportunity to extend its membership also to the European and American communities and elsewhere.

The growth of Mouridism is somewhat dependent on the dynamic increase in its numbers. The incorporation of new members in international contexts would provide the order with the basis of support necessary to sustain its hierarchy traditionally founded on the agrarian economy. As N'Diaye continues, "The progression of Mouridism would only occur with the adherence of believers from very different perspectives" (N'Diaye 1990).[31] The Mourid would like to incorporate more and more Europeans and others into the world of their religious practice. To this end a great effort is needed to translate the message of the founder into a form that will be accessible to Europeans. In order to do this the countries, their particular cultural practices and conceptions of the world, must be studied and known by the Mourid in every detail: "The first step in a process of popularization is to uncover the customs of the host country. If the country has a mass media, one must utilize this to spread the message. If the country is reflective, one must privilege discussion" (N'Diaye 1990).[32]

It is important to note that Mouridism has in fact a mission in immigration, and that this mission rests on the familiarity of the Mourid with Europe and with the cultural practices of the countries in which the Mourid live and work. This in no way entails the notion of a temporary residence in these societies but, rather, posits a continual relationship with Europe and many of the other destinations of migrants and the Mourid. In another passage from the same article, N'Diaye encourages the Mourid reader who wishes to carry on this mission to present the message of the Mourid, which is essentially, in the author's judgment, that of the Koran and the prophet Mohammed (that is, of Islam) to the non-Islamic world:

> The primordial problem is that of educational training. One must press against these two blockages in order to succeed in popularizing the thoughts of Serigne Touba. One must not stop at merely cultural expressions but actively invest one's efforts. This will facilitate spreading Mouridism throughout the world. Such advancement is only possible by being open to other viewpoints. But if one succeeds in sounding the necessary education, this will permit future popularization to reach the level of the universities, to learn the sociology of the countries in which their message will be delivered, while always respecting the local cultural realities as well as their visions of the world.[33]

The leaders of the Mourid order are the descendants of the nobles of Wolof society. In fact, all of the founding Marabout come from the old nobles of the Wolof. Under their direction the Wolofization and Islamization of Wolof society were accomplished. This same order is currently carrying out another type of mission, this time in the major cities of the world and under the direction of essentially the same order. Urban expansion has meant for the Mourid a global expansion through the migration of the *talibés* throughout the world rather than a diminution of its members. At least temporarily, the Mourid are attempting to export both labor and Islam.

The House: Senegalese in Turin

One of the first houses of Senegalese in Turin was established in the early 1980s by Ibrahim Wade, a former peasant-turned-trader, another trader, Abdoulaye Sow, a Laube master artisan and wood-worker, along with a third trader. "At that time in all of Turin there were only a few Africans";

according to tradition, the first Wolof conversion to Islam was made by a Wade (Waad) in the line of the second king of Walo in the end of the thirteenth century (Behrman 1969). The founding of the house in Turin, then, follows a religious heritage of the Wolof. The fact that Wade is actually Tidjan does not in fact detract from this but, rather, provides a point of common Muslim reference: "I called for others to come and they came from all over Italy, and they came to stay in the house. The more there are, *va bene.* Everyone works and doesn't cause trouble. There is no problem."

Now Wade lives in a room with twenty-two other persons. Originally, the house, which has three stories, had only the three founding residents, the traders. Now the house is the residence of more than 120 persons confined to living in only six rooms. While a trader for five years, Wade sold watches, glasses, and earrings and never had a real problem with the Turin police. His two wives and four children live in Senegal. He would like to bring his young wife, nineteen years old, to Italy where she might work, but it is difficult to find a place to live and, for a family of small proportions, almost impossible to find a landlord willing to "rent to foreigners." His eight dependents, including his father, who at seventy-five is too old to come to Italy, rely on the remittances he sends home and has sent for years.

Ibrahim Wade, like many other Senegalese peasant-trader-workers is multilingual and speaks Nar (Arabic), Wolof, Italian, and Serer. Although he can read some Arabic, he is not literate in any language. There is a great deal of pride attached to the fact of establishing the house in Turin and Wade, who was taken on as a welder by a local construction firm, has earned a place of respect at prayer meetings and in the daily activities of the house. He defers, however, to everyone else and offers the hospitality of this house to all who need it; there is always room. A Wolof, Wade lived only in Turin where he has had official residence since 1988. This is significant in that official residence is usually given when the resident can demonstrate employment in the official labor market and give a stable place of residence. Wade is recognized as the founder of the house and, although a Tidjan, he practices regularly with the Mourid Da'ira, which has facilitated the communal practice of praying circles in Turin.

Wade's household is the most crowded Senegalese residence in Turin and is the community with which I was involved the most during my fieldwork. The Senegalese in Turin during 1990–1991 were predominantly male, partly due to the difficulty of finding adequate housing in Turin, while other cities had a much greater proportion of women among the population. Women, however, participated in the daily life of the community and in the visiting and ceremonial networks. Women also had an important role in linking cities in Europe and African centers through travel. The house of the Senegalese in many ways was the counterpart of the compound or family residence in other parts of Europe or in Africa where children, parents, partners, and siblings resided. At times, this world was vivified through the showing of photographs or the telling of stories; at times, it remained a silent yet present world.

The house that Wade established was in a critical location for the internal trade of the Senegalese, both in France and in Italy. Communities of Senegalese extend the whole length of Italy and the islands with communities in Lecce, Milan, Livorno, Pisa, Florence, Rome, near Naples in the agricultural belt, and in other cities in Sicily and Sardinia. Turin was a crucial location for a community since it stands right on the line from Paris and has a large industrial belt surrounding it, giving a greater range of possibilities than agricultural regions that have been in Italy centers of foreign workers; the collection of various agricultural products such as tomatoes, for example, has almost completely been abandoned to migrants. Turin was a city that figured preeminently in the winter rest of the ambulant Senegalese sellers who travel the summer circuit along the seacoasts in Italy, and thus large portions of the population are found in such towns as Rimini. In the summer of 1986 the Senegalese were seen almost nightly on the customary beach Ferr' Agosto, the Italian holiday season taken by almost everyone at the seaside resort towns. The traders would sell sunglasses, tanning products, lighters, and other items and were referred to as *morochini,* a general term for ambulant sellers. As Cruise O'Brien and Coulon have pointed out, in Senegal the trader would move rather fluidly between city and country: "You go to town during the dry season, peddling what you can; but if the rains don't come at sowing time or come in insufficient quantity, you stay where . . . you are . . . in town." In the same way that trade was mediated by agriculture and street peddling in Senegal, in Europe it supplemented occasional work in construction, agriculture, and industry (Cruise O'Brien and Coulon 1988).

The establishment of the house occurred a short distance from the banks of the Dora, one of the rivers that runs through Turin and defines the Borgo Dora, once the farthest reaches of the reticular octagonal of

Turin. Just a few passes from the Arsenale di Borgo Dora and Piazza Borgo Dora, now the site of the weekend Baloon market and of a temporary home for homeless foreigners in Turin, lies the house of Wade. The Baloon is part of the great market of Porto Palazzo, which extends out from the historic center into the reaches of the borders of the city. The Baloon winds down streets leading directly in front of the old arsenal building now converted into a shelter for migrants. The little *piazzale* just at the shores of the Dora that stands before it fills with the sounds of migrants talking and smoking into the evening, and on market days it becomes a make-shift frontier of stalls. At this end of the market by the bridge over the Dora and just before it ended out into Corso Vercelli, on occasion migrants, often Senegalese, would join in and attempt to sell a few things in the market. They were often chased away from the other side in Piazza della Repubblica proper; here their transgressions were tolerated in a way.

The quarter of Barriera Milan stretches out at angles from the former Strada d'Italia and leads to the superhighway to Milan at one end of the city. In the local view, the whole region has been abandoned to small industry, the foreigners, and various factions of Piedmontese and southern residents (Passerini 1984, 44–49). Two of the characteristics of this quarter are the prominence of Third World migrants and the housing decline that has remained unchecked since the end of the Second World War. The area is defined in many ways by one of the unfortunate arteries that divides the eighteenth-century arcades of Porta Palazzo from the expansive urban residential quarters of this half of the city. One could hardly find a more contested domain of the city than this, either architecturally or culturally.

Coming into the house from the streets, one is disoriented a bit at first. Following with the eyes the line of the stairs that trail off to the right and the flight of mailboxes—many broken—lining the right wall of the entrance, this place seems abandoned at times. Just up the first landing on the left toward the river side of the house lies a wooden doorway almost obscured by the texture of the stone wall leading up to it. One could pass this door many times and never be aware of its existence, but it was here that the landlord lived. This door was rarely open, giving the house the feeling of closure that although false seemed complete. Up the stairs were the first rooms. Off to the right and above these was the only toilet in the house that consisted of a porcelain covering in the floor. This room served as a kind of dressing room at times, and the area just in front of the door of the bathroom, as a place for washing clothing. A large bucket was placed in the center of the space, and clothes were washed by hand, as others stood waiting their turn to wash or talking to pass the time, or brushing by the close space in order to pass into one of the adjacent rooms. There was no shower or bath.

During the early days of the migrations before many had work, the beds lining the walls would be full of people sleeping, wrapped in blankets with just their noses showing a little bit. Sleeping and reading were the only ways of being alone in the place. Meetings were often held in the landing rooms, and ceremonial foods were prepared and distributed there as well. Several of the rooms had faucets that were the only source of water. The landing provided the only space for bathing and, at times, the bathroom was a place one could pour water over oneself as a makeshift shower. The smell of the damp stone floor was always about, and on occasion there would be an excursion to a public gym to take a bath. Turning to the right from the final landing was the room in which the Marabout slept, and on the left, one of the main communal rooms in which a stove (a series of burners) was arranged in order to cook meals. On ritual occasions this room would serve as the center of meals and ritual presentation of food (see figures 4 and 5).

In the same manner that the great housing projects of Mirafiori Sud, Falchera, and Le Vallette were once moved by the rhythm of the great factories, the house of the Senegalese is drawn into the times of work and times of inactivity. The importance of work in the Mourid ideology, *khidma,* is perhaps one of the elements in the commercial expansion of the Mourid,[34] yet the economic pressure on other Moslem members of the "community of faith" (as the young Marabout Djilly Fall Mamour once called much of the Turinese Senegalese) seems to cause a decided discomfort with inactivity (Martinengo 1990). Babacar, who was one exam away from a technical degree in Senegal when his job in an Italian design firm in Dakar disappeared with the transfer of the project back to Italy, once said while we walked through the Baloon market, "I must work, I just can't sit around here [the house] all day. I must find something else to do. I am a man and I must work." Babacar has been coming to various parts of Italy since 1982 and has been involved in the trade of *roba Africana objets d'art.* "I had to do something. I have six children and I couldn't find anything down there, there was nothing. It would have been a shame to try and sell *roba Africana* in Africa." Babacar is part of a growing, would-be middle class, which for

Fig. 4. Senegalese (Bambara) woman preparing for Muslim ceremony. (Photograph by
Heather Merrill-Carter, 1990)

various reasons finds itself expatriated.[35] Babacar and other educated
migrants like him from Mauritania, Morocco, Eritrea, and Somalia feel
hemmed in, in their own countries by lack of political and educational
freedoms, the entrenchment of local systems of patronage, and religious
intolerance.[36]

The house in many ways became the center for a host of activities
including the Da'ira, the urban religious organization of the Mourid.
The Da'ira would meet weekly in one of the larger rooms of the house,
and Senegalese would come from all over Turin. The house had another
peculiar feature: the presence of one of the grandsons of Cheikh Ibra
Fall, Djilly Mamour Fall, of one of the leading branches of Mouridism,
the Baye Fall. Although a Senegalese association had existed in Turin for
more than five years, the young Senegalese did not trust an organization
founded by intellectuals, which they thought did nothing for them and
did not take their interests to heart. So there was the call for the establishment of a Da'ira that could represent them and place them in direct
relationship with the Khalifate-General of the Mourid order.

The house attracts attention from the Italian authorities. The house
of Senegalese in Turin has become a shorthand for the problems of the

Fig. 5. House after bombing and fire dispersed Senegalese residents. (Photograph by Heather Merrill-Carter, 1995)

"migrant" in Italian society (Grillo 1980, 1985).The house was known to the neighborhood, becoming famous in local urban folklore. People told the same stories about the making of the house that they had told about the making of the housing blocks of southern Italian migrants— those documented in the work of Goffredo Fofi in his classic study of Turin, *L'Immigrazione Meridionale a Torino* (1964). The politics of space is one of the primary forms through which various social orders, classes, and states envision the contemporary manifestations of power, privilege, and difference.

The Circle of the Angels

The Da'ira is a circle, a circle of the community of faith, and this circle is one taught to Cheikh Amadu Bamba by the angels. It is this circle that surrounds the singers in the prayer circle of the Da'ira practice when they recite their *dhikr* and walk around the space.[37] In many ways the mystical events of Amadu Bamba and the many features of this mystical world are a part of everyday Mourid life. Many times in passing these mystical events are referred to in everyday speech: "His power was so great that he went to Jerusalem on his own power," or "The colonialists tried to subdue him and he was exiled seven times." Such declarations link the life of the Mourid in diaspora with the sacred orbits of the life of the founder. The most striking example of this is in the discussion of one of Amadu Bamba's grandsons, educated at the religious *darra*, or religious school, of the order, and a resident of Turin.[38] The power of Amadu Bamba extends into the spiritual realm as well as that of the role of saint. His grandson asserts, however, that his power was so great that Jinns were his disciples:

> The angels are more powerful than the Jinns. . . . the Jinns can only reach one sky, but the angels can go to seven skys and the angels know many secrets. They know secrets from God. The Jinns know only the things of the world from all around the world; they know many things. The Jinns have a great deal of knowledge about technology. Technologies come from the Jinns. My grandfather had disciples that were Jinns.

The Marabout also have Jinns associated with them, and they are said to attempt to control their anger when they become too emotional about an issue because their Jinns may become involved. The Marabout, especially one from the dominant lineages of the Mourid Order, is feared for the power of his mystical sanction. It is very difficult for Senegalese to disobey the order of the Marabout. In Turin, the Marabout attempted to act as the intermediary between the community of faith and the outside. This meant job recruitment, housing, education, and all other aspects of the organization of the migrant in the new environment. Moreover, many thought themselves out of favor with the Marabout should they lose a job or have a particularly difficult period trading. If the Marabout does not speak to someone in the house, for whatever reason, that person is treated by other Mourid as though he or she did not exist. No one, save close relatives, dares to speak to the person who seems to incur the wrath of the Marabout.

Marabout are assumed to have mystical powers that stem from their knowledge of the Koran, certain forms of mystical knowledge, and the grace, *Baraka*, that flows through their familial line.[39] Marabout are assumed to be able to perform miracles and alter the course of worldly events. The Marabout may intercede for the follower in a whole range of activities. Many Senegalese wear amulets prepared by the Marabout for protection, especially when traveling abroad. These amulets have the power to enhance the success of trading, make one invisible, or protect the wearer from harm or arrest. Marabout may give blessings to their followers, but they may also cause harm to those who disobey their wishes. The mystical sanction of the Marabout is widely feared. One migrant once told me, "If I was at home in Senegal, I would have no fear of the Marabout here in Europe, but here without the protection of my family, I can do nothing. At home there are Marabout just as powerful as those here. Here I have no protection. I will give my presents to them; I want no trouble. . . . The Marabout could take his prayer beads and read something from the Koran and you would be dead." The Khalifa represents a tremendous achievement of mystical and religious powers for many followers. Although there are many Marabout, there are few who attain the status or power of the few hundred who direct the major orders. These Marabout, their families, and retainers wield considerable influence both through the orders that they direct and through the influence that the order may exercise in other spheres (Behrman 1970). The sons of the heads of these powerful lineages are often the extension of the order internationally throughout the diaspora populations.

The character of the Marabout in immigration is somewhat different from that of the Marabout outside of Europe. The Marabout is often a figure who is problematic for the West, given the basis of power and the association with both pre-Islamic and Islamic traditions. Often the object of media attention, the Marabout is a controversial, if not enigmatic, figure for Western sensibilities. Moustapha Diop points out that while the Marabout who devotes himself solely to ascetic pursuits poses no problem, the Marabout who steps beyond this purely religious role raises issues not unlike those posed by modern Western religious figures: "The figure of the Marabout is indisputably given in the religious imagery of the Sahelian populations; he is a venerated and feared figure, but also one that is sometimes subject to mockery, derided as a charlatan or unbeliever" (Diop 1989).[40] The images of the Marabout as a religious personage and charlatan are images that the Senegalese also use to talk about the Marabout. Some are clearly charlatans who merely want money and power, while others are true men of God who marshal Koranic knowledge and the grace of the true religious ascetic.

Diop delineates two types of Marabout in France who have distinguished themselves through religious and business activities. There are Marabout who, arriving with the massive black African migrations in

France, have become the focal points of religious education. This first category of Marabout linked to the religious practices of the great orders was in France the first generation of Marabout in migration: "This category derives from Maraboutic families long experienced as students of the theological sciences, councillors, directors, and secretaries because they are disposed to the power of writing, and the man of God in relationship to the invisible world" (Diop 1989).[41]

The second category includes those Marabout who have taken up the world of commerce and become *petits commerçants* in France. Some act as the intermediary of the *gestionnaires de foyers* and offer services of consultation in business negotiations and transactions involving their communities (Diop 1989). In short, the possibilities of both religious activity and business endeavor are very diverse in France, while these areas remain merely emergent in Italy. While Senegalese immigration to France, along with that of other Franco-African migrants, has continued apace since the 1960s (yet halted since 1983) and has resulted in more than 30 percent employment of these workers in industry and services in France, Italian immigration is only just beginning to penetrate the world of work. Migrant workers in Italy benefit from no social services specifically set up to serve their needs. Such basic problems as that of housing are difficult to solve. The formation of a stable community like that of France is, under current conditions, very difficult to foresee. Employment opportunities and bilateral agreements have in the past facilitated a more complete range of advantages—economically, culturally, and socially—for French migrants (Diop 1989).

Marabouts from Senegal regularly visit their followers in France and the United States. This visiting has now also been extended to Italy. Marabouts come to visit their followers and to pray with them and often make collections for the local communities of Senegal. This has produced diffuse feelings of Muslim solidarity, to some extent bringing members of various orders together in the celebration of Islamic practice. In addition to this there is an increasing awareness of the broader Muslim community, international religious movements, and the positioning of Islam in Europe. The nature of Islam in Europe is a subject entertained by the European media, particularly in Italy. This discussion has centered on the building of both a Milan and Roman mosque. Although Senegalese are not viewed in commonsense Italian ideology as primarily Muslim, they must come to terms with at once an anti-Muslim bias and a more encompassing notion of what it means to be

Muslim in Europe. It should be pointed out that the relationship between Catholic and Muslim Senegalese in many cases is a close one. The young people of the Turin community find themselves in a dynamic social situation in which many Muslim communities may come together and enjoy the solidarity and unity of being Muslim in a predominately non-Muslim country.

II
States of Grace

4

The Art of the State:
Difference and Other Abstractions

> The Nation-State . . . is a continuing project, involving collective experiment and experience. It is also an arena for a multitude of lesser projects, of many kinds and on many levels. The central problem of the Nation-State . . . is to maintain a reasonable balance between the national project and those projects of lesser scale.
> —L. A. Fallers, *The Social Anthropology of the Nation-State*

Toward an Anthropology of the Modern State

The state is envisioned through official documents. From the cartographer's maps of the national territories to the presentation of columns and graphs in daily reports, the state must create and re-create a vision, or visions, of its own existence. The document, an artifact of the state constituted by routine data compilation and interpretation, is a nexus of complex underlying cultural significations and classificatory practices that give life to the art of the state. Like the cartographer's map of the nation, the document maps vast territories of the imagination cast between the identified and the unknown, life and death, and normalcy and divergence. The simple statistical profile of the nation, which has become essential to the daily rhythm of the state, charts this imagined terrain, marked by such practices as numeration, the designation and demarcation of the health of the population, and the delimitation of criminality. The document is a kind of cosmological window on the modern state, and through it we may examine the most taken-for-granted quarters of its routine practices (see Trouillot 1995). The document may grant or deny the state of grace that allows for safe passage through its world.

The anthropology of the modern state involves, as L. A. Fallers states in the epigraph quoted above, the "continuing project" of the nation-state and the constellations of discourses and practices that construct the state as a locus of collective meaning, allegiance, and knowledge. Since at least the seventeenth century, this process has apparently proceeded through the coalescence of local identities and communities in the project of state formation and "nation building" (Sahlins 1989). And yet just as easily as national projects and local territories and communities may converge in a dialectic that gives birth to the nation-state, recent events have shown the resilience of "imagined communities," of communities invented and constructed on the basis of various systems of distinction and local knowledge (Anderson 1983). In the contemporary context the state is no longer merely a location in which the project of creating the identities of its citizens takes place but is, rather, the locus of multiple practices and traditions, both local and of the noncitizens who pose difficulties for the state's imposition of social and cultural boundaries, which render the process of inclusion in a society both comprehensible and coherent to its population (Kearney 1991).

European societies today face one of the greatest challenges in the short history of the European social formation of the nation-state: the presence of non-European immigrants. The difficulties besetting those attempting to posit a conception of Europe as a kind of historical and natural whole are compounded by the increasing heterogeneity of European societies. I view this increasing heterogeneity as part of a process that includes the chronological progression of European colonial, postcolonial, and neocolonial relations, which have resulted in the creation of a vast transnational and interwoven world of great cultural, economic, and social diversity.[1] Conceptions of territorial jurisdiction over a certain territory and of the political boundaries of the modern state pale in comparison to the creation of human relations, which rest on the recognition and significance of imagined communities, rarely contiguous with the ideology or tenets of modern nationalism (Appadurai 1990). In Turin, a young Senegalese Mourid religious leader once spoke to me of the many Senegalese migrants in the town: "Ask them about the state. They don't even know what the state is—they only know God." The Senegalese state became an important entity to many of the migrants only when they made the trip to Dakar in order to obtain the passport and the airline ticket that brought them to Europe.

The state project is often articulated through the the curriculum and what Antonio Gramsci calls the "whole social complex" of the schooling process (Gramsci 1971). For many states, however, this diffusion of knowledge remains poorly integrated into the daily lives of its citizens. For many of the Senegalese migrants with whom I worked, the state-operated French schools were a symbol of French neocolonial domination and of the rule of an urban intellectual (Cruise O'Brien and Coulon 1988). Many of the rural-based Senegalese migrants—by this I mean the subproletariat Senegalese Mourid trader in Dakar and elsewhere—may distinguish the arch of his or her world as existing outside that of a so-called urban intellectual. The state project of Senegal may be ideologically inferior to that of the Muslim Brotherhood, which imposes its logic on the world of signification and order in which some Senegalese live, both in Senegal and in the elsewhere of the diaspora.

The coherence and persuasiveness of the state project may also have similar effects on European national social orders and classes that enjoy privileged access to schooling and other benefits of Western democracies. In Italy, persistent historical and social asymmetries between the North and South of the country and between the cultivators and the industrial proletarian, north and south, have resulted in a series of social problems that still face the contemporary nation-state (Bagnasco 1988, 1990a). In much of Europe, for the first time in contemporary postwar history, the legitimacy of its governing majorities is being challenged at the polls by those who have felt themselves to be excluded from the running of these countries in the past.[2] There is no doubt that this crisis of legitimacy, which has been discussed by many observers of Italian politics since the 1970s, has coalesced in a strong antigovernment voting bloc that has recently dealt a devastating blow to Italy's governing party of the past fifty parliamentary governments, the Christian Democrats.[3] The era of Giuliano Amato marked the advent of a housecleaning in Italian government, as no major leader took on the task of guiding the nation through the scheduled debates over governmental reform. It is unclear what form the postreform government may take or what role the old power brokers of the party system may play. The new experiments will undoubtedly be directed by increasingly technical players, those without political futures. The technical government is truly what Gramsci once called the "government of functionaries," a kind of automatic state (1971). This is the curious pose of the Amato period: with his ministers swept away and pending reforms, the government appears to run itself in the transition to the fifty-first postwar government and beyond. In spite of the scandals of the Tangentopoli—capital of the kickbacks—in Milan, investigations and resignation of ministers, bankers, industrialists, and party leaders, the most day-to-day activities of the state, its routines, continue: the unquestioned background, asserted in every line entry, is reaffirmed in every dossier.[4]

Ideological Projects of the State

Several themes or tropes, including work, criminality, and health, are features of particular discursive and administrative practices that took shape during the formation of the contemporary state. These themes are an integral part of state intervention and legitimation, and the popular vision of various state ideologies. I consider these themes sites that focus certain complex sets of discursive practices, ideologies, coercion, the articulation of disparate social classifications, the implementation of policy, and other practices. These constructs, like other artifacts of the eighteenth and nineteenth centuries—community, democracy, population, and the nation-state—condense vague traces of ideologies into particular visions of society and polity (Nisbet 1966). Crucial to the interplay of consensus and coercion in all state cultural forms, these sites are an integral part of some state projects. State practices—including numeration, intervention in the health and composition of the social body, the construction and diffusion of state ideologies through a vast array of social sites (schools, the workplace, and the media), and the many interventions of the state in the domain of work—all form part of an extensive repertoire (Gramsci 1971).

There are several projects essential to the modern state: numeration, surveillance, collecting information,[5] classification, and intervention, which may be examined in an anthropology of the state. Perhaps the nation-state's most important activity is the continual orchestration of its own existence. Key in the initial phases of state assertion is a monopoly on various forms of state coercion. According to Max Weber, the state is the "human community that . . . claims the monopoly of the legitimate use of physical force within a given territory" (Gerth and Mills 1977). This capacity to resort to the use of force is particularly important in the weak state, which can rely on little popular consensus. There is a more portable form of power, however, that has no need of the trappings of force—in a word, routine. Routine data collection of state administrations informed by the methods of the social sciences helped to create a new configuration of coercion in the modern state.

Gramsci to Foucault: Coercion, Othering, Ideology, and the State

The pretense of modernity, of the scientific nature of the foundation of modern democracy, gives the coercion of the state its legitimate basis (Gramcsci 1971, 243–44). There is a great emphasis in the work of Antonio Gramsci on ideological dimensions of state power and on the struggle for control of this power by various political authorities and social coalitions. The state for Gramsci was equivalent to a "hegemony protected by the armour of coercion," or, rather, the exercise of a political and social hegemony over both political and civil society. The great array of state agents and the ever growing cadre of functionaries of the state for Gramsci constituted a kind of "government of functionaries" of political society who exercise particular legislative and coercive functions of the state. Only through the restructuring of state life by a party that might represent the interests of the subaltern or popular masses might the state attain a true state character and state life be rendered more "spontaneous."[6]

The possibility of the rule of the state by an alternative social group or party would allow the individual to "govern himself without his self-government," thereby entering into conflict with political society—but becoming its normal continuation, its "organic complement." For Gramsci, each member of society is ultimately a legislator. The organic intellectual may in turn represent the interest of the subaltern classes as an extension of this legislative power at the governmental level, once the state takes on its true quality:

The maximum of legislative capacity can be inferred when a perfect
arrangement of the organisms of execution is matched by a perfect
preparation of the "spontaneous" consent of the masses who must
"live" those directives, modifying with those directives and with the
objectives which they propose to achieve. If everyone is a legislator in
the broadest sense of the concept, she or he continues to be a legislator, even if she accepts directives from others—if as she carries them
out, she makes certain that others are carrying them out too; having
understood their spirit, she propagates them as though making them
into rules specifically applicable to limited and definite zones of living
(Gramsci 1971, 266).

Everyone contributes to the modification of the "social environment" in
which she "develops" and thus tends to establish "norms," "rules of living and of behavior." According to Gramsci, it is this aspect of the life of
each and every person that may be said to participate in the "legislation"
of society. Although the "greatest legislative power belongs to the state
personnel," the agency of this second nongovernmental order may offer
an alternative view of the world of the state. This, of course, follows
Gramsci's preoccupation with the nature of state power and the exercise
of leadership or hegemony that might precede the taking of governmental power.

Gramsci argues that the period after 1870 ushered in a transformation of the Italian state that resulted in the creation of "massive structures of the modern democracies," including extensive state organizations and "complexes of associations in civil society," which became the
"trenches" and the "permanent fortifications" of the modern state. This
is in fact quite accurate. The dimensions of this massive state apparatus
constructed in the wake of a progressive or, rather, progress-oriented
scientific social movement in Europe were to become increasingly associated with the development and articulation, albeit disorganized, of
a number of investigative practices. Investigative practices were transformed through concerns with environmental explanation, following
Hippocratic preoccupations in both medical and physical sciences and
an increasing concern with methods of observation, the health of populations, and economy—in short, with an interrelation of data of all
kinds. Growing apace from the 1770s or so through the late 1800s was a
concern with the rationalization of nomenclature and classification of
every sort, particularly in medical sciences, and a concern with precision
in the formulation of investigative questions. The "encyclopedist scientific thirst for cataloging all forms of information about the material

world," as Stuart Woolf and Jean-Claude Perrot note, was increasingly challenged through an interplay of data comparison. The medical investigations of population, for instance, led to an undermining of theories that posited a relationship between organism and environment (Woolf and Perrot 1984; Copans and Jamin 1978).

The state is synonymous with a project of state affirmation and control. Gramsci once described the state as "the entire complex of practical and theoretical activities with which the ruling class not only justifies and maintains its dominance, but manages to win the active consent of those over whom it rules" (1971, 244). For Gramsci, the activities of the social sciences were essentially "political" in nature. The success of the evolutionary and positivist theories of the nineteenth century merely led to a legitimation of the vast structures of the state, viewed as following a "natural" process of evolution over the backwardness of less rational forms of government and society. The nineteenth-century views of the state as the natural outcome of an evolutionary process were opposed by Gramsci with the philosophy of praxis, or Marxism, that viewed man in relation to a historically determined social complex, "the totality of social relations," and certain sets of conditions. For Gramsci, the state may be conceived of as an "educator" who imposes a particular conception of the world and as an instrument of the continual acceleration of the rationalization and standardization of its population. Here we may take *rationalization* to refer to the continual implementation of state ideology that attributes state activities to rational projects or to progressive strides over backwardness and disorder. The "cultural policy" of the state, Gramsci once wrote, "will above all be negative, a critique of the past; it will be aimed at erasing from the memory and at destroying"; at every point an oppositional posture exists to popular forms of memory and self-assertion or "spontaneous consensus" of subaltern classes (263). The state, he writes, "urges, incites, solicits, and punishes," once the condition is attained in which "a certain way of life is possible." That which falls outside of this sphere is then "criminal action or omission" and must be negated by the "civilizing activity undertaken by the State" (247). Meritorious activities are rewarded while "criminal actions" are punished, and thus "public opinion" attains the form of public sanction (247). The rational tenets of the nineteenth century became a kind of passion for some practitioners of anthropometric and statistical design, a passion that ushered in new forms of distinction and new ways of envisioning the world.

Criminality as Social Mapping: Others and Social Unrest

Banditry was in the first place a revenge upon established states, the
defenders of a political and even social order.
>   —Fernand Braudel, *The Mediterranean*
>   *and the Mediterranean World in the Age of Philip II*

To the peasants . . . the myth of the brigands is close to their hearts
and a part of their lives, the only poetry in their existence, their dark,
desperate epic.   —Carlo Levi, *Christ Stopped at Eboli*

From the sixteenth century onward, the problem of popular disturbances
plagued European societies. Banditry was the correlative of an increased
impoverishment that was to continue throughout the sixteenth century
into much of the seventeenth. In the cities the poor became a permanent feature; such categories of persons as vagrants, beggars, and gypsies
were regularly expelled from the cities only to return and begin the cycle
again. The vagabond soon became a popular literary trope; these figures
began to enter into European literature as early as the latter part of the
1600s (Braudel 1966). These wanderers and unfortunates were sometimes associated with the underworlds of the towns. The popular disturbances of the sixteenth and seventeenth centuries continued on a regular
basis in Italy, and such areas as Calabria, Abruzzi, and other southern regions experienced problems of brigandage right through Italian unification. The fringes of the young Italian state were peopled with brigands
who posed themselves as defenders of the peasants against the gentry
and the state. Their activities continued through much of the 1860s in
spite of military intervention.

During his obligatory exile in a small southern Italian town during
the Fascist period Carlo Levi described the brigands as the heroes of the
peasants. In 1935, at the beginning of the Abyssinian War, Levi was ban-
ished to Lucania, a village that even today remains remote to both Italian and foreigners. This experience placed him in contact with a world
rarely seen by members of his class:

> The brigands unreasonably and hopelessly stood up for the life and
> liberty of the peasants against the encroachments of the State. By ill
> luck they were unwitting instruments of History, and History, quite
> outside their ken, was working against them; they were on the wrong
> side and they came to destruction. But through the brigands the

peasants defended themselves against the hostile civilization that never understands but everlastingly enslaves them; instinctively they looked on the brigands as heroes. The peasant world has neither government nor army; its wars are only sporadic outbursts of revolt, doomed to repression. Still it survives, yielding up the fruits of the earth to the conquerors, but imposing upon them its measurements, its earthly divinities, and its language. (Levi 1963 [1947])

This "peasant Italy," as Levi calls it, vanished at the end the Second World War, when these remote villages of the South were deserted by the internal and inter-European Italian labor migrants, who became the largest industrial proletariat in Europe. There is a lyric quality in the discussion of the South of Italy that often forms an integral part of the discussion of the *Mezzogiorno*, or land of the midday sun: the assumption is that time somehow passed over the South and left this Italy outside of time. Levi writes of the peasants of southern Italy in another passage: "There should be a history of this Italy, a history outside of the framework of time, confining itself to that which is changeless and eternal, in other words, a mythology"; "every outside influence has broken over it like a wave, without leaving a trace" (Levi 1963 [1947]). This trope of the changeless South, however, is a contemporary part of popular imagination and forms the basis of the current view of the South. The *Carabinieri,* an Italian police force established in 1814, was crucial in the fight against brigandage in the South of Italy (Haycraft 1985). More than a threat to the legitimacy of the young liberal state in the early 1860s, the activities of the resistance to the state in the South were an affront to the sensibility of the political elite. Influenced by the "positive" developments of modern society and ever aware of "primitive" forms of social evolution (Woolf 1979b), the ruling elite articulated a vision of the south that was to be normalized in its most intimate routines, rituals, and administrative forms (Grossi 1981). The activities of the brigands in the South, Martin Clark notes,

forced the northern ruling class to abandon any idea of regional autonomy; they ensured that the army would be organized "nationally"; and they contributed greatly to the North Italian belief that Southerners were a separate and inferior race. . . . The educated, progressive, "European" view of the world was clearly not shared by the bulk of the Southern population. A sense of unease, of fear, of dark subterranean hatreds waiting to be unleashed, was never absent from political debate thereafter. (Clark 1984)

Integral to the "internal pacification" of the population was to be the designation or classification of "potentially recalcitrant groups" in an increasingly extensive body of administrative practices, relegated to the appropriate policing or regulatory agency (Giddens 1987). The extension of state regulatory and administrative practice in the early nineteenth century converged with an enthusiasm for the methods and procedures of the social sciences. This young science provided the state with its most characteristic coercive projects. The popular disturbances of the brigand were sometimes labeled "social deviance" and were dealt with summarily by military forces such as the *Carabinieri* for the threat that such groups posed to the nation.

This convergence of a new coercive complex of the modern state, the classification and exclusion of certain populations and inclusion of others in its configuration, has no doubt been taking form since the seventeenth century (Giddens 1987). Michel Foucault calls this process "sequestration," a process through which the control of vagrancy, crime, and the care of the sick becomes the "social concerns" of the European ruling classes. Subsequently, the separation of the various "unfit" populations became a routine practice (Foucault 1979a). This partitioning of individuals and spaces—of the distribution of productive functions into particular spaces such as factories, of persons into spaces that both "isolate them and map them," the quality of surveillance, and the arrangement of spaces of production, care, and training—is of great importance to the development of the administrative complex of the modern state. Foucault points to administrative measures that individualize medical, economic, and political objects and become cultural forms of state routine. It is clear that during the transition to the modern state, "a new nexus of coercive relations was established" through the articulation of a centralized power that could classify and control various forms of "deviance" or difference (Giddens 1987).

The tension between two Italian social orders, the North's European Italian progressive elite and the many contours of an alleged southern atavistic and primitive world, was an essential part of the conception of the national project of Italy from the moment of its unification. The difference between north and south in Italy, Luigi Barzini once wrote, "permeates every detail." Official Italy (which some call "legal Italy" in order to contrast this legal world of laws and statutes and the powers of the state with the "real Italy" in which people live and in which the reach of the state and its "civilizing activity" have had limited success), in the course of one hundred years has "succeeded merely in unifying names, labels and titles, but not reality," Barzini observes.[7] The regionalization of the Italian economy, the great heterogeneity of its populations, their many histories and traditions, the resonance of the South with social unrest and calls for land reform—all of these changes were carefully mapped by young architects of change of the new nation.

The structural imbalances of the Italian economy have become a permanent feature of the nation's historical development (Bagnasco 1977). The displacement of poor agricultural laborers from rural communities began in the early 1870s and continued apace through the early 1900s:

> The dualism of the Italian economy, marking off the south from the rest of the country, most of the countryside from the cities, deepened within the manufacturing sector through the development of a modern, mechanized, mostly capital-intensive industrial sector. This structural imbalance had a depressive effect on the growth of internal demand and above all on employment. As population grew, emigration, initially mostly from the rural areas of northern Italy, shifted increasingly and decisively to the south. From about 100,000 a year in the early 1870s, overall emigration rose to 300,000 annually by the 1890s and over 500,000 annually in the years of rapid industrial growth after 1900. (Woolf 1979a)

According to one popular song that recalls the brigand tradition, the *Piazza del Sud* or southern townsquare is where one goes to "speak of departed friends and relatives that have passed away." The song notes the devastation of southern regions with the loss of much of the productive population. The figure of the migrant is firmly implanted into the popular imagination of Italian modern social lore. In the mountain passes of the North that cut into the foothills of the Alps, only a stone's throw from the French border, the villages remain virtually empty until summer, when Italian migrants return from France for holiday to their old home village.

The Italian internal migrant experience has perhaps been one of the most contested and difficult situations to come to terms with since the host country, Italy, was not a foreign country or destination and was yet clearly implicated in many forms of neglect and discrimination. The massive migrations during the initial 1950s through the 1970s from the impoverished South to the industrial areas of the northern triangle

(Milan, Turin, and Geneva) were some of the most dramatic and unsettling. The social world that took shape in the wake of these displacements ushered in an era of protracted labor struggle and gave birth to rigidly segregated quarters along regional and class lines in many northern cities. Still, there is a kind of ceiling above which southerners seldom travel. The expansive housing projects of the great cities like Turin and Milan are a testament to the "southern question," which today appears as an urban question. Unemployment and an abandonment to the urban reality of post-Fordist life are the key features of the new generation, the sons and daughters of one of Europe's largest urban proletariats.

In the contemporary context some of the same classifications that have remained a part of the mapping of Others in European society since the sixteenth century, such as beggar, vagrant, and prostitute, have become figures by which to map the social contours of a new stranger in Italian society.[8] The separation of the unfit requires clear criteria that are often sought in the assurance against various types of "risk" associated with the stranger. Various forms of criminality and disease were initially voiced as concerns in the recent immigration of Third World peoples to Italy. The Martelli Bill, the first immigration legislation of postwar Italy marking the shift of Italy from the list of *sending* nations to that of *receiving* immigrants, contains a clause that allowed the exoneration of medical fees for newcomers for the first year of the law's tenure. This provision was passed into law for fear that African and other immigrants might introduce the threat of AIDS and syphilis, conditions reportedly prevalent in sending countries. The newcomers' lack of clear means of support places them at risk for possible recruitment into criminal organizations. The migrant therefore is often seen as contributing to a rise in criminal activity in *lavoro nero*. *Lavoro nero* covers a wide range of activities from the sale of heroin and hashish to off-the-books construction work or domestic service. Such provisions as the Martelli Bill, however, regulate through a parade of documents, medical records, police reports, and the fetish of racial, national, and other distinctions the development of a transnational labor context that requires an increasingly portable form of "partitioning." In Europe, as in the United States, this is provided by the play of biopolitics, race, and the passport.[9]

The "marginal" became for the state (or states) a permanent structural feature. In part the apparatus of the state (Italian or other) is constructed on the basis of the existence of this other reality. The off-the-books work world, *lavoro nero,* of the Italian and other economies is a permanent feature of Western capitalism. Migrant labor is drawn into the national system here and yet remains apart from its welfare and other benefits. This stranger becomes, as Meyer Fortes once wrote, "the prototypical 'other,' the alien outside the fence of custom, belief and rule that marks the limits of the moral community to its members" and in turn creates a justification for the many policing functions of the state (Fortes 1975; see also Kearney 1991). The identification of this marginal world and its contours in the contemporary context are part of an ideology of protectionism that acts in many ways to still the rise of labor activism, while imposing exploitative work regimes in this marginal world and giving national workers cause to be more cautious in their demands. Rather than risk calls for reform, which during the 1980s resulted in the curtailment of the labor movement and the reaction of middle-strata management and workers against the disruption of production through the many strikes, national workers focused simply on holding on to what they had.

Calls to end *lavoro nero* are complicated by the fact that the disappearance of this off-the-books work world means that the social cost of labor must be confronted by the whole society and labor costs of the new workers must also be considered. Such issues as welfare benefits, pension plans, and housing are in fact international issues since these programs are paid for through deductions from workers' paychecks and are confronted by the entire European Community (EC). Thus the maintenance of the marginal world at once precludes a crisis in the state of postmodern capitalism and signals the welfare states' inability to maintain production and reproduction of labor within the same national boundaries. The contemporary closure of Europe marks the creation of a single European community in which some nations take on greater policing functions for the entire EC. Countries previously designated as senders of labor, largely to the EC and other core economic centers in the world market, have become the receivers, if not importers, of labor. Countries such as Italy, Spain, Portugal, and Greece fall into this category. In turn, the boundaries of these nations increasingly become those of the transnational EC rather than those of a single nation, creating in fact the myth of Europe.[10]

Numeration: State, Statistics, and Other Abstractions

Bureaucracy is a circle from which no one can escape. Its hierarchy is
a hierarchy of knowledge. The apex entrusts the lower circles with insight into the individual while the lower circles leave insight into the
universal to the apex, so they deceive each other reciprocally.
                                                        —Karl Marx, *Grundrisse*

Population is an abstraction . . . if we leave out the classes of which it
consists.   —Karl Marx, *Grundrisse*

Karl Marx notes in the *Grundrisse* that such concepts as population,
nation, and state are "imaginary concrete" creations of seventeenth-
century economists—conceptions drawn from the tenets of liberal
democracy and the contours of the market that delineate in a condensed
form an entire theory of society. Through a series of general principles,
these "living aggregates"—"labor, demand, the division of labor, exchange and value"—are held by the economist to be "true" and lead to
the creation of the state and international exchange of world markets.
For Marx, such abstract conceptions as the living aggregate of population were merely errors of reasoning in the thought of G. W. F. Hegel.
"Hegel fell in this error" by assuming the real to be the result of "spontaneously operating thought," a mere "combination of many determina-
tions," a process of synthesis of diverse elements. Through this method
an illusion was born that conferred "concreteness" on the object of
thought. The state, then, for Marx is in many ways an illusion, an ideological project that imposes its concrete reality through systems that
confer legitimacy: "The method of advancing from the abstract to the
concrete is but the way of thinking by which the concrete is grasped and
is reproduced in our mind as concrete. It is by no means . . . the process
which itself generates the concrete" (cited in McLellan 1977, 351–52; see
also Corrigan and Sayer 1985).

The state is thus an ideological project that is realized through the
governmental practice of routine cultural forms that affirm and extend
the "totality" of its social and political relations. Various national manifestations of the state are therefore merely particular instances of the
universal processes of capitalism. The "present state," Marx argues, is
merely the instance of an arbitrary imposition of boundaries and frontiers, not a universal form like capitalism that may be analyzed accord-

ing to its actualization in diverse, historically situated contexts and societies. The present state is therefore an illusion (Gordon 1991).

For Michel Foucault, population as a preoccupation of the contemporary state was an innovation of the seventeenth century, when this new nexus of coercive and administrative powers of the state began to take their characteristic modern form. Population became one of the targets of governmental intervention, and with developments in the social sciences, through such methods as statistics, an increasing body of information was available on the specific contours of the population. The practice of what Foucault calls "the art of government," which privileged the "family" as its basis for economic reasoning, turned now to the population as a model site of intervention, subordinating the family, now seen as an element of the population. A new form was born, "governmentality":

> The perspective of population, the reality accorded to specific phenomena of population, render possible the final elimination of the model of the family and the recentering of the notion of economy. Whereas statistics had previously worked within the administrative frame and thus in terms of the functioning of sovereignty, it now gradually reveals that population has its own regularities, its own rate of deaths and diseases, its cycles of scarcity, etc.; statistics show also that the domain of population involves a range of intrinsic, aggregate effects, phenomena that are irreducible to those of the family, such as epidemics, endemic levels of mortality, ascending spirals of labour and wealth; lastly it shows that, through its shifts, customs, activities, etc., population has specific economic effects: statistics, by making it possible to quantify these specific phenomena of population, also show that this specificity is irreducible to the dimension of the family. (Foucault 1979b)

For Foucault, as for Marx, the ideological aspects of the state, and this shift from the art of government to an emphasis on economy and population or the practice of political science and political economy, has led to a tendency to overvalue the problem of the state. The rendering political of every aspect of governmental practice has in part enabled this complex to continue. According to Foucault, we live in the "era of governmentality" that originally developed in the eighteenth century. It entails the "governmentalization" of the state, the consolidation of various "techniques" and "tactics" of governing, internal and external to the state. Contestation over the "continual definition and redefinition of what is within the competence of the state and what is not" has become a crucial feature of state practice. The state lacks the "individuality," "unity," and "rigorous functionality" often attributed to it through a focus on certain functions, such as the state's role in the articulation of productive forces and the reproduction of the relations of production. For Foucault, the "state is no more than a composite reality and a mythicized abstraction, whose importance is far more limited than many of us think" (1979b). The principal forms of knowledge of the state and the particular ensembles of its institutions are the state's key figures for Foucault and constitute a process that cannot be confined to the immediate contours of the state as a vehicle of a specific function or "functionality."

Statistics: The Compass of the Social Sciences

> They cannot represent themselves, they must be represented.
> —Karl Marx, *The Eighteenth Brumaire of Louis Bonaparte*

> Nations . . . cannot be imagined except in the midst of an irremediable plurality of other nations.
> —Benedict Anderson, "Narrating the
> Nation, Race and Nationalism"

In his preface to a description of the Italian subalpine city of Turin, Davide Bertolotti wrote, "I believe that the proper description of Turin should be a kind of statistics." He noted that the beauty of the city lay in its "regularity" and the complementarity of its many parts, giving it a most modern aspect (Bertolotti 1840). Bertolotti's account, which details the various contours of Turin[11] through a description of its "popolazione, igiene e meteologia, storia and monarchia, esercito" (population, hygiene, meteorology, history, monarchy, and the army) among a host of other preoccupations and points of interest, harkens back to the designs of Aristotelian descriptions of states. Details of the customs, manners, and the formation of public administration, systems of justice, and the arts, along with a description of the contemporary character of the state and its relationship with other states, were among the concerns that Aristotle dealt with in his account of some 158 states. Although much of the Aristotelian "statistics" (a science of information important to statesmen, as it was to come to be known by German scholars) were lost, much of the collection of information no doubt helped in the for-

mulation of a theory of the state (Wetergaard 1932). Such collections
were a part of the early political life of Italian cities, beginning with the
work of Francesco Sansovino (1521–86) and Giovanni Botero (1540–1617).
Sansovino's work even included a chapter on "utopia" and gave accounts
of some twenty-two states, including ancient Sparta and Athens.[12]
Stuart Woolf notes that the development of statistical activities, which
chart the regularities of the modern state, began to take form in Europe
roughly between 1770 and 1840 (Woolf 1979b). Some ideological dimensions culminated in a preoccupation with statistics as a "science of facts
of state" and began to take shape around shared notions about the functioning of society filtered through an Enlightenment lens by means of a
"matrix of natural historical taxonomy." The nineteenth-century preoccupation with "environmentally anchored medical representations of
society" and the influence of population density linked to the incidence
of disease and the "medical-positivist theories of inherited class distinctions" began to create an interest in the quantification and numeration
of phenomena among a wide range of social interventionists from private associations to government agencies.

Between the coming into being of new juridical entities and the
emergent investigative practices of the social sciences, an elaborate cosmology, or state-ology, was taking form. Because of its role in the rationalization of society, the state was accorded a privileged place in an
elaboration of "progress" by a loosely organized cadre of thinkers and re-
formers. Many of the architects of modernity were actually on the outside looking in, in relation to state posts and powers. The consolidation
of the influence of medical practitioners or statisticians in state ideologies is fairly recent. The hegemonic visioning of the social world in its
medicalized or quantified form is the product of a long historical struggle. This recalls Marx in the *Brumaire* when he wrote of the peasantry as
one might write of the investigative practices emergent in the eighteenth
and nineteenth centuries and their sponsors as an emergent class of
specialists: "Their representative must at the same time appear as their
master, as an authority over them, as an unlimited governmental power
that protects them from other classes and sends them rain and sunshine
from above" (cited in McLellan 1977). This great concern with data collection led some to a shift in methodology from the "haphazard cataloging of *curiositis*" to the use of the tool of statistics for the observation
and classification of society (Woolf 1979b). This desire for the *rigor* of
positive information about social phenomena runs from Auguste Comte

(1798–1857), the originator of sociology, to the invention of criminal anthropology by Cesare Lombroso (1835–1909), and last, to a group of re-
formers and explorers who would discover in Italy the nature of the unknown fledgling state, for example, Carlo Cattaneo (1801–1869).[13] The
tropes of continuity between environmental phenomena and inherited
class distinctions and the relative proportions of the cranium were the
foundation of the scientific positivism of Lombroso; his criminology
used the new methods of statistics in order to purify the nation of elements that inhibited the progress of the country and threatened the integrity of the social order.[14] In conscription records from the military,
Lombroso sought lists of crimes and prison records, housing densities
and information on schooling; the symptoms of the "born criminal"
and the prostitute became two of the most popular forms of "deviancy"
antithetical to bourgeois nineteenth-century ethics (Gibson 1986). In
the prostitute and the criminal, all forms of medical contagion, social
and sexual deviance, and notions of the undeserving poor were combined in such a manner that both figures conform to the dominant
medical-positivist theories of society. Entering into the constellation of
common sense, these images have become part of the many fragments
derived from scientific thought that characterize the often almost lyric
forms of Othering and stereotyping that are common in European societies today.

The anthropological-statistical method of Lombroso was based on
the anthropometric methods of the Belgian meteorologist, astronomer,
and statistician Adolphe Jacques Lambert Quételet, who came to Paris
in the 1820s in order to create the "true science of man."[15] The outlines
of this new science of the body, *antropometrica,* were delineated through
the practice of the exact measurement of the body and elaborated
through the publication of several papers and essays, including "Sur
l'homme et development de ses facultes" in 1835, "Physique sociale, ou
essai sur le development de facultes de l'homme" in 1869, and "Anthro-
pometrie ou mesare de differentes facultes de l'homme" in 1871. According to Bernardino Farolfi, anthropometric methods became from the
beginning of the 1800s "the most direct instrument of the knowledge of
bodies and the processes of the first industrialization and socialization
of bourgeois society" (Farolfi 1979). The field of observation created
through the use of the techniques of anthropometry helped to isolate,
segregate, and individuate bodies through both social and civic enclo-
sures of youth, women, the working class, the aged, the infirm, and the

socially dangerous prostitute and criminal. By way of the bodies of these persons, in the first part of the century, through the gaze of doctors, philanthropists, and functionaries, the somatic was accorded the representative qualities of an entire social order. Quételet's measurements were drawn from the factories of Manchester, the poor of Paris, the insane asylums of Norway and Belgium, and the records of the Italian military. The anthropometric notions derived from this process gave credence to a vision of universal probabilistic homogeneity. This impulse to reduce heterogeneity to a common feature underpins the intrinsic instability of the national project and thus lends itself to affirmation of scientistic assurances (Farolfi 1979). In fact, the influence of Quételet and French Napoleonic administrative statistics was to be integral to the development of statistical practice in Italy.

Quételet, through an investigation of marriage patterns and birth and death records, invented statistical tools that focused on the "normative" in its relationship to the "pathological" and thus imposed a conception that privileged social regularity "along a continuum from normal to pathological" (Rabinow 1989). Paul Rabinow argues that the work of Quételet represents a step away from moral, psychological, and metaphysical theories derived from notions of natural law toward a notion of society as a phenomenon, "an object sui generis, with its own laws, and its own science." Normalcy and pathology were, then, a function not of an individual's moral state but, rather, of a social whole. Reform was in turn a matter not merely of individual moral fortunes but of "the social milieu," within which an actor's "actions were formed and normed" (Rabinow 1989). Statistics of the state were sometimes seen as not only the compilation and inventory of national resources but as the basis for the formation and articulation of national cohesion and identity. Reform was soon an integral part of the national project of the formation of "national subjectivities" and authority structures: "Statistics in the service of the state epitomized the political process in which decentralized local enquiry—to supply knowledge as the basis for action—was the necessary route for the reinforcement of central authority" (Woolf and Perrot 1984). And again: "Statistics, from the choice of field of enquiry to the conceptual classification of the questionnaires and the collection and re-elaboration of data, was indelibly marked with the imprint of Authority" (Woolf and Perrot 1984).

In 1861 in Italy, with the formation of the new Italian nation, even before military control was assured over the new territories, the first census was conducted by the Ministry of Agriculture, Industry, and Commerce.[16] The results of the inquiry were presented to the king and were said to prove the undeniable diffusion of the "national and unitary concept" throughout the young state (Romanelli 1980). The census was, moreover, "a new way of voting." It served as a proof of national unity—it was a kind of national statistical plebiscite, *una controprova statistica del plebistico nationale*. Raffaele Romanelli has argued that the young state sought to affirm its authority and to extend and search for a popular consensus through its diffusion of statistical activities literally mapping the whole of Italy (1980). The extraordinary compilation of detail was, however, in spite of its great volume, rarely the basis of governmental action. Those reports that depicted the government in a poor light were suppressed. Reports and inquiries into the condition of public security in Sicily and train service in Sardinia and the South were among the first reports sealed by the government; in fact, the second report disappeared completely, according to F. S. Merlino, a parliamentarian of the period. S. Jacini, another parliamentarian famous for his investigations of various land-tenure practices and poverty, complained in 1870 that the parliamentary archives were full of "precious relations and parliamentary studies, today covered with dust and forgotten," which reveal in each volume a surprising intellectual effort and care.

From the germinal stage of maintaining sources, however, the state was a protagonist of the first order. From the medical record to the census schedule, the very act of compilation rested on a knowledge that until then had been missing as a normative and political phenomenon in the daily lives of the general population (Romanelli 1980, 774).[17] Although Italy's passion for the collection of information far exceeded that of France, this may be, as Woolf suggests, due to the weak articulation of the new state in local areas and its constant need for the cooperation of local elites (Woolf 1979a). The great suspicion of the general population toward the many inquiries in fiscal matters and the conviction among them that such inquiries were, in any case, futile (along with a great "weariness at the repeated questions") often led local and national administrators into some difficulty (Frascani 1980).

From Document to Cosmology

Piedmontese legislative models and the traces of the Napoleonic era in Italy, which in some regions remained profound, led to the creation of a set of routine practices in Italian administration, inquiry, and government. Piedmontese hegemony set the tone of much of the legal pursuit of the young nation, its law providing the precedent for many of the important investigations in economic matters including the first medical geography of the Italian population in 1885. Piedmontese legislation of 1865 was the prototype for the formation of a core constellation of statistical projects of the prefecture system and offices coordinated with it; the information was designed to enable authorities to "envision" and control the communes, provinces, and the vast and somewhat poorly integrated state apparatus (Fried 1963). The Italian prefect had a great deal less power over local matters than his French counterpart. The Italian prefect's power was articulated through local elites and was exacted through the use of repressive measures and police functions.[18] The prefect was the furthermost point of the state's powers and acted in all matters concerning the state. This post in Italy was shifted frequently in order to maintain a strict allegiance to central control and for this reason was often considered part of the practice of "parliamentarianism," a directly articulated rule of the central state.

The prefect was, then, the embodiment of the dictum of the times— that the collection of knowledge was for the purposes of efficient administration, *conoscere per amministrare* (Frascani 1980). The mapping of the nation through the methodologies of the social sciences constituted a crucial way in which the liberal, anticlerical political class "envisioned" the social body through the lens of an increasingly coherent anthropometric and medical "cosmology."[19] During this period there was some concern about a lack of knowledge of the great variety of the nation's landscapes and economic and social resources. This unknown Italy became a preoccupation of the political classes, who wished to bring it into view of the "legal" Italy (Grossi 1981). Unknown reaches of the nation were coming to light in the columns of figures affixed to the reports of doctors and prefects and compiled in ministerial portfolios as affirmations of control and as the extension of the national project to even the most remote areas of the territories.

Count Cavour once said, "Studies that may be applied . . . are the primary needs of the modern epoch" (cited in Gambi 1980).[20] Indeed, statistics were seen, in the words of one provincial prefect, as "the primary guides and companion of the social science . . . the compass of the statesman" and, on another occasion, as the "sounding-line of the social sciences" (cited in Gambi 1980). The enthusiasm for the methodology of the social sciences went even further. In the view of this prefect as well as Count Cavour, the primary architect of the modern state, it was important to train the general population in the techniques of these most modern practices; failure to do so would, in the words of the prefect, "betray the interest of the Country and leave the working classes in the dark" (in Gambi 1980). Every datum became a matter of national import, and the documents that contained this knowledge through figures, rates of growth, records of deaths and births became cosmologies.

The nation-state may be viewed as the site of a particularly complex construction of a European cultural taxonomy, which entails the mapping and compilation of disparate data according to certain spatiotemporal coordinates and the construction of various media, such as maps, documents, emblems, histories, kinship ideologies, and language. And yet this abstact information has little relationship to the living and dying in local communities whose systems of meaning do not submit to quantification. The dialectic between incorporation and distancing is an integral part of the construction of the nation-state as a crucial site of coercion, control, and the coordination of economic and political phenomena. The trope of the European state as a time maker in a continuum of temporalization was a crucial feature of both premodern incorporation ideology and postmodern "modernity" metaphors associated with the eclipse of the nation-state as a key site of economic phenomena. If we look at spatiotemporal features of the constitution of the state as tropes of continuity and legitimacy and tropics or tropes of history, and in terms of replication of these tropes or polytropy in other forms and contexts, we may view the routine practices of the state as cultural forms informed by broader cultural processes. The document is the manifestation of a particular "mapping of things," which in turn reveals an encyclopedic constellation of discourse, not merely figurative, of the state (Fernandez 1991; Friedrich 1991; Fabian 1983; Eco 1985).

Knowledge and the Art of Statistical Caricature

The prerequisites of the prefect's knowledge formulated largely for economic reasons in Piedmont in the 1860s became a model for subsequent investigative practice. The territorial thinking of the political class and the European enthusiasm for the political administrative philosophy of *conoscere per amministrare,* knowledge for the purposes of action, along with a renewed preoccupation with the health of the population led in

1885 to the first medical inquiry into the Italian population (Rabinow 1989; Frascani 1980). The study, executed prior to a full-scale medicalization of society, is interesting for its attention to the categories of the administrative practices set out in the 1860s for the prefect and its disregard for many of the concerns of the emergent professional, the doctor. The compilation of knowledge of economic conditions, articulated by commune and region, was closely linked to the dictates of public order and security. The management of the many public assistance institutions in this manner became the direct responsibility of state representatives since control of these institutions assured the stability of public order and the eradication of problems of *mendicità,* or begging, which threatened the sensibilities of the upper classes. Along with describing general physical qualities of the region and the moral and economic nature of the population, and drawing comparisons between the country and urban areas, the prefect was to provide any other information that might prove enlightening to his superiors. The historically situated physiognomy of the regions was compiled through the comparison of yearly differences in rates of growth. The territories were enveloped in the monotony of figures, comparative tables, the presence or absence of resources, in the endless counting that became an etiquette of state. Populations became the abstract object of investigative requirements; soon, every act of administration, every effort of the functionary created a corresponding datum (Romanelli 1980). The document became to the state what money is to capital, an artifact constituted by the underlying cultural significations, classifications, and practices that bring them into existence.

Interest in the relationship of environmental factors to the distribution of disease and the efforts of the emergent medical practice to construct a "medical geography" of the nation culminated in the 1885 medical inquiry. The diversity in the incidence of illness led some medical investigators to call for state intervention in the field of medicine for the good of the nation. The medical profession stood precariously between the beneficent agencies of the philanthropist and the church, on the one side, and the anticlerical liberal elite of the state, on the other. Most doctors were not in the employ of the state and no comprehensive medical-administrative structure for the classification, administration, or treatment of disease had yet been created. Harvey Mitchell notes for France that the combination of the initiative and voluntarism of the physician and the medical cosmology or knowledge of the eighteenth century coupled with the support of this emergent cadre by the patronage of the bourgeoisie in France resulted in a decided dichotomization of medical care, where the great medical interventions, therapies, and treatments were to focus on the bourgeois environment of the urban world, neglecting those less fortunate (1979). This group of physicians in Italy called for the implementation of elementary medical practices, such as the control of waters and water sources, waste disposal, mortuary practices, and the investigation of dietary practices of the peasantry, and the distribution of health services to stem the spread of disease. The medical elite was very attuned to the possibility of "enhancing" its position vis-à-vis a state constellation of functionaries; this was accomplished in large measure through an increasing demand on the medical community to be the arbiters of all forms of medical information (Mitchell 1979; Frascani 1980).

The Milanese doctor Gaetano Strambio complained after the completion of the Italian medical inquiry of 1885 that the country had lost an opportunity to "collect the data necessary for an elaboration of a proper medical geography" of the nation (Frascani 1980, 954). The mapping of medical phenomena was sought out in the environmental contours of the countryside and assumed to have some relationship to the socioeconomic conditions of the nation. These concerns of medical men slowly took shape as a social project with implications for the entire community. One of the important developments of the early 1800s was the increasing medicalization of the military. Modeled on the Prussian and French armies, the Italian military took on the model of the Quételetian ideal of the "average man." New conscripts were held in comparison to an ideal of the model soldier. According to the military ordinance of 1854, the conscripts were to be examined in accordance with the requirements of a good constitution indicated by the vividness of the eyes, an erect neck and large chest, muscular arms, and a general harmony between the various parts of the body (Farolfi 1979). Furthermore, the exact manner in which the conscript was to be examined by the doctors, nude from head to toe, was outlined with an indication of the manner in which the feigning of fraudulent physical disorders would be treated through both the isolation of the conscript for observation in a military hospital and the criminal prosecution of those involved in the simulation of disorders, including doctors who knowingly affirmed spurious diseases. The doctor was, then, merely a functionary of the convergence of various repressive measures—not a protagonist in the first instance but a player in the orchestration of coercive powers (Farolfi 1979).

The 1865 Piedmontese ordinance from which the medical inquiry was derived did not even mention a role in the system of health for the doctor but spoke, rather, of the functionary's right to intervene in conditions of clear contagion, *cagione di insalubrità* (caused by lack of hygiene),[21] and in the control of certain beverages and other articles of consumption assumed to be harmful (Frascani 1980). The convergence of the physicians and the new techniques of the medical-statistical inquiry marked a qualitative shift in the role of the medical profession in the state project. The challenge to theories of environmental factors and the disposal of the many categories of medical knowledge and classification of the medical cosmology now in the service of the state made the study and articulation of this knowledge a primary concern of the state toward the latter part of the 1800s. Despite the tremendous resistance of the population through popular medical practices and an overwhelming weariness of the respondents to the questions of the functionaries, resistance to these new claims to scientific competence of state and medical officials was lost in the monotony of the data (Frascani 1980; Gambi 1980). This enthusiasm for the tabulation of the population has, in a sense, rendered the population superfluous; its pulse no longer perceptible, the population becomes an object of intervention. What Henry James once said about art can be said of statistics: statistics "is an embalmer, a magician, whom one cannot speak to fair" (James 1954). Such abstractions as statistics allowed the political class to view society as if it were an object with regularities like the orbits of bodies in the constellations, observed in the manner of the bourgeois's view of a painting in Honoré Daumier's *Connoisseurs*—with the all-knowing gaze of a specialist, in self-sufficiency, confident in an affirmation of regularity and control.

State (Desert) Crossings

The balance of precepts of rationality and control, which were to converge in the new state in Italy, along with new methodologies of the social sciences helped tip the scales of the nation toward a modernizing project or, rather, toward the modern. These investigative practices became such an integral part of the state project and the commonsense worlds of its populace that today we only vaguely envision a world without the table, the graph, or the population census. Foreign populations in the influx of migrants from the Third World in Italy have been at times viewed according to the many sites of information constructed during the eighteenth and nineteenth centuries in Europe designed to envision and map unknown worlds of the peasantry and the dangerous classes. Commonsense preoccupations of many Italians, with the continuous influx of foreign populations into the country, lack of government intervention, and knowledge of the phenomena have often culminated in a concern for the protection of national economic fortunes, pay scales, and jobs. These preoccupations resemble some early investigative themes, such as tropes of the moral texture of the newcomer, regional dispersal, social unrest, and, finally, medical and health concerns. Yet the methods of the modern European state proved initially inadequate to the new object of study, the Third World migrant. The categories of numbers, regions, and economic variables could not chart the far reaches of a population hidden in the world of work. With the close collaboration of employers who wished to evade the payment of taxes and medical benefits to workers, the workers themselves sought wages to place in a complex remittance economy that the welfare state was incapable of understanding, counting, or regulating. Beyond the marginal estimates of the migrants' numbers on the tables of the minister of labor, transnational migrants are only visible in the sensational tracks in the papers, and in the investigative reporting of the newscasts that place "blacks" just where commonsense dictates. The migrant, the men, and women with whom I worked, and the countless others like them, are invisible—their lives do not turn line entries on official documents into biographies. Thierno, a young Senegalese in Turin who dreams of becoming the next Ousmane Sembene once told me, "There has been a lot of talk about the colonialization of Africa. Now we have come to colonize it over here, and they don't like that." The *they* in this sentence tells the whole tale. *They*, the state, the Europeans, the world that constructs itself as the center of all things, cannot imagine themselves/itself as the *they* of another. Estimates take the place of actual numbers, and the estimates of the number of immigrants in Italy were enough to spark an increasing preoccupation with the supposed criminality of this underground economy and the presence of migrants and newcomers.

That which does not lend itself to quantification, medicalization, and control in the boundaries of the nation-state is suspect.[22] A residual assumption in the incorporation of the methodologies of numeration in the eighteenth and nineteenth centuries is that "all that the statesman's compass surveys may be controlled," may somehow be fixed by the columns, tables, and graphs that represent the illusive object of inquiry. The state "urges, incites, solicits and punishes," as Gramsci reminds us (1971, 247). But between the solicitation of the state and its punishment lies a vast realm of agency in which the state ceases to exist or, rather, is refracted by countervailing constructs, significations, and processes. For the transnational community, the state is at best refractory, an instance of a particular prism of alternative claims of allegiance and location. This brings us to an old anthropological dilemma of Max Gluckman, who posed types of social organization between the poles of tribesmen and townsmen, attempting to keep the categories distinct while retaining some explanative power. We may perhaps say today that the state is a peculiar tribe that appears to be in the process of being effaced as a distinctive unity, that is, as the distinct unity that it was once conceived to be; the transnational, however, is not new, and may be said to be a new phenomenon only in terms of its scale. In short, the movements of capital, people, and media of communication have rendered the world a very small place indeed.

5
Media Politics and the Migrant

Each day has its own slogan, its own vocabulary, its own emphasis.
—Mikhail Bakhtin, "Discourse in the Novel"

In most of our ordinary encounters, the assumptions of similarity
and dissimilarity are accepted without question. It is only in the ex-
ceptional encounter that they come into question.
—Vincent Crapanzano, *Tuhami: Portrait of a Moroccan*

The Politicization of Italian Society

One of the best ways to enter the complex world of Italian politics is to
walk to the corner *giornalaio,* pick up a local paper, and begin to examine the Italian political cartoon usually prominently displayed on the
front page of the paper. This chapter and the next are dedicated to this
daily encounter with media and deal with the question of how to read
an Italian political cartoon. The path to the heart of Italian political
humor and critique presented here leads through some of the folk models of Italian culture, society, and the media. A kind of shift has taken
place in the nature of an Italian political configuration that may be seen
through the crucial play of images that mark this transition from the
culture of politics that dominated the postwar years to that of a politics
of closure that has dawned in the early 1990s. The politicization of Italian society is unusual among Western democracies: virtually every as-

pect of Italian society has undergone a form of politicization. This profusion of politicization is a legacy of Italian Fascism, which organized every part of Italian society from the state's relationship to business "corporatism" to the field of leisure (de Grazia 1981). Regardless of political ideology or position, this legacy has certain stylized characteristics.

The immigrants' incorporation or lack of incorporation into Italian society must be accounted for in this symbolic world of Italian politics. Inasmuch as the incorporation of immigrants involves their presence in the world of work and the social life of its many urban centers, this incorporation must also involve an enclosure of immigrants into ritual and symbolic significations of Italian society. This entails a process through which immigrants are ritually incorporated in discourses of Italian society. The immigrant becomes in the early period of this process a ritual object of discourse that evokes the boundaries between the world of the immigrant and that of Italian society. In this liminal world the immigrant is increasingly drawn into political discussions and representations. Part of the privileged position of the immigrant in the symbolism of the Italian social world derives from the ambiguity of the immigrant's social status and position. The immigrant is between a clearly defined social status and class distinction and presents the problem of a perspective beyond the politicization of Italian society.

According to Umberto Eco, the presence of Third World migrants poses a cultural question to European societies that will either accept the migrations as a prelude to increasing multiculturalism or deny, through restrictive policies of closure, the inevitable presence of Third World peoples in Europe. This presence signals the emergence of another world, "another season of culture" (Eco 1990) and must be given a clear political identity and, failing this, a clear social identity. The presence of the immigrant must be managed within the framework of Italian society. This leads to the difficult issue of race and non-European cultural traditions. Immigrant incorporation proceeds, if at all, through the juxtaposition of images of transmigrants and certain figures of a historical Italian system of distinctions that associates the South of Italy with an exotic and other world, Africa, and with an imputed lack of "development" and a low level of literacy. Commonsense models of the Italian state must be examined in their relationship to the world of Italian politics.

Such themes as criminality and a contemporary disaffection with the majority parties in Italy have given a renewed strength to a previously fringe right-wing movement. This disaffection is linked to the manner in which the state is viewed as ineffectual in the face of growing social unrest, economic change, and the seemingly uncontrollable invasion of the Other. The fight against the "criminal" world in the form of the many organized crime networks and the many manifestations of an *economia sommersa* (an underground economy) has contributed to a popular view of the government as weak and unable to extend its control over all of Italy. This is similar to the criticisms of the liberal government that preceded Fascism. The call for "law and order" has been one of the platforms of the right-wing factions in Italy. This coupled with a call for reform of the *partitocrazia* or party rule of Italy's many public institutions and corporations has resulted in an increasing protest vote against the major political powers that have run Italy during the postwar era (Cowell 1992).

The realignments of Europe in the post-Soviet era have resulted in some odd configurations in Italy. The battle for the representation of the Italian masses now takes place between the Right and the various factions of what is left of the Italian Communist Party coalitions. The newly named Communist Party, which has shed the name Communist in preference of Democratic Party of the Left (PDS), has even lost members to the right-wing leagues of the North. The gulf between the intellectual leadership of political parties in Italy and the masses of followers has always been a problem. Palmiro Togliatti, the Communist leader who built the Italian Communist Party after the Second World War, once said that perhaps only Antonio Gramsci, the first theoretician of the Italian Communist Party, knew how to speak to the workers. Rightwing groups have a decided popular register through which they continue to gain a popular following (see fig. 6). The slogans and platforms of these groups sometimes even use local dialect in order to transmit their message. The profusion of political parties in Italy in recent years perhaps is one of the most convincing indications of the disaffection with the Italian political process; some fifty-four parties in the early 1990s span the political horizon. The most successful newcomers are the Lombard League and the Northern League, groups whose anti-immigrant and antisouthern message seems destined to undermine the strength of both Christian Democrat and Communist factions in northern Italy. The electoral strength of the leagues in the North has made the national political situation increasingly difficult; as in Germany, the emergence of this network of right-wing parties may become a permanent feature of the political landscape (Cowell 1992; Kinzer 1992).

Fig. 6. MSI Fascist Party political poster during local elections in Turin, 1990. The caption reads, "We say what you think. No to immigration."

I argue that this rise of the right-wing fringe is based in Italy and elsewhere in Europe on both antidemocratic separatist movements, various forms of localism, the assertion of often suppressed local traditions, anti-immigrant postures that mobilize social orders most affected by industrial restructuring of the labor market, and the lack of access through education and political connection to majority power holders. Anti-immigrant right-wing factions have been gaining support across Europe since the rise of Jean-Marie Le Pen, who first made himself known to the European Community through an early success in French elections in 1984 when his National Front walked away with more than 11 percent of the vote for the election to the European Parliament. Many of the anti-immigrant groups use the same basic slogans with merely a particular national twist.

Since the 1980s in France the issue of immigration has been highly politicized. The centrality of the issue of immigration began in the years from 1981–86 in French political life, the first period ushered in by the Secretary of State for Immigration, François Autain and the second ending with the legislative elections of 1986 by the then new Secretary of State for Family, Population, and Immigrant workers, Georgina Dufoix (although the title had changed, this was the same office). Although the repressive measures of the control of borders were a constant, the emphasis in France took on a decidedly human rights concern with a focus on the fundamental rights of immigrants and with such problems as family reunification and freedom of association. There was even some discussion of the possibility of immigrants voting in local elections. Such a proposal has also been considered by political parties in Italy to which the idea is attractive and would fully integrate immigrants into a ritual politics with wide-ranging implications (Wihol de Winden 1991).

Senegalese, Literacy, and the Media

Early in the morning most people in the house that contains more than 120 Senegalese in six rooms were already out to work. Sometimes employers would wait around until five in the morning for the young men to cross the misty streets and join in the work groups assembling there a short distance from where the Dora River crossed the quarter. These were laborers who did not officially exist, who would not show up in population counts or on local registers. A few miles away at the heart of the local government in the center of the city, officials would tell me stories about the abusive labor practices of the past as if they existed in another world. They would deny those abusive practices of the moment in an effort to subdue their worst fears: that in Turin, the bastion of a particularly powerful culture of work, an alternate and illicit labor market was emerging, peopled by the most precarious laborer, the migrant.

This was a very sad time for many of the migrants. For those who had no work the beds that lined the wall of the rooms were a kind of refuge. Some would sit and talk through the day while others slept and others talked about the possibility of work. Many Senegalese in the early part of 1990 still worked as ambulant sellers in the streets of Turin, although an increasing number of persons found work in construction and small industry. Around the middle of the month, for instance, Babacar found work as a mason in a town near Turin; others were being taken on in local firms as welders or masons.

One morning as I arrived at the house of some Senegalese in Turin the imposition of this silence was dramatically demonstrated to me. It was at a time when many of the Senegalese had been in Turin for only a short time, and many were still tied to ambulant street selling as their only means of income. One of the master craftsmen, Abdoulaye, a Laube wood-carver, had been out selling his objects of African art, mostly sculptures that he finished by hand at home. One of his friends told him that he had seen his son in the newspaper. Abdoulaye's son had been beaten by a group of Italians near the Gran Madre, a quarter along the Po River.

This incident occurred in an area of Turin in which tensions between foreign migrants and local youths increasingly became a problem. The beating of Abdoulaye's son happened on 16 March 1990. He was attacked by a group of six Italian youths while coming out of a bar near the Gran Madre, a great church sitting just past the bridge that connects Piazza Veneto to the long arcades of Via Po. Later that same month, three Senegalese were beaten in the same area by a group of young Italians who were eventually charged with attempted homicide. The attackers were suspected of having ties to neofascist groups. The motivation for these incidents was allegedly the association of drug selling with African and North African young people in the area. The three Senegalese who were beaten earned money (about a dollar or whatever the motorist offered) by washing the windows of motorists who happened by. The Gran Madre leads to a motorway to Milan in one part of the city and to the South to the highway to Genoa. A well-traveled area in the morning and evening commute, the roadway is filled with motorists allowing the window washers ample time to accomplish their tasks. Allegedly, some of the window washers were also selling drugs to motorists. Shortly after this, the local government attempted to discontinue the practice of window washing altogether. In protest of these incidents, and the government's attempt to take away the window washers' only means of sustenance, a member of the local government, one of the only Black Communist Party officials, washed windows with the others on the motorway (Patruno 1990a, 1990b); Conti 1990).

In the circle of beds Abdoulaye was sitting on his bed fully dressed and visibly upset. He had Babacar translate for him from Wolof to Italian. Babacar's Italian was not very good at the time, so occasionally he would slide into French, the language he was most comfortable with (Babacar was from a major Senegalese city and had been educated in French schools). Abdoulaye, though Peul, spoke Wolof, which for him was already a second language, and he spoke a variety of Pidgin with some words from English, Wolof, and other Senegalese languages. Abdoulaye spoke no French and at this time no Italian. He had undergone religious training by the Marabout and in all of his sixty-eight years had never had any form of formal education.[1] Finally, Babacar said, "He just wants to know if his son is all right, and where he is," and Abdoulaye handed me a newspaper, *La Stampa,* the Turin-based paper, which had a picture of his son on the cover. The article had no news of the health of Abdoulaye's son save an indication of how many days his wounds would take to heal, a standard bit of information. I translated the article into Italian and then Babacar translated it into Wolof. None of the Senegalese in the room (about ten or so) read Italian well enough to read the article. As the Senegalese went to work, however, particularly those who gained employment in the official work world, their language skills improved dramatically. Many Senegalese who were literate in neither Wolof nor French gained literacy through Italian language classes taught for foreigners. Just a few days before this incident occurred Abdoulaye's brother, who sells his sculpture in the street, sitting on the corner of the bed that the brothers share, was joking with Babacar who sat on another bed across the room: "The only Italian that I want to know is, 'How much will you give me?' That's enough Italian for me."[2]

"Why does this man, the man who wrote the article, not say where my son is? Is he still in the hospital or is he at home?" Abdoulaye asked me to see if I could talk to the man who wrote the article and try and get this information for him. Abdoulaye had passed his whole lifetime without the newspaper's ever once mentioning the smallest detail of his life or those of the persons closest to him. Now the intimate details of his life were the knowledge of strangers, closed between the pages that he must hear in translation. Senegalese share with the greater portion of Italian society no direct access to the modes of representation or voice in Italian media.

Italian Media and Political Satire

One of the classical vehicles of political satire has been the cartoon. Since at least the nineteenth century the political cartoon or drawing has accompanied the text of newspapers and journals throughout the Western world. The political cartoon, according to Charles Press, encourages a certain political action on a social question. In the good political cartoon "the aroma of genuine sentiment seems to be floating about in the air somewhere" (Press 1981). Using a form of masquerade and not saying in a direct manner what is to be said, the cartoonist or satirist through an argumentation of images can critique the latest social fashion or political discourse (Fernandez 1986). A particular organization of the contradictions of the day is often at the heart of the humor of an image, intermixing social, political, historical, and cultural dimensions. Calling on the knowledge of many contemporary contexts, the satirist may stress weak elements or express hidden contradictions in order to convey to the reader a given humorous conclusion. The juxtaposition of utopian themes (Jameson 1991) or abstract ideological features with elements drawn from more immediate or mundane social conditions, or the contrast of the ephemeral and the commonplace, may be an essential part of the manner in which these often comic images convey meanings. And yet the "elastic environment" of other significations, of meanings that go beyond official discourse, that recoil from its judgments and distinctions, and that predicate contrary themes and notions is often a part of the satirist's images and its traces.

The satirical cartoon is a particularly pronounced feature of Italian contemporary journalism. In the newspapers of the late 1960s and 1970s one cartoonist in particular, Giorgio Forattini, gained notoriety for his critiques of the government. Forattini, a cartoonist for the newspaper *La Repubblica,* is perhaps best known for his caricatures of such political figures as seven-time prime minister Giulio Andreotti, Enrico Berlinguer, late leader of the Italian Communist Party, and others. One of the characteristics of *La Repubblica* is its sleek format that often carries a Forattini cartoon on the front page of the paper. *La Repubblica* is owned by the publishing firm Mondadori, the same firm that has published many of postwar Italy's most popular literature. The Mondadori Group also has interests in broadcasting and magazines, publishing the popular weekly news magazine *Panorama. La Repubblica* is run by one of Italy's most famous editors and journalists, Eugenio Scalfari. By 1980 Scalfari had established the paper as one of the most important political daily newspapers in the country. The importance of figures like Scalfari and his role in the political life of Italy is greatly tied to the significance of the journalist in Italy. In 1978 Aldo Moro, then president of the Christian Democrats, called Scalfari to his office and gave an interview that opened up communications with the Communists. A Socialist at odds with the leader of the Socialist Party, Bettino Craxi, Scalfari has developed a paper that is independent of the traditional party rhetoric and that seems to many to offer a fair and informative version of the political landscape (Porter 1983).

Of the multiplicity of voices that comprise official discourse in Italy in the media and to some extent in the government, two have greater historical, cultural, and political depth than others: the Catholic world and the Italian Left.[3] While the former has been associated with the Christian Democratic Party, which has in effect dominated Italian government during the postwar era, the latter may be associated with what was formerly known as the Italian Communist Party. It is important to note the distinct humanistic and literary traditions that are associated with these two major influences in contemporary Italian society. There is a prevalent Catholic humanism that is embodied in the many charitable organizations linked to the Church. There is also a lay humanism and literary tradition associated with the Left, a kind of cultural humanism represented by such writers and social thinkers as Norberto Bobbio, Alberto Moravia, Natalia Ginzburg, and Carlo Levi (Mancini and Wolf 1990).

Television broadcasting began in Italy in 1954 and then expanded further in the 1960s; its influence was not greatly acknowledged, however, until the late 1970s and 1980s, when the medium began to be shared by the state-run *Radiotelevisione Italiana* (RAI) with private concerns and independent stations. During the 1970s there was still only one channel in Italy, and this was the Christian-Democrat-dominated RAI 1. It was only with the weakening of the majority party that other political parties were allowed to acquire channels: the RAI 2, run mainly by the Socialists and the RAI 3, controlled mainly by the Italian Communist Party (Haycraft 1985). Large corporate concerns and holding companies now control some of the private stations and many of the national newspapers. Influenced by the work of Antonio Gramsci, the Left was initially attentive to "cultural phenomena" and to the process of consensus building, while the Catholic world was concerned about the "hedonistic and materialistic values that television culture might introduce in Italy" (Mancini and Wolf 1990). The educative function of the mass media was seen by some of its administrators as primarily a question of maintaining a certain "morality," of "informing without corrupting," as a former president of the Radio and Television Vigilance Committee put it, often ending in what left-wing critics viewed as outright censorship (Mancini and Wolf 1990). Increasingly, the television is seen as *lottizzati* or parceled out among the three large public channels of the government RAI stations. With a fairly low readership of journals, magazines, and books of those over thirty-five, the television is for many an article of consumption and of political allegiance. Although the creation of a mass audience gives the form some semiautonomy along with a "consumerism" that the ubiquitous "spots" or commercials present, many themes such as criminality, and the growing cost of the state are also accorded television time. In spite of the continual representation of the *classe politica,* the political leadership, there have been a reaction against this political world and a rejection of much of its pretense. This rejection is seen particularly in recent moves away from the traditional party system.

The Italian Newspaper

> The most striking characteristic of Italian daily journalism is a preoccupation with politics.
>   —William Porter, *The Italian Journalist*

It has often been noted that "most potential readers . . . find the prose of daily journalism difficult to read"(Porter 1983). The Italian newspaper is a site of multiple discourses on society, economy, criminality, government, political parties, and the historical asymmetries that pervade images of Italy in the many distinctions between North and South. Until quite recently, the Italian newspaper had been the preserve of an educated elite, and the pages of the newspapers are still the locus of many discussions of art and "culture" that are directed at an educated and "cultivated" elite (Nowell-Smith 1990). Italy's literacy rate has always been low compared to the standards of other European societies. Until the middle of the nineteenth century Italian as a common language was only widely spoken in Tuscany and Rome; even the Italian monarch spoke only a dialect or regional language (Porter 1983). Even for those with a functional literacy, the political portions of the newspapers are difficult to read since they contain a very dense political language. At least a secondary education is required to even be able to plod through them. Political cartoons, however, are read easily by just about everyone.

There are still no mass-circulation newspapers in Italy. The only paper that sells more than half a million copies daily is *La Gazzetta dello Sport,* a Monday paper devoted almost entirely to sports (Nowell-Smith 1990). Many of the features of what might be called a popular or mass culture exist only in the form of magazines and cartoon books directed at mass audiences, and the many local (provincial) papers that until recently published twice a day and contained primarily local news (Lumley 1996a). Papers like the Turin-based *Stampa Sera* put out a 4 P.M. daily that contains mostly local news and is as close to a "popular" paper as any Italian newspaper. Since the late 1980s, however, there has been an increasing ambiguity that influences many national papers. In an effort to expand readership and no doubt to perform some sort of educative function, many papers of which *La Repubblica,* a Rome-based paper founded in 1976 with a circulation of or near four hundred thousand, is an example, attempt to serve as an elite intellectual news source and a mass newspaper simultaneously.[4] This attempt to encompass the multiplicity of discourses of the so-called political classes and the restricted languages, nuances, and insider allusions that this entails (with the mass appeal of the slogan and of the commonsense world of daily life) has resulted in a certain discontinuous journalistic practice. Journalistic style is somewhat affected by this division. As recently as 1986, *La Repubblica* was said by many on the Left to be one of the most well-thought-of newspapers in Italy; today, it is considered a hybrid of mass communication and intellectual elitism.

The problem of language has been a crucial feature of Italy history. The great profusion of Italian has only really occurred with the expansion of television after the late 1970s. The prominence of regional dialect in Italy is difficult to grasp but essential to the understanding of the great gulf between those who speak Italian and those who command the language only with some difficulty: "It is difficult for Americans to sense a tight linkage between language and position in society; difficult to believe that a citizen could read a line or two of discourse and instantly decide it was for somebody else, not for him. But it is true in continental Europe and in Great Britain" (Porter 1983, 16). In Italy the various registers of discourse are often kept quite separate. The dialectical voice is more often seen on the printed page of a local or provincial newspaper than a national daily of the capital (Dardano 1986). Only thirty years ago standard Italian had been adopted in daily conversation by only about 18 percent of the population. Today, it is estimated that in large urban centers about 60 percent of the population speak Italian exclusively, while in small population centers dialect is spoken in most contexts. Official projections of the Istat, an Italian government statistical service, estimate that by the year 2000, six in ten Italians will prefer the use of dialect over that of standard Italian in contexts ranging from the home to the local town hall. Although today eighty-five in one hundred persons are said to be capable of speaking standard Italian opposed to three in one hundred a century ago, it would seem that more persons in everyday conversation prefer to use at least the flavor of dialect (Garbesi 1990). The young people of Turin, for example, use a slang that incorporates many words with the flavor of Piedmontese and other dialects; on the other hand, young people from Turin will joke in dialect but seldom will speak it exclusively in public.

Maurizio Dardano (1986) has examined the relationship of various lexical differences between political discourse in Italian daily newspapers associated with a register of eloquence and intellectual rigor and discourse linked to a popular register that incorporates dialect and the more familiar rhythms of spoken language. These two poles of discourse are very similar to the conception of the critical and naive reader discussed by Umberto Eco (1985) and are, I would argue, crucial aspects of the tension in the Italian press for at least the past twenty years. This can be seen in television news coverage when people speaking dialect are often interviewed at length and in the Italian native speaker, who after continual exposure through television to different dialects has some basis for understanding—at least some portions of discussions without translation. In the early postwar years some films that contained dialect carried subtitles in Italian to emphasize the need for equal access to education and other benefits of the modern state (Dardano 1986).

In the case of the representation of the immigrant, an increasingly dialectical voice is heard in the newspapers. The lexicon that describes the immigrant is drawn form the register of informal spoken language, and so such terms as *vu' cumprà* (you buy), which was in the early period of the incorporation of the immigrant a term used extensively to connote the itinerant Moroccan or Senegalese street seller, are drawn from dialect.[5] One of the interesting things about this term is that its derivation is unclear. Some Italians attribute it to a generic southern dialect, others to the Calabrian dialect. The explanation for the origin of the term in a southern dialect is crucial to its ritual significance. The dialect or regional accent is especially an indication in popular ideology of a poor education and an inability to speak the Italian language properly. So the immigrant is said to have picked up this phrase from a southern dialect since he or she presumably was unable to speak the Italian language (Lerner 1989). This explanation is of course absurd and yet it is offered by both the educated Italian elite and popular ideology with equal regularity. The phrase *vu' cumprà* is no easier to say than its Italian equivalent, and the derivation of the term follows an impeccable Italian logic that has everything to do with the relationship of dialect to Italian and very little to do with immigrants' language competency. The term merely reflects a popular register close to spoken language and moreover close to the traditional dialect; in contrast, standard Italian associates dialect with low literacy and the stigma of the lower orders of social classes and southern communities. Even a national political official may be ridiculed by an Italian educated elite for the inability to pronounce certain words or to speak with eloquence and restraint. Even such writers as Alberto Moravia, Ignazio Silone, and Natalia Ginzburg have been criticized for not writing well enough in a sophisticated Italian and for introducing informal usage in literary texts. At the same time, these writers are national and international fixtures of contemporary fiction writing.

It is perhaps more appropriate to note that the term *vu' cumprà* comes out of an informal register, one increasingly incorporated into the newspapers and reinforced by many public opinion surveys conducted and re-presented by the news media. Other such popular notions about immigrants in commonsense ideology were presented in the media, such as a fear of the migrant association with the AIDS problem and with a sexuality without taboo or bounds. Images range from the "foreign Casbah" of Mazara, a Sicilian city with a large population of migrants, to the blaming of the *vu' cumprà* for hard economic times in the northern seacoast town of Rimini. In short, in early 1989 the popular register had become a rich source of tropes that encompassed the immigrant in Italian political discussions (see Lerner 1989; Lonni 1990).

The right-wing neofascist Leagues of the North have given new meaning to the use of dialect and familiar expression (see figure 6). The use of Piedmontese is promoted by the local Lega Nord, an offshoot of the leagues, and so in Lombardy and Piedmont the use of local dialect is held to be an act of local pride. The dialect is at once an affirmation of localism and a claim to a great historic tradition of the North, the monarchy, and the process of industrialization seen to be an artifact of the North.

During an interview at a local private television channel organized by a local parish priest, Don Sergio Federigo in Turin, in which I participated with local residents and Senegalese, this dialect issue and its association with the new Right came up in off-camera discussions. The interview concerned the selling of drugs in the area. The participation of the Senegalese in this antidrug effort involving the local community and the Catholic Church was a novelty. Don Sergio Federigo attempted to ameliorate the situation in the quarter by engaging the participation of migrant groups when possible, in spite of the fact that there was considerable opposition to his efforts within the church. The association of all foreigners with drug selling in popular ideology in the area of Porta Palazzo in Turin had resulted in some difficulties for the Senegalese residents of that community. In an effort to demonstrate the Senegalese solidarity with the local community and in an effort to identify the "foreign" element in the community with some of its most prestigious institutions, the local priest asked for the participation of the Senegalese in a television broadcast on the drug problem in the quarter. I was also asked to participate, having been involved with the Senegalese and other immigrant groups and their efforts to improve their image in local media. One participant in the interview was a local resident who ran the Catholic-affiliated CARITAS, an organization that is involved in charitable activities, notably the administration of dormitories and kitchens that house and feed immigrant communities in Turin. This participant had a very strong Piedmontese accent. The priest, from Friuli, joked that he could let his accent come through during the interview and surpass the local Lega Nord in their appropriation of Piedmonteseness. At this, the director of CARITAS turned to the priest and said, "We want nothing to do with those people. They are there at every turn. When we go to the commune they are there, everywhere trying to *strumentalizzare* [exploit] this problem, but it has nothing to do with racism. We want our community back." A local resident, a woman who did not want to be identified on television for fear of reprisals by the drug sellers, said that she and others on their antidrug committee had been approached by local neofascist groups who offered to organize gangs of youths to throw the young foreign drug sellers out of the quarter. "Give us a few days, and we will take care of this problem," she was told (Shack 1979).

Language mastery is an important sign of social class and status in Italy. Significant Italian regional linguistic distinctions make the judgment and classification of language mastery particularly important in everyday life. Some accents and dialects are more prestigious than others; mastery of Italian is preferred over the use of dialect in many social contexts. Although dialect may be used to assert adherence to a certain group or region, the use of Italian in formal situations is preferred. In this manner migrants who approach the preferred mastery of Italian are classified differently from the way that those with a poor command of the language are seen. The familiarization of practices associated with literate capabilities considerably enhances the prestige of the migrant and increases the social possibilities of the migrant within Italian society (Bourdieu and Passerson 1977).

The migrant participates in an international labor market and, what is equally important, in an international cultural interchange that is continuous and, although much less tangible than the labor market, ideologically very effective. Proficiency in European languages, educational backgrounds, and work disciplines has been a crucial part of this introduction and exchange with the so-called West. The migrant with greater language mastery has greater access to all dimensions of Italian society, and the interlocutors of the migrant with a high language mastery are often those Italians with a heightened grasp of their own language and culture. For those newcomers to Italy who perform labor requiring little conformity to verbal standards that range beyond the most practical language mastery, the social world appears very different (Bourdieu and Passerson 1977). One Senegalese migrant, a recent arrival to Italy who was educated in French schools all his life and was working in construction in Italy, once complained: "This language is so difficult, Italian. At work my boss is Piedmontese and so he speaks Piedmontese. Another is Sicilian and he speaks only Sicilian. With all these languages, how am I to learn Italian?" The migrant may be classified according to grammar, tone, accent, and delivery, which are the established order in Italian society (Bourdieu and Passerson 1977). The new arrivals must then resort to channels of gestural dispositions and traditions that lack the social prestige of verbal mastery (Efron 1974).

From its inception in the 1900s through the 1980s there was little effort in the national newspapers to win popular support. The journalists, a formal professional elite,[6] produced papers "written in an esoteric, over-literary style, full of allusions[,] written to be decoded by the élite, not absorbed by the public" (Clark 1984). The connection between the professional journalist and the politician is almost a tradition in Italy; many practice their journalistic skills while in office. Political figures from the president of the republic to the secretaries of the major political parties in fact regularly contribute to newspaper columns and articles.[7] Many of the political parties run national papers, while others are closely associated with business interests. The absence of a real popular press seems to have helped to create the double nature of the contemporary Italian paper, which in the late 1980s began to include both dense political articles and features of popular interest. Labor disputes with paper owners have, however, led to some reductions in many papers,[8] notably *La Repubblica,* which has reduced its local section, which contains items of more popular interest, while it has not greatly reduced its cultural sections or the production of its weekly glossy political magazine (Schlesinger 1990). Sports pages and *fumetti* (comic strips) remain some of the most popular reading materials in Italy.

The influence of televison has been greatly enhanced by the activities of such figures as Silvio Berlusconi, a Milanese entrepreneur who has successfully entered into the television market in Italy through his holding company Finivest, one of Italy's top seven firms. Moving toward a kind of globalization of the television format, Berlusconi has introduced popular television programming from world markets. After Berlusconi bought out the rights to three major private television networks, Canale 5, Italian 1, and Rete 4, these networks have changed the way television is viewed in Italy. Since the early 1980s Berlusconi has captured a major share of both the television viewing audience and the all-important

advertising revenue through the introduction of films, serials, and cartoons. Recently, his attention has turned to world markets in France and
Spain and to a fight with the Mondadori Group for control of *La Repubblica,* one of Italy's most successful daily newspapers. If Berlusconi
succeeds, he will control one of the largest Italian private media empires,
following only the government-owned RAI and the Agnelli Group, which
controls FIAT. Berlusconi has very powerful political connections and is
a close friend of Bettino Craxi, leader of the Italian Socialist Party who
has intervened in governmental affairs for Berlusconi on several occasions, virtually saving the entrepreneur's investments. Berlusconi owns
in addition to the television interest a sizable portion of the right-wing
Milanese newspaper *Il Giornale* and the most widely read periodical in
Italy, a television program guide, *Sorrisi e Canzoni* (Schlesinger 1990).

The impact of television on the nature of readership is perhaps wor-
thy of some comment. The transmission of the news through the national RAI stations and the many programs of Italian entertainment that
are available present the news in a readily accessible format devoid of the
elite accent of the papers. One former member of the secretariat of the
Italian Communist Party in Turin, an active member for more than ten
years, noted that one of the great differences of the role of the organizer
in the early 1960s was that of informing the members of the party and
debating the significance of various developments: "Now they turn on
the television. They don't need me to tell them what's going on—they
know as soon as I do." This secretariat member split with the party after
the Labor defeats of 1980 when he felt that the "Stalinist" structure was
not responsive to the new elements in the party or to the needs of Labor.

Television has also made itself felt through the presentation of an
increasingly global pattern of consumer possibilities and lifestyles. This
is also true of the newspaper: the third page, or cultural section, of the
newspaper has declined from its earlier literary style to take on a more
journalistic tone. Some complain of the "Americanization" of television.
Many of the series that dominate Italian popular television are American
sitcoms and soap operas: The American soap opera *The Bold and the
Beautiful* is one of the most popular shows on Italian television. The
popular films of Italian cinema are another favorite; the comedy film
surpasses all other forms in its popular appeal. The imminent expansion
of the movie theater will soon permit an even wider consumption of foreign cinema.[9] Many complain that the classical Italian film genre that

produced such recent films as *Tree of the Wooden Clogs* and *Three Brothers* and the modern classics of Fellini such as *La Strada* and Vittorio de Sica's *Bicycle Thief* will wither with the impact of foreign popular films (Grundle 1990).

Film going became the most popular form of entertainment in the fifties and sixties for all Italians, appealing particularly to classes previously excluded from mainstream social life. The cinema in these years was one channel of inclusion and entertainment that crossed over the whole society. In other European countries of the same period the film-going audience declined slightly. Images of poverty began to disappear in the late 1950s and were replaced by a vision of a "better material future" (Grundle 1990). Already the movie video market in Italy, less than two years old, has made a tremendous success in the marketing of largely foreign films. Much of Italian film going is now subsidized through film clubs and work benefit schemes.[10] The worlds of film and of television create an "imagined community" (Anderson 1983) that promotes a national language and an image of the Italian "we"; it underscores this through the wider heterogeneous audience of which Italians are not a primary audience, but one of numerous subsidiary audiences, in a transnational presentation of texts from American television productions to Russian ballet or Romanian symphonic concerts. Many of the themes once restricted to an elite readership are now available through the coverage offered on television news channels and talk shows. Political figures dominate news coverage. In Italy the political debates once restricted to the editorials of national newspapers are now enacted in the daily television news, a battleground for campaigns, labor disputes, and factional positioning (Ignatieff 1985).

The distance between the model reader of the mass communication text (which Umberto Eco suggests is always a double one), a critical reader, and the other, more naive one is conflated somewhat in the contemporary newspaper (Eco 1985; 1979).[11] The critical reader is aware of the various strategies of the author and evaluates the work partly as an aesthetic product and therefore enjoys the manner in which old themes are reworked to give the appearance of novelty. The journalistic language of the newspaper is most difficult in its stylistic and in-group tone. This leads William Porter (1983) to write: "Given the general low level of education, the gulf [journalistic language] creates between writer and reader in Italy is greater" than in other countries. The naive reader is drawn along a system of "previsions and expectations" that the author's strategies lay out for them. The critical reader, according to Eco, is encouraged to evaluate the innovation of the variation. In mass communication critical and naive readers are drawn ever closer to one another as the product becomes more and more abstracted from the possibility of a restricted textuality. The model critical reader is one who has privileged access to the kind of knowledge and nuance that the strategies of an author reveal. A great deal of the possibility of the critical reading comes from the knowledge of certain conventions, special languages, and histories.

The context of the contemporary mass media product, however, relies on a kind of intertextuality or an interchange and dialogue between texts that presupposes the possession of knowledge from other media— both extratextual knowledge from the world and television, and references to the continuing series of a daily chronicle (Bagnasco 1990b). Headline slogans such as "The war between the poor," referring to the confrontation of poor Italians with Third World migrants ostensibly competing for the same resources, bring the notions of popular ideology into the political debate over the allocation of state and private monies. In a sense, in what Eco calls a "post-post-modern aesthetic," all "readings" become critical, as only the manner in which the media product is formed becomes of interest. The simultaneous presentation of the "cultivated" and the "popular," once restricted from the pages of mass communication, marks the advent of a new "democratic era," which accords "populism" a place in national representations. Thus the genre mixing of the sophisticated reader and the popular reader presupposes a kind of blasé knowledge of the way mass media functions, as Fredric Jameson notes (1991). The mediocre nature of its product, in short, is increasingly attributed to the profit margin. The large papers are said to be unable to sustain themselves on the small elite readership that until the 1980s almost exclusively consumed Italy's many newspapers, journals, and magazines. Most of the Italian papers actually lose money and must be subsidized by either political parties, government agencies, or private funds, usually industrial concerns like the FIAT groups or the growing mass communications managers. The Monday newspaper is still the most successful in terms of its sales. This is said to derive from the fact that it contains the copious sports pages. The newspapers have chosen a hybrid form, a mediocre product. This knowledge is then "built into its consumption," according to Jameson (1991, 350–51). This hybrid has the mass appeal of the popular paper, while attracting the traditional intellectual reader. Jameson has argued that there is an increasing identification of the media with the market; the notions of profit and production are then attributed to the very medium through which the daily chronicle is presented.

This oscillation between the cultivated, intellectual left-wing newspaper and mass communication has resulted in some confusion over just how the media needs to cover the issue of immigration. For the first time in the postwar era, the Italian media is faced with the problem of representing notions of race across its television screens and on the pages of its magazines and newspapers, and perhaps the novelty of the problem coupled with the profound monotony of commonsense notions of race has produced an image of people of color filtered through the lens of localisms and xenophobia.

The democracy of the media in its embrace of mass forms of expression has a double aspect: no longer subject to the dualism of the cultivated and naive addressee, the media manages to represent a kind of internal democracy between social orders through the juxtaposition of popular and elite discourses and through the representation of a new equality of the market that embraces the two. This "utopia of the market," according to Jameson, exists in the confusion of "foreigners" or outsiders to the West in the form of a vision of the West through its products. This may actually be more appropriate to diverse social orders or classes within the West itself:

> Driven out of the Third World by our own counterinsurgencies, and lured out of the Second by our media propaganda, the would-be immigrants (whether spiritual or material), not understanding how little they are wanted here, pursue a delirious vision of transubstantiation in which it is the world of the products that is desired like a landscape, and not one of them in particular: Products . . . being themselves allegorical emblems of the whole, mesmerizing properly aesthetic Postmodern structures in which the identity of the media and the market is perceptually reenacted, something like a high-tech special effects dramatization of the ontological proof. (Jameson 1991, 353)

This "delirious vision of transubstantiation" seems more appropriate to the world of Italian consumerism, which in the wake of Italy's economic boom has led to a consumption of the "emblems" of class symbolism, rather than to the Third World consumer. The expansion of the mass markets in Italy and the relative prosperity of recent years have produced a host of new consumer patterns.

Imagined Communities

> Discourse lives . . . on the boundary between its own context and another, alien, context.
> —Mikhail Bakhtin, "Discourse in the Novel"

The idea of Europe—a Europe tied to particular geographical spaces, certain vernacular languages,[12] and the many tropes of continuity embedded both in the very stones of its churches and monuments and in notions of historical, cultural, and social genealogies of its various nations—seems to be everywhere in ruins. The manner in which the contemporary European Nations are imagined, in Benedict Anderson's phrase, is at the root of the problem (Anderson 1983; Chabod 1961). Problems with the resurgence of racist and xenophobic sentiments plague the European landscape. In Italy, just one year after the passage of the first comprehensive immigration legislation since 1931, separatist right-wing groups called Leagues captured a wide range of voters with their passionate anti-immigrant platforms. The Italian historian Valerio Castronovo has suggested that "this dangerous rebirth of localism" of right-wing groups threatens to efface "national cohesion" (cited in Battistini 1991). The Pope has recently spoken out against "reactions of rejection" of Third World migrants in the European Community. Legislation has recently passed in France that will institute the practice of constructing "zones of transition" to house (near airports and seaports) the myriad immigrants and potential political refugees who daily request entrance into France (La Rocca 1992).

The issue of "clandestine" immigration has been for some time a point of concern throughout the European community, and, in fact, the vision of the newly emergent Europe, whose inner boundaries will be enveloped by common trade networks and the spirit of exchange as money and goods flow freely through the former frontiers, is predicated on an ability to enforce a kind of enclosure of the European Community, especially to Third World immigrants. Italy had been pressured by the rest of the European Community for some time to draft a comprehensive legislation dealing with immigration. The call for controls was launched by the right-wing leagues and, more important, by the Italian Republican Party, a center right-wing political party headed by La Malfa. The conflicts that were ignited between the Republican leader and the vice president of the Republic and sponsor of the new immigration legislation, Claudio Martelli, placed the bill at the heart of a struggle to define the future government position on the "foreign question."

Responding to the pressures of right-wing calls for the abrogation of the immigration legislation because it was too lax, Martelli proposed to use the armed forces in order to patrol the extensive Italian coastlines against the increasing clandestine immigration. "We cannot accept another clandestine immigrant," Martelli declared. "I am not exaggerating. The armed forces must intervene to stop new waves of immigration. For six months I have repeated that the philosophy of the law is yes to *regulation* and no to clandestines" (cited in Pepe 1990). Martelli's call for the intervention of the armed forces was parodied by a cartoon in *La Repubblica,* which ran 5 April 1990 (see chapter 6), that through caricature questioned this authoritarian solution to the "immigrant question" and the viability of support for Martelli's immigration initiatives in a changing political climate. The anti-immigration stance was to become a crucial issue in the so-called movement to the Right, particularly for the Fascists.

Party, State, and Popular Memory: Fascist Regalia and Socialist Leadership

> People can say what they want, but you see that school over there and the train station, all of them built by Mussolini. And Mussolini made you proud to be an Italian.   —Milanese cab driver, 1986

On 5 April 1990, a *La Repubblica* cartoon (see fig. 7) depicted Italian Socialist Party member and former Prime Minister Craxi in Fascist regalia circa 1935, chasing the figure of a black woman who has the face of Claudio Martelli, sponsor of the immigration legislation. The figure of Craxi masquerading as Mussolini is now a somewhat standard part of the political satire of contemporary Italian politics (see chap. 6). The comparisons come from Craxi's former role as prime minister and refer to the decisiveness of his leadership style. Craxi cut a differ-

Fig. 7. Cartoon appearing in *La Repubblica,* 5 April 1990. The caption reads, "You will ruin all my plans, Little Black Face."

ent mold in the political world as "a man whose desire to impose his will quickly drew comparisons with Mussolini" (Friedman 1988). The comparison in the case of this particular drawing is not altogether fortuitous, however, for there is another feature of Mussolini's political and cultural role that in the immigration context strikes a chord with a popular legacy of Mussolini—in the notion of what it means to be Italian.

The Postunification Liberal Government (1861–1922)

In the conventional view government was plagued with bitter conflicts of factional and sectarian groups within and outside of parliament. The postunification state is often seen as one so strangled by internal conflicts that it is virtually immobilized by political dissension. Thus the postunification state was a weak state, one with an insufficient articulation at local and provincial levels throughout Italy. The state was, in fact, an amalgam of elitist propertied classes with a combination of an anticlerical ideology and a strong tendency toward a progressivism—the vision of a progressive, technologically advancing society and economy, the proponents of selective public works, better communication and railways, and the elimination of the encumbrances of communalism on landholding rights (Grossi 1981). Collective property holding was viewed as an anachronism and was opposed by this class of nineteenth-century landholders whose discourse on forms of property was to remain dominant and thus legitimated by the new state. Although many of the collective lands existed in the South, a great number of them were in farming communities of the North. This struggle of the state's definition of property and the discourse that opposes it in the form of various areas of collective holding in Italy are still going on; as a recent conference in Emilia-Romagna, which was organized by Paolo Grossi in an attempt to marshall some opposition to the state's seizure of these lands, made this quite clear, alternative forms of landholding embody the principles of alternative forms of governing. Although the elite classes enjoyed the mechanisms of the appropriation of national lands and the codification of the types of property and the public works that were or were not to be undertaken, for the masses little significance of the state pressed on the day-to-day world. Alan Friedman argues that it was with the "rise of Mussolini that the masses were forced to develop a sense of being Italian" (Friedman 1988). This is undoubtedly the popular view; it was Mussolini's aim that with the imposition of teaching Italian rather than dialect and with the assertion of the national government into every region of Italy the unification of Italians would begin. Benito Mussolini was a former schoolteacher and journalist, and his most lasting popular memory shares in the quality of both of these professions. His imposition of Italian in schools helped to introduce a common language throughout Italy.

From the 1900s onward the Italian newspaper became an important feature of the social and political landscape and figured importantly in the persuasion and mobilization of public opinion (Clark 1984). The Milanese *Il Corriere della Sera* became a kind of official opposition paper to state policy in northern Italy. Large national papers did well and included women's interests and sports sections. *La Gazzetta dello Sport* was founded in 1896; this type of sports paper remains the most widely sold in Italy. The press, moreover, became a crucial platform for the launching of political discussion and conflict: the leading journalists were in fact politicians. Journalism was to take on its national role as a "delegitimizing" ideological arena of the national government. Both Mussolini and Gramsci built their political careers and expressed some of their most important positions through the national institution of the Italian newspaper (Clark 1984).

The fact that Mussolini was a former journalist only underscores his relationship to mass forms of communication. Fascism marked a crucial convergence of the initial appearance of mass forms of communication and political mass mobilization. Mussolini once resolved one of Italy's great contemporary economic crises by issuing the following statement to journalists: "Do not mention the World Economic Crisis" (in Barzini 1964, 144–45). Measures that gave a sense of national cohesion, however, were dealt out with this same forthright manner, and these form the contours of Mussolini's popularity. He eradicated the *Lei* formal form of address from all grammars and imposed the Fascist salute in place of the handshake. Foreign words were abolished or Italianized. Such problems as banditry and malaria were in effect renamed and appeared in official documents under the cover of other sanitized terms. The style of Mussolini's leadership was in certain respects "journalistic" (Barzini 1964).

The public speeches for which Mussolini is famous, in a style borrowed from romantic figures like the nineteenth-century poet Gabriele D'Annunzio, were to usher in a new period of the inclusion of the masses in the spectacles of modern politics. Popular Fascism promised land to the land-hungry peasants of southern Italy in a distant African empire; the slogans of "Vive duce" (long live the duce, another name for the Fascist leader) were followed by "A noi, a noi" (land to us). Mussolini is one of the innovators of the modern forms of mass mobilization. The intervention of the state in all aspects of private life, as with the formation of leisure-time activities sponsored by the Fascist state, accomplished "a political extension of the state" into the most mundane

activities of the populous. The state was in this manner "deeply embedded in civil society," giving every activity the quality of a national ceremony. The joining of the political to every aspect of society helped to
create an artificial "sense of overriding 'national' identity"(de Grazia
1981, 21). Italian society during Fascism was saturated with ideological,
political, and cultural motifs from the classroom to the sports arena.
Some writers are famous for the lack of mention of Fascism in the face
of this overwhelming representation of its themes; for example, Sandro
Penna's poetic writings of the period leave no trace of the regime. All of
this occurred, however, in the light of a rather unresponsive public: the
public sentiment about the regime except for some brief protest is difficult to access.

Thus Mussolini is one of the key historical figures who has problematized what it means to be Italian and what in fact the Italian state is;
in the popular view, under Mussolini the state was strong and had the
respect of other nations. And so Italy's role in Europe and its role in the
lives of each and every one of its citizens are implied by the mention of
Fascism. Some explanation of the views of the contemporary situation is
needed in order to proceed. First of all, the contemporary state is viewed
in much the same way that the postunification state was viewed, that is,
as essentially weak. In order to exercise authority within the state, therefore, one must call on sources of organizational or economic power independent of state mechanisms proper. In the contemporary relationship of politics to the media in Italy, some say that the political class
dominates media representations; some people suggest that politicians
talk altogether too much, that the media is, in short, saturated with their
views. We may then acknowledge the correlation in popular ideology
between the monotony of Fascist propaganda (which was virtually un-
opposed) to the discourse of Italy's so-called political class, which by
virtue of its privileged access to the media may be said to dominate if
not monopolize public attention.

Some Models of the Modern Italian State

There are several models of the Italian state that pervade popular imagery of the contemporary government and that reveal a discourse of
the notion of governability from unification forward. First, there are the
views from political commentators and historians. In these popular views

Italian politics is often seen as a kind of quasi-Hobbesian landscape in which the bitter conflicts of the political class or elite are fought along religious, factional, and ideological lines. Further, such battles only serve to demoralize public support of national institutions and to undercut all possibility for the formation of a lasting basis of consent. This is essentially the postunification model that resulted in the great politics of "accommodation," which one might compare to the five-party coalition, the party system led by the Christian Democratic majority, which has recently dissolved over the issue of immigration. This image of Italian politics was seen in the climate of postwar Italy as a kind of pessimism and at times an outright fatalism concerning the vitality and resilience of the possibility of governability in Italy.

The central figure in this dismal political science is the Italian party system. The rule of the party is so pervasive at every level of local and national government that politics is reduced to a competition for various resources of government to be allocated according to party loyalty. The power of the party system, which is sometimes called the *partito-crazia,* is grounded in the allocation of various state jobs and government posts of the *sottogoverno,* which entails a vast system of civil service positions, state-run corporations, and banking concerns. A complex system of patronage, which is often referred to popularly as a kind of "mafia" or "racket," is cited as an integral component of the political structure of postwar Italy. Thus the crisis of representation and legitimacy is often found in the titles of works that treat the contemporary image of Italy: *La Crisi Italiana* (The Italian crisis), *Italy in Transition, Conflict and Consensus, Il Governo Difficile* (The difficult democracy), and *Republic without Government* are among the texts that detail the collapse of the possibility of government in Italy.

This notion of the "difficult democracy" comes from a statement that Aldo Moro, former Christian Democratic leader, made near the end of his life: "We know that our system is characterized by limited change of government and is therefore, in contrast to other European systems, a difficult democracy" (cited in Spotts and Wieser 1986). In the postwar era there has been no change in government: the Christian Democrats have virtually controlled the Italian state. A political figure like Andreotti, virtually in power for more than forty years, has had no analogous counterpart in the democratic world. The fate of Aldo Moro himself underscores the difficult democracy of the postwar years. One of the key figures in postwar Italian politics, Moro was kidnapped and assassinated by the infamous Brigatte Rosse. His bullet-ridden body was left in the trunk of a car abandoned on a Roman street about halfway between the headquarters of the Christian Democrat Party and those of the Italian Communist Party. A photograph taken by the Brigatte Rosse of Moro shortly after he was kidnapped remains one of the most haunting images of Italian political conflict. The photograph shows Moro holding an Italian newspaper with the headline "Moro Is Dead"; in the background the symbol of the Brigatte Rosse overshadows the small figure of Moro.

However labyrinthine the political landscape has become in Italy, the governments have rolled along with uncanny regularity, and each new crisis has been met with unique—at times, unprecedented—political and parliamentary strategies. Things seem to proceed in some manner. Looking at the Italian political system is somewhat like viewing Michelangelo's prisoners—one is not quite sure if the figures are liberated from their apparent encasement in the stone or, rather, imprisoned within the very substance that gives them form: *eppure si muove* (but it does move).

This model, however, and the concern with the apparent instability of the Italian political structure are integral parts of folk visions of Italian society. It is somewhat ironic that the careful limitation of state control and centralization in certain quarters, which was resolved in the devolution of powers to regional and local agencies, only extended the powers of the state. The devolution of governmental powers formerly held in the national governmental structure in the 1970s was part of a kind of "politics of accommodation": the regions, themselves creations of the 1970s, ushered in the Communist and Socialist control of state-dominated agencies at the local level. With the changes of the 1970s the national state became in effect a regional state. While the critics of the postunification state complained of its weakness as one of the crucial components in the balance of power of the various religious, political, and social groups in unification Italy, their contemporary counterparts complained about the overwhelmingly powerful state apparatus and the need to gain some amount of control over the profusion of the bureaucratic and administrative nightmares associated with the function of the modern state.

The modern state is one of the largest employers in contemporary Italy. Some of the largest corporations in the world are state-owned corporations administered by functionaries of the Italian government. The control and regulation of the massive state-owned holding companies, some of which number among the largest in the world, are subject to continual internal negotiations and conflict within the government and political party structure. During the postwar years a considerable bureaucracy of state-employed elites emerged. During the 1960s less than a quarter of university students came from working-class backgrounds, including artisan and peasant farming traditions; furthermore, these students were more likely to drop out before graduation (Clark 1984). In fact, of the many clerical workers and managers of the postwar boom, which became a preoccupation of many political observers in Italy, very few came from the working class. In the postwar era, Italy's elite was no longer based on property but on what Gramsci called the "government of functionaries," the army of state managers and office holders. As Martin Clark notes:

> The richest men in the country were members of the "State Bourgeoisie," managers of State industries and agencies—secure in their jobs and guaranteed in their positions. Even many "professional" workers like doctors, architects and teachers, were employed by the State in all but name. . . . And where did a State job come from? Political connections, of course; but also from education. The new class— or "New Class"—structure of post-war Italy had little obvious justification, but what little it had came from the formal titles of higher education. Fiat was managed for years by a "*professore*"; successive governors of the Bank of Italy, or chairmen of nationalized industries, were also known as "*professore*," or at least "*dottori*." . . . These titles were often the only claim men had to their income, status and power. No wonder they insisted on using them. They furnished the essential social distance between the élite and the vulgar throng. (Clark 1984)

Given this massive state structure and the need for a politics of accommodation, such a politics could draw the disparate factions together, across the complex range of political parties—from what was formerly the largest Communist Party in Western Europe and the various lay parties to one side, and the Catholic-dominated Christian Democratic Party, which has essentially dominated postwar government, on the other. Additionally, affiliation with any of the parties is seen as one manner in which to enter into the world of recommendations and employment: "Without the Parties, you are nothing. If you want to do anything, you must have one of them behind you. If you stand outside , I'm sorry," as one Turinese official quipped.

One of the popular images that conveys the weakness of the contemporary government is the attention given to the issue of criminality in recent years. In the late 1980s the coverage of the various Mafia organizations was one of the most consistent elements in the news, with stories on kidnappings and the great trials of the leaders of reputed criminal organizations in Italy. In this view, the contemporary state is powerless to extend its authority over the many local centers of power. Maps depicting the extensive influences of the various Mafia organizations give the impression that Italy is engulfed by the enclosure of the *piovra* (octopus), an allusion to the title of a popular television miniseries that ran on Italian channels until it was canceled over the controversy of the realistic depiction of the Mafia.[13] So the second model of the modern Italian state may be likened to the later period of the liberal regime (1861–1922) in which the leadership was unable to contain both popular dissent and various forms of criminality. This model, which we may call "criminality against the state,"[14] poses for the Left the problem of a weak and indecisive government that cannot contain the economic crisis and that has for forty years been unable to extend its control and reform over the country. In contrast, the right wing sees a weak government that needs to wage a campaign against the locus of criminality and corruption, which carries the South, an unproductive area of violence and waste.

6
Other Crossings:
Socialist in Fascist Clothing

Hundreds of books, tracts, newspapers and magazines have dealt
with the Negro to produce a cumulative image so absurd, so removed
from reality that it belongs more to caricature, calumny and lampoon
than it does to descriptive analysis.
—James Walvin, "Black Caricature"

Black Caricature

I am given no chance. I am overdetermined from without.
—Frantz Fanon, *Black Skin, White Masks*

Stereotypes are fictions that live through masquerading as naturalized
and seemingly indispensable parts of our worlds.[1] Although historical
creatures, stereotypes may be crystallized as portions of common sense,
the taken-for-granted bedrock of popular ideologies and/or fashions. In
the light of asymmetrical collective capacities to represent, know, and
self-identify, the continual interplay of such notions in social context becomes the terrain on which visions of social reality are constructed, contested, and on occasion forgotten through time.

Black caricature has a long and tortured history (Walvin 1972). The
tropes of caricature are drawn from a host of sources passing from early

speculative writings, to travel accounts, and finally, and not always in this order, to fantasy. Such images appear to the public gaze in the form of cartoons or often as literary caricature (Walvin 1982). The discursive portrait of blacks in caricature includes such themes as black sexuality, views of blacks as "creatures of nature," and a vision of Africa as a far-off, exotic, yet disorderly place. In the realm of black sexuality it is seen as a kind of "damaged sexuality," one that is presented as a form of pathology, although articulating the exotic realm of fantasy of a sexually repressed turn-of-the-century world (Gilman 1986b, 360). This gives rise to discussion of pathological sexuality in which blacks (read primitive or Other) are seen as closer to nature and natural processes. As Brackette Williams has recently suggested, such "stereotypes focused attention on the subordinated or 'othered' males' lack of control over their lower passions, and so they may be attributed with a lust for the 'pure' women of other races, especially those 'belonging' to the dominating race sharing their political terrain" (Williams 1996). This image of the perverse sexuality of the Other has increasingly inhabited contemporary rhetoric of the Right, in the building of the male and female Othered subject. In such views, the Other is then seen as given to bestiality, lustful and unrestrained sexual behavior, and the abandonment of the orderliness and restraint of repressed sexual regimes (Fryer 1984, 137–38).

Constructions of male and female subjects as forms of categorical Otherness borrow from the repertoire of black caricature appearing in diverse forms through the play of time. Bodies often become privileged sites for the representation of frontiers of normalcy and Othering, casting the definitive markers between the world and that which lies beyond insoluble to taken-for-granted cultural understandings (Gilman 1993). Crucial to the formation of the Other-as-subject is the eroticization of the other that this newly created subject may symbolize across the boundaries of gender, race, and sexuality.[2] Although the discursive features of black caricature have also traveled in the guise of the sociological imagination, myths of black womanhood and black male sexuality have figured prominently in contemporary notions of black cultural inferiority, family disintegration, and social (dis)order (Morton 1991).

Black caricature and the multiple images that make up its repertoire resonate among European caricaturists (Walvin 1982; Lester 1986). Blacks were a favorite subject of the graphic cartoon of the eighteenth century:

The physical features, social characteristics, verbal intonations and the alleged "natural" abilities of the Blacks were frequently reduced to a grotesque shape by English caricaturists from Hogath to Cruickshank. The mythology of the Blacks—as a species and as individuals—was perpetuated by cartoonists who added to and exaggerated some of the existing stereotyped images. (Walvin 1982, 59)

Contemporary cartoonist and literary practices carry on this tradition, often employing black images as the essential emblem of difference. European graphic caricatures of blacks began to emerge particularly after reactions against French detachments of soldiers from Morocco, Madagascar, and Senegal and during the so-called Rhineland Occupation of 1919, in compliance with the conditions of the Versailles Treaty after the First World War (Lester 1986, 113–14; Hermand 1986, 67). There was widespread resentment of the presence of these troops, and following alleged incidents of misconduct of the occupation forces a propaganda campaign was launched on both sides, German and French, over the controversy. Claude McKay, one of the poets of the Harlem Renaissance, considering the Rhineland controversy in a sharply critical manner, places the Germans on the faultlines of the problem:

To perform that onerous duty [of Allied occupation of the Rhineland] France called upon her dependable African soldiers. And that action started a bitter, vicious propaganda which poisoned the minds of thousands of Germans and ultimately culminated in Hitler's mad onslaught against the Jews. (McKay 1933, 324)

German protest materials were widely circulated in Europe and the United States. Yet allegations of sexual abuse and violence had formed part of the racist portraits of American and other black soldiers during the period; suffering under a "Jim Crow regime," as W. E. B. Du Bois pointed out in *The Black Man in the Revolution of 1914–1918*, was part of the untold "history of the black man in the Great War"(Lester 1971, 107 passim).[3] In a report to the secretary of state by General Henry T. Allen, commander of American forces in the Rhine, the Rhineland conflict was laid down to the German media and political maneuvering: "The wholesale atrocities by French Negro colonial troops alleged in the German press, such as alleged abductions, followed by rapes, mutilations, murder and concealment of the bodies of the victims, are false and intended for political propaganda" (cited in Barker 1921, 598).

One of the core features of the Rhineland controversy, according to

Rosemarie K. Lester, was expressed by an anonymous writer for a pamphlet distributed under the title "Colored French Troops on the Rhine," and here stated in a racialist tone:

> It is not the behavior of the colonial soldiers that causes their greatest and most righteous indignation. It is rather the circumstance of . . . one civilized European nation, actuated by the fiendish desire to humiliate . . . letting loose on another civilized European nation a mercenary host recruited from a semi-savage and far inferior race with which to attain its horrible ends. (quoted in Lester 1986, 117)

W. E. B. Du Bois notes that German propaganda directed toward black soldiers in 1918 had taken a different tack. "Can you go into a restaurant where white people dine?" one leaflet dropped near St. Dié and Ranon-l'Etape queried; in Germany the statement went on to say blacks were treated "as gentlemen and as white men," in an attempt to persuade black soldiers to disengage from the fighting (Lester 1971, 113). The delicate play of racial ideology in the "sense of the present" inherited, according to Stephen Kern, in part from the era of the Great War, has no doubt yet to be written (Kern 1983, 292–93).

Italian Fascist posters produced near the close of the Second World War revived some of these issues, by alluding to the alleged acts of violence of the foreign detachments during the Rhineland occupation. Such works follow the spirit of what Peter Fryer has called "vulgar racism," a racist form created for popular consumption often by the press (Fryer 1984, 189). Struggling for the "real" in such a climate is extremely difficult as incidents of sexual abuse and other forms of violence and claims created out of these incidents at times escalated to pure fiction (Lester 1986).[4] The imagery drawing on the encyclopedic repertoire of black mythology particularly that of black sexuality would inspire Italian Fascist propaganda and German racialist caricature many years later.

From the extensive range of black images certain themes may be drawn into political discourse and fuel debate; this submerged racialist discourse may crystallize in such periods of crisis as that concerning political issues of contemporary colonialism and decolonialization, immigration, and the incorporation of Others into European and other societies. Although participating in the silence of the images and a continual repertoire of mythologies such as black sexuality, black indolence, and a purported natural closeness of blacks to nature, each period shapes its commonsense images according to contemporary forms, norms, and requirements of representation.[5]

Contemporary serial novels, popular print media, television, and advertising images and messages consumed daily in the new Europe traffic images of the Other as exotic, sensual, and primal. Although as in Italy many communities of immigrants and Others of color have lived in relative obscurity, until quite recently they have been "good to think" in the imaging of the European (Lévi-Strauss 1962; Lester 1986, 118). Often captured in discursive patterns that are of importance to sectors of fragments of European societies, the sometimes "abysmal ignorance" of the Other provides a kind of flat discursive field on which to view historical displacements and inequalities and through which to examine the parameters of significant collectivities (Lester 1986; Domínguez 1994).

African imagery has been most recently represented in popular world print and media as humanitarian crisis or international intervention in the wake of local conflicts. Such opportunities provide viewers with images often influenced by what James Walvin has called the roots of racialism—"an unbroken line" of stereotypes that contain Africa, in a kind of free-form discursive space, placing its contemporary visage into an encyclopedia of knowledges about Africa and things African (Walvin 1982). Rosemarie K. Lester has described this process in contemporary Germany where German blacks constitute a small yet highly objectified part of the population. Lester calls "the cannibal cartoons and grotesque negro caricatures" that enjoyed a marked popularity in the 1950s and 1960s "the evergreens of German 'humor'"(Lester 1986, 123). These cartoons often included elements that "ridicule African dress and hairstyles" and accompanied stories that highlighted the "sensationally exotic." She notes the many ways in which the reproduction of a certain stereotype of Africa is cast in racialist tonalities of colonialist portraits during the years of decolonialization:

> Negative African imagery, the cheaply ironic language used to describe everything African (and that meant black), the viciously racist cartoons—all that pervaded the popular media (all the more important in the 1950s since TV was still in its infancy)—was still present in school books as well as in children's and young people's literature . . . and, consequently, was very much part of public consciousness during the time in which German blacks were taking their first steps into society. (Lester 1986, 123)

Unfortunately, there has often been in all this little control of the representation by those represented. An image is a strange property: although it can be consumed, it can never, it seems, be possessed. Black caricature is often in the sweep of time drawn into the most heated debates; it forms the basis for political discourse on the nature of society and race. And it may be used to justify the most diverse actions from colonial campaigns to the desire to rid the country of immigrants. The general trend to identify the degenerative or atavistic elements in society and eliminate them is a part of the development of modern conceptions of society, normalcy, and nation. Atavistic elements have been associated with criminality and various segments of society viewed as outside of the purview of the fully social, a process I call *Othering.*

Images of the Third World, Localismo, and Demography

> The truths of a Nation are in the first place its realities.
> —Frantz Fanon, *The Wretched of the Earth*

The Italian journalist Giorgio Bocca's *Gli Italiani sono razzisti?* (Are Italians racist?) brought some attention to the problem of the immigrant of color in Italy (Bocca 1988). The relationship between Italians and foreigners of color had, according to Bocca, already been transformed by the 1970s: migrants were "no longer a curiosity or a passenger. . . . they are a presence which creates new economic and social situations."[6] One of the decisive moments in the media presentations of the phenomenon of racism in Italy was the impact of *Le Penismo Francese.* The success of the Le Pen movement in France and its affirmation in French electoral politics sent the Italian media in search of an analogous figure in the Italian political world. Italian media, according to Bocca, began to be engaged in a continual parade of issues of alleged racism and conflict:

> Giornali e televisioni riportano, quasi quottidianamente, episodi di razzismo o di presunto razzismo e non è facile capire quanto appartenga a un reale conflitto etnico e quanto al meccanismo imitativo e ossessivo della informazione di mass (Newspapers and television report almost daily episodes of racism or presumed racism, and it is not easy to understand when this is a result of real ethnic conflict or when it is a result of the imitative and obsessive mechanism of mass information). (Bocca 1988, 37)

In popular imagination the Third World has become a synonym for economic underdevelopment, political upheaval, famine, overpopulation, and disease. The images of the relief efforts of the Red Cross and the political violence of Liberia and Somalia tell us through images that the Third World is a place quite different from the world in which we live. We see no inauguration of benevolent organizations, no statesmen in the halls of parliament—just the constant murmur of statistics of world watch organizations that document the overpopulation of a continent of the imagination, a construct. Not the Third World is offered but proof that it exists (Jameson 1990). One afternoon while I was watching television with Senegalese migrants a program came on about the relief efforts of the Red Cross in Ethiopia. The room filled with a flurry of protests: "This is the way they see Africa, always starving, and this is all they show, always the same." A person who is starving will do anything to survive—so goes popular Italian ideology, and so it is clear that people coming from the experience of despair will take the first thing that offers itself, and thus it is only understandable that they should become involved in the criminal world. If immigrants are "good to think," they are also good to prohibit.

Distance is deceiving. At the very moment that the Third World is projected onto the television screens of European viewers it is assumed to exist in a far distant reality, yet the very image calls for some consideration of the so-called crisis of the Third World, of the acknowledgment of the pressing difficulties of its relationship to the First World. The contours of this crisis are well known to the viewer:

> Every structural feature of the crisis—the arms race in the Horn of Africa, the injustices of the world commodity price system, the failure of Western development agencies to invest sufficiently in soil reclamation, land reform, and resettlement projects, the grotesque preference of local rulers to fight their civil wars instead of attending to the needs of their peoples—all these have been documented on television. If the viewers have taken for granted that the Ethiopian starving are in some degree, their business, it is because the pictures have been preceded by more than a decade of documentaries on Third World development, which, while tending to favor the ideology of Robert McNamara at the expense of Frantz Fanon, have at least made plain some of the structures of neo-colonial economic and political dependency. (Ignatieff 1985, 63)

The notion of a Third World in an ideology of bourgeois humanism is a crucial part of the idea of the Ethiopian crisis; the call to pity
evades the historical relations of exploitation that link the West with the
crisis. What is left is a kind of modern tragedy in which the victim becomes a vehicle of a new type of victimhood, one that is universal and
capable of depiction through the medium of television as a "media
event," whose coverage calls for the mobilization of those distant to the
events. The passage of the few seconds of the image at once creates a
heterogeneous "community" of viewers—an audience that receives proof
of the existence of the Third World and confirmation of its famine and
distance. These images carry another notion, one that challenges certain
taken-for-granted thoughts about the West, that is, the idea that there
are too many people in the Third World, that the excess of persons on
the planet is somehow responsible for this new form of victimhood. The
persons who fill the screens of the documentaries propose the problem
of sheer presence (Bortot 1983).

In the pages of the Italian paper *Il Giorno* on 11 November 1989,
under the title "Toward the Discovery of a Country That Is Changing Its
Skin: The Army of Those Who Have Escaped the Inferno of Poverty,"
both Claudio Martelli, the vice president of the council of ministers,
and then minister of labor, the late Carlo Donat-Cattin, set the tone for
a parliamentary examination of the problem of immigration: "Immigration is the proving ground . . . perhaps the most significant of the world
vocation of the European community," according to Martelli (*Il Giorno*
1989a). Donat-Cattin called immigration the most grave social problem
that would be before the members of parliament for the next twenty
years. Italy must prepare both the proper means of receiving the immigrants and adequate employment for the arriving migrants, warned
Donat-Cattin. It is not clear just what Europe's "vocation" may be in the
face of non-European migrants. It is, however, clear that at every opportunity Italian parliamentarians noted the role of the wider European
community in facing the problem of immigration. Earlier, on 3 November *Il Giorno* ran an article under the same general title, "The Discovery
of a Country That Is Changing Its Skin," the article titled, "The Sea of
Clandestines." The article treated several of the centers in Rome that
deal with migrants providing Italian lessons, meals, and other services
such as the Saint' Egidio Center, which is run mainly with the support
of volunteers in the Trastevere section of Rome. The "army of those who
wish to live among us" is growing, according to the article, and large

cities like Rome are the centers that most readily open up the job market to the newcomer. The journalist from *Il Giorno* continues by giving an image of the growing heterogeneity of Rome, depicting the city as a giant octopus:

> The Capital, like a giant octopus, swallows up more easily foreign workers, refugees, political exiles, regular and clandestine, and offers ethnic solidarity to the new arrivals, facilitates contacts, creates opportunities, and makes almost normal by means of the age-old practice of tourist and religious requests, the presence of thousands upon thousands of persons of diverse races, skin colors, and religions.[7]

The *piovra* is associated with the great octopus of the many systems of organized crime in Italy, and the image is particularly poignant now since the problem of criminality in Italian cities has become so pronounced. The city is viewed here as an octopus, which at each of its folds holds the world of the migrant and is in each instant linked to a potential world of illegal activities. The article points to the difficulty with the controls in Italy of the influx of immigrants and the failure of the government to develop a clear policy on the phenomenon by the end of 1989. The Milanese sociologist Umberto Merlotti is quoted in the initial paragraph of the article as saying, "notwithstanding the 1943 law, no other country has conducted itself in the manner of Italy, where it is possible to enter and to remain practically without any controls whatsoever" (*Il Giorno* 1989b). In the same article the statements of the director of the Agnelli Foundation, Massimo Pacini, are more to the point as he mentions the two key horns of the dilemma maintaining a comprehensive European approach to the problem of immigration and clarifying the state's relationship to immigration:

> Occorre allora il controllo alle Frontiere per essere conerenti con la legislazione comunitaria. Anche il mar Mediterraneo può essere controllato. Se non lo facciamo, rischiamo di restar fuori dall'Europa (It is necessary to have controls at the frontiers in order to be in accord with the legislation of the European community. Even the Mediterranean can be controlled. If we do not do this, we risk remaining outside of Europe).

> I problemi per lo Stato e la società italiana inizieranno al momento del varco della frontiera. Dobbiamo impedire che l'immigrato vi entri da clandestino e dobbiamo assicuragli un complesso di provvidenze che eliminino alla radice quegli aspetti drammatici di miseria e di

marginalità che troppo spesso hanno accompagnato e accompagnano i flussi migratori spontanei, non gestiti e sovente clandestini (The problems for the Italian state and the society begin at the moment of the crossing of the frontier. We must prevent the immigrant from entering as a clandestine, and we must assure them a complex of precautions or measures that eliminate at the roots those aspects of dramatic misery and marginality that all too often accompany and have accompanied the spontaneous migratory flows that have not been managed and that are often clandestine).

The problem is one that is seen in the calculations of such social observers as Pacini and Merlotti, which rely on certain projections about the population growth of the Third World. The Agnelli Foundation in November 1989 came out with some estimates of the need for labor in Italy in the coming years. According to some observers, the "demographic explosion" forecasted for the countries that face "the southern rim of the Mediterranean" could not possibly be contained in the countries of origin alone; this population excess might then overflow into Europe (Livi Bacci 1990; *Il Popolo* 1989). This abundance of population, however, would satisfy Europe's need for labor due to a decline in the growth of European populations. The idea that this demographic explosion might somehow solve the labor needs of Europe, Pacini has warned, is a dangerous proposal based on the apocalyptic visions of demographic evolution on the planet. Pacini maintains that by the year 2000 the employment needs of Italy, should the population decline slightly as expected, may not be sustained by the future labor market.[8] The advantages of short-term immigration must be considered in light of the long-term public costs of such measures to the society. This warning recalls the social problem of the 1950s to the present in Turin, where the head of the Agnelli Foundation is based.

Much of the early speculation of the growth of population was focused on the contrast between the north and south of the Mediterranean. According to Lucio Magri, this focus on population growth is part of a new racism (Magri 1989). The population of the southern rim of the Mediterranean is said to "grow dizzily and will continue to grow for decades. The geographic distances and the cultural barriers will shrink and we will be at the beginning of a great and unstoppable (*inarrestable*) migratory flow from the south to the north of the world." These migrations are similar to those that have occurred at other times in history. The migrations differ in the manner in which they are received through

the lens of the neoracism that seeks to control the "invasion" from without by controlling the frontier while attempting to control at the same
time the "contamination" from within. This evaluation is an essentially
antidemocratic one, according to Magri: democratic forces must give
the opposite emphasis to the crisis. The erection of barriers is both ineffectual and inappropriate to the spirit of a democracy, he continues:
"We owe some form of compensation to a world that for too long we
have exploited and exploit; we must do what is necessary to render this
migration bearable to those who are forced to make it and create a tol-
erant and multiracial society" (Magri 1989). Few voices have been as
pointed as that of Magri, who directs the gaze of bourgeois humanism
toward an accounting of the costs of the relationship of the Third World
to the so-called First. The contradictions of democratic measures as opposed to those of an antidemocratic nature may have more to do with
the exigencies of the European labor market and a particular manner of
conceptualizing the problem than with projections of zero growth in
Italy in the coming years:

> L'idea di una cittadella di benessere che si arocca e difende rispetto a
> un mondo che degrada è, oltre che abietta, irrealistica e stupida, com-
> porta comunque una sorta di degredazione autoritaria e elitarisitca
> della stessa civiltà che si pretende di difendere. Ma, posta così, la
> questionse si rivelerebbe anche insolubile: non esiste alcun tipo di
> sviluppo economico o politico possibile che premetta di assorbire
> uno spostamento che possa alleviare in modo apprezzabile la spinta
> demografica e la povertà del Terzo Mondo (The idea of a citadel of
> affluence that takes up a defensive position against a world in decline
> is, other than being contemptible, unrealistic and stupid and entails
> in any case a kind of authoritarian degradation and elitism of the
> very same civility that one pretends to defend. But posed in this way
> the question would appear insoluble: there exists no form of eco-
> nomic or political development that would be capable of absorbing a
> displacement that could alleviate in an appreciable manner the de-
> mographic impact or poverty of the Third World). (Magri 1989)

Massimo Livi Bacci, the noted Florentine demographer, is a proponent of a vision of a "demographic silent revolution," which in thirty years
will change the face of the Mediterranean, *mare nostrum* (Chiaberge
1990; Pacini 1989; Nirenstein 1990). "We are destined to end up in the
minority, this is certain," notes Bacci. By the middle of the next century
the southern end of the Mediterranean will constitute two-thirds of its

population, more than "160 million mouths to feed," according to Bacci. This all, of course, depends on the involvement of the various governments concerned and their respective policies regarding birth control (*Il Giornale* 1989b). These remarks target countries like Morocco, Tunisia, Egypt, and other nations, primarily in the early comments of some demographers.[9] Visa requirements for those entering from Morocco, Gambia, and Senegal were in place shortly after the passage of the Martelli Bill in 1990 (Sarrocco 1990; Freeman 1986). Italy will, however, continue to need the manual labor provided by the abundance of workers who will emerge from the south of the world during their productive years between fifteen and sixty-five, according to Bacci. The newcomers will take the jobs that Italian youth are no longer willing to perform; this is just the kind of thesis that Pacini considers "dangerous," since it suggests a labor-market justification for migration.

The dichotomy between the West and the rest of the world in such a pessimistic demographic vision, however, attributes high fertility regimes to those less developed and low patterns to the postindustrial world in an altogether-too-simplistic manner. The underlying assumption of an eminent economic boom into which the Third World worker may be inserted ignores the needs of the European labor market, which is increasingly diminished in the manual categories. Also, the assumption that the workers from the Third World will fill positions of relatively unskilled employment is built on the fallacy that Third World workers are for the most part unskilled. In fact, Third World workers may be confined to manual labor regardless of their qualifications, due to both their weak position in the labor market and their lack of familiarity with host country labor legislation. Exploitation of foreign labor requires both a myth of the abundance of labor and an effort to conduct labor outside of the official labor market, in Italy's *lavoro nero*. In an official labor market foreign workers under the terms of recent international agreements are accorded labor legislation and protections equivalent to indigenous workers (Seccombe 1985). It is access to these benefits of the Western European welfare state that creates the problem for the state already overburdened with a massive welfare apparatus erected in the wake of Italian labor movement triumphs of the 1960s and 1970s. Such problems as those arising from foreign worker contributions to pension plans and national health systems must be resolved through international accord (Freeman 1986).

The evolutionary models of the growth and development of civilizations, a standard in some nineteenth-century theories of society, are the common sense of today. To some extent both Malthusian notions in political economy and Marxist notions of semievolutionary schemes, in which societies like India were on the periphery of the analysis of capital proper, have contributed to a pessimistic vision of the Third World.[10] The free-floating anxiety that notions of the Third World seem to evoke in popular imagination can perhaps be best compared to Thomas Malthus's concept of a world of poverty—an alien world that appeared so antithetical to nineteenth-century moral imagination (Himmelfarb 1983). This other world was one in which poverty was an endemic condition and in which the poor are considered a relatively homogeneous class. In the Malthusian "continuum the poor are always being pulled down toward the very poor, and the very poor toward the abyss of starvation and death" (Himmelfarb 1983). With the poverty of the immigrant in popular imagination, as in the popular derivations of Malthus, work is forced to labor by the dictates of poverty. The ambulant street sellers, the *vu' comprà*, are the embodiment of this logic. These street sellers, who sell lighters and tissues and items of African art, are associated with a form of criminality and with a world of poverty and despair.

Demography is not a neutral issue but, rather, is saturated with multiple discourses about the nature of society and the world at large—discourses that through the seemingly objective statement of fact, through the presentation of projections of population growths and economic forecasts in local newspapers, may enter into a set of discursive practices that frame and contribute to its context and signification. In the Malthusian popular imagery of the immigrant, the notion that the overpopulated Third World will overrun Europe is one of the key metaphors of a discourse on immigration and a central preoccupation of such right-wing groups as the Le Pen followers in France, the National Front in England, and the right-wing leagues of Italy. The Italian MSI Party has taken up the anti-immigrant slogan of "Italy to the Italians." The poverty of the Third World gives rise to a teeming population that, once unleashed on Europe, will cause the demise of European society as it is known today, according to this ideology. This anxiety is often depicted in the press through the use of an image of the residences of the immigrants of color in the urban world of Europe. Giorgio Bocca fixes the appearance of these media images in the late 1970s and specifically in Genoa, where police cleared a former maritime housing complex of migrants who refused to accept return-trip tickets to their respective countries: "From that day we knew in a manner that we could not evade that the poor of the Third World were embarking on our shores and that they did not intend to leave" (Bocca 1988, 38).

Race, Difference, and Their Antecedents: Images of the Mezzogiorno

The right-wing MSI has declared that Jean-Marie Le Pen in France speaks with the voice of "the profound France." During the elections in 1990 the party carried a series of posters, some of which depicted a young black ambulant seller on the street. The caption read in a slogan borrowed from the French Right, "We say what you think. No to immigration" (see fig. 6). The right-wing Italian leagues unite their antisouthern position with overtones of a renewed racism made legitimate by the new respectability of racism. This has brought the problem of Italian ethnic discrimination to the forefront of public discourse (Bocca 1988).

Some members of the right-wing leagues, which now even include former Communist Party members in northern Italy, call for the nationhood of northern Italy, looking to neighboring former Yugoslavia separatist movements as a model (Kopkind 1991). A recent proposal for legislation in Italy called for the official recognition of minority languages including German, Sardinian, Albanian, Franco-Provençal, and Ladino-Friulano. If passed the measure would assure the teaching of dialect in schools and their status as official local languages. This has been opposed strongly by such figures as Italian historian Valerio Castronovo as a dangerous rebirth of "localism" that stands to efface "national cohesion"(Battistini 1991). Although the call for the representation of the minority languages in 1971 would have seemed to be an issue of mere cultural representation, the atmosphere today is clouded by the right-wing leagues' cry for separatism and local purity. The leagues have been very successful recently with another issue, the opposition to immigration and the call to throw immigrants (most of them African and Arab) out of the country. This culminated this past summer in the expulsion of thousands of Albanian political refugees: "Almost everyone in Italy wanted them shipped home at once, although some accompanied their cries of 'good riddance' with murmurs of regret" (Kopkind 1991). These problems of localism and xenophobic sentiment create a difficult political and social climate in Italy, which today faces its first encounter with immigration. Just one year after the passage of the first comprehensive legislation dealing with immigration in Italy since 1931, separatist right-wing groups in the leagues have captured a wide range of voters with their passionate anti-immigrant platforms.

The manner in which the antisouthern Italian bias of such right-wing groups as the northern Leagues converges with an anti-immigrant stance in Italy requires some explanation. The historical, socioeconomic, and cultural divisions between the North and South in Italy have been a persistent feature of the contours of the Italian peninsula since unification. Massimo d'Azeglio's often quoted line cuts to the heart of the problem: "We have made Italy—now we must make Italians." His comment suggests that the Italian unification of the Risorgimento made Italy and that it was left to the postunification liberal regime to make Italians (cited in Clark 1984). This comment was echoed by the Italian historian Stuart Woolf, who said that the "painful experience of mass migration south to north" might be considered to have accomplished "the real unification of the Italian people" (Woolf 1979a). The process of making Italians is, in fact, the very thing that is being contested by the separatist right-wing groups, and the legitimacy of the state to make Italians is, in fact, already contested in the manner in which the southerner is viewed by northerners through the lens of an antisouthern ideology.

One of the key features of the right-wing characterization of the South and the southerner in Italy turns on the economic conditions of the South in its relationship to the industrial North; discussions of Italy frequently involve the issue of the "economic backwardness" of the region and the industrialization of the North. The dichotomization between the developed north and the underdeveloped south is in fact the classical axis along which the contemporary imagination of the Italian landscape has been formulated. Until quite recently Italy's backward economy was one of the features that characterized it to the European Community. Cultural dimensions, although seldom mentioned, were given the dignity of an explanation and were relegated to the stereotype.

The contrast between the expansive development of the economy in the North and the slow and stilted progression of the backward economy of the South evoked the most varied explanations and assessments. In light of the diffusion of ideas of the physical sciences, some pointed to the impact of environmental imbalances in society and economy. The differences in regions and peoples could be attributed to race and physiognomy or could be the basis of some phrenological aberrations. In fact, a curious amalgam of possible explanations existed. Cesare Lombroso (1836–1909) was professor of psychiatry and criminal anthropology in the University of Turin and the architect of modern criminology. Impressed by the developments in the evolutionary theory of civilizations and the findings of phrenology, he employed these two components in the development of an "evolutionary theory of racial development" (Pick 1986, 62). Lombroso made a carefully calibrated scale of the degree of "social savagery" of various portions of the Italian population and as early as 1859 published a paper on "cretinism" using data collected in southern Italy during his stint in the Italian army. Lombroso thought that the use of statistics and photography would enable him to isolate the "features of a criminal sub-species which plagued the Italian race and state" (Pick 1986, 62).

The "southern question," as it is traditionally called, is complicated by the attribution of essential characteristics to the populations of the region to explain economic backwardness. "The South," writes Daniel Pick, "was cast as a form of other world, racially different, a space to be explored, penetrated, contained, colonized"(1986, 62). The form of the other world that the south took on was inexorably associated with the implicit racial ideology developed by writers like Lombroso during the nineteenth century. Underlying the works of Lombroso was the creation of a certain type of Italian and the elimination of those who would be defined as outside of the "pale of polity and society" (Pick 1986). The definition of the ideal political subject for Lombroso was made on the basis of the racial and regional distinctions arrived at through scientific and technological findings. One student of Lombroso's wrote in a treatment of the differences between the North and the South of Italy, *Italiani del Nord* and *Italiani del Sud:*

> Not all the parts which compose Italy's multiple and differentiated organism have progressed equally in the course of civilization; some have remained behind, due to inept government or as the sad result of other factors . . . whilst others have progressed strongly. Unfortunately the Mezzogiorno and the islands still possess the sentiments and customs—the substance if not the form—of past centuries. They are less evolved, and less civilized than the society to be found in Northern Italy. (quoted in Pick 1986)

Alfredo Niceforo, this student of Lombroso, was merely expressing an attitude that defined the relationship between North and South in terms of levels of civilization achieved respectively by the two regions.

The folk expression "Africa begins at Rome" carries with it this same racialist ideology of the nineteenth-century thinker in the form of a slogan. In the early 1970s when a group of lawyers and social activists in the town of Matera in southern Italy wished to protest the treatment of the area by the central government in Rome, the protesters claimed that they had more in common with Africa than with Rome in an attempt to highlight the contrast of development and intervention. Matera, famous as the place of internment of the anti-Fascist Carlo Levi, is also the home of a series of cave dwellings, the *sassi,* or stones that housed families until an order by Fascist government officials forced people from their homes. Mussolini was concerned that the image of Italians living in caves would send the wrong message to the outside world. The cultural world of the inhabitants of the *sassi* and their various traditions—for example, leaving a stone on the opening to the dwelling of a young woman as a sign of the engagement and calling out the post over the overlapping levels of the landings that cascade down the hillside—have all been long silenced in the name of modernity. To such regions as that in which Matera is found, Rome is a distant shore, a vague figure in the historical drama that has swept up the interlacing mountains and the promontories facing the ocean, while the caves in Matera still hold the traces of Byzantine fresco as evidence that this world, not the Roman one, came closest to its caverns.

After the liberation of the kingdom of Naples by the forces of Giuseppi Garibaldi in 1861, the newly appointed governor of the region, Giuseppi Farina, wrote to the Piedmontese Count Cavour: "This is no Italy! This is Africa: the Bedouins are the flower of civic virtue beside these country bumpkins" (in Pick 1986, 83). The substance of past centuries imagined in the form of the infusion of "Arab" blood in Sicily or in the primitive attributes of the peoples of the islands was articulated through the scientific theories of men like Lombroso and his followers. Lombroso eventually drew a map of the distribution of criminal traits and transposed this onto a map of the nation. He associated Italian districts in Italy that showed the "maximum number of births" with various forms of criminality: the Italian South, far in advance of the number of births in the North, in this manner demonstrated an elevated criminal activity. The excessive heat of southern regions was thought by Lombroso to cause "all Malthusian precautions to be forgotten in the act of procreation" (Lombroso 1968[1911]).

The contemporary concern with criminality that is said to originate largely from the South presents its own mapping of Italy, one that is incorporated into the social and cultural justification of the right-wing leagues' rejection of the South and call for a separate state. This modern mapping of criminality follows the opposition of presumed criminal networks to the state, the Cosa Nostra of Sicily, the N'Drangheta of Calabria, and the Camorra of Naples. Each is said to specialize in a particular criminal enclave: "The Sicilians dominate the heroin trade, the Neapolitans the cocaine business and the Calabrians kidnapping" (Friedman 1988).

The profusion of the ideas of Lombroso in Italy came about through the founding of a scholarly journal in 1880, the *Archivo di psichiatria, antropologia criminale e scienze penali*, which was to be one of the most influential showcases for the theories of the Italian positivist movement (Pick 1989, 120). The techniques that Lombroso employed revealed to him not only a criminality that he thought of as one of the crucial elements in the weakening of the nation, but also the existence of an ancestral past, a primitive form of society that through the criminal or the less civilized was brought into the heart of modern society. Thus Lombroso argued for the elimination of the unproductive, the weak, and the evolutionarily unfit: "Even when honor, chastity, and pity are found among savageness, impulsiveness and laziness are never wanting. Savages have a continuous horror of continuous work, so that for them the passage to active and methodical labour lies by the road of selection of slavery only" (in Pick 1986, 66). The vision of the South and its economic backwardness in the rhetoric of Lombroso was mixed with notions of the primitive as well as with criminal anthropology with its designation of a hierarchy of races that went beyond the confines of Italian society. Whites for Lombroso were at the top of the hierarchy. From the perspective of such a theory of racial evolution like that promulgated by Lombroso and his followers (Pankhurst 1969), there is a continual threat to society of the atavistic elements that lie within it and, moreover, from the primitive world that surrounds the European world. According to the notions of Lombroso the external threat to European society and to the emergent form of the nation-state was seen to emanate from the dark continent or from the many atavistic elements within the Italian nation itself. These theories were formulated so that some form of intervention might preclude the advent of the threat, streamline the evolutionary process within society, and contain the external threat altogether. Lombroso's criminal anthropology sought to contain the threat of the Other and thus to unify the dangers, holding it within a single taxonomic and historical model, in order to keep it outside of the state, outside of the fragile coherence of Italian unification (Pick 1986, 66).

The Use and Abuse of Images

A Senegalese migrant once pointed to an Italian political poster and remarked, "They use our own images against us." The climate has changed somewhat in Europe (*International Herald Tribune* 1990). It now appears legitimate to reawaken racist sentiments and slogans, which attain a more accepted response in certain circumstances than the previously fringe position of far-right ideology during the postwar years:

> I sondaggi di opinione avrano un valore relativo ma quando ripetano che sette su dieci vorrebbero rimandare gli immigrati di colore a casa e bloccare ultiriori arrivi, quando esprimono sentimenti di diffidenza e di ostilità, dicono con sufficiente chiarezza che sono finiti sia il colonialismo rurale "a fin di bene" del fascismo popolare sia bella egualanza della repubblica democratica; sia la "Facetta nera" fascista che il legionario portava a Roma "liberata" per farne una piccola italiana, sia il metarazzismo, il supermento sdegnoso del razzismo dei grandi conformismi democratici (Opinion polls are of relative value, but they repeatedly report that seven out of ten Italians want to send the immigrants of color home and to block further arrivals, and they express sentiments of diffidence and hostility and say with sufficient clarity that both the rural colonialism "a fin di bene" of popular fascism and the equality of the democratic republic are finished. And the end also of whether it is the "Little Black Face" fascist that the Italian legionnaire brought to Rome, "liberated" in order to make here a little Italian, and half-caste-ism, or the disdainful antiracism of the great democratic conformists). (Bocca 1988)

Ruth Benedict once wrote that "the history of national racism . . . is the history of chauvinism"; the many racist slogans are the "camouflage" of political conflicts and mask the underlying "aggressions and alliances" of the racist (Benedict 1947). It is no accident that the new racism is articulated through the search of contemporary neofascist organizations for a common basis of Europeanism in the "invidious distinctions of race," to use Gerald Berreman's phrase again (1976). The distinctions that divide Italy into myriad localisms also segment Europe in popular ideology, and it is just these sentiments that are reasserted today. The antidemocratic voice once again rises up against the "democratic con-formists" of postwar Europe. Benedict notes the transformation of the image of Italy that was necessary in order to justify the Rome-Berlin al-liance during the Second World War:

> Orthodox racism of the prewar and First World War period had been
> full of contempt for the Mediterranean race, but the Rome-Berlin
> Axis had to be given a racial basis. Much was made, therefore, of the
> German-ness of Northern Italy and the fact that classic German
> racists had ascribed all achievements beyond the Alps to infiltrations
> of northern blood; Chamberlain and others had outdone themselves
> in claiming as "Nordic" such Italians as Dante, Petrarch, Giotto,
> Leonardo, and Michelangelo. The same Italy which in 1915 France
> had welcomed as an ally because they both were racially Latin, Ger-
> many now welcomed on the basis of their common Teutonic blood.
> (Benedict 1940)

The new racism draws on the alliances of a right-wing fringe: Le Pen followers in from Paris speak to right-wing rallies in Turin just prior to Italian elections encouraged the anti-immigrant stance of their col-leagues. Mussolini once said that "one could think of an empire, that is of a nation which directly or indirectly guides another nation without the need to conquer a single square kilometer of territory." Could this be some community or nation defined in terms of its "superiority" or claim to ascendancy on some other ground? The empire of the colonial era is today an empire of signs, of invidious distinctions, and disposi-tions that may mark, as Bocca suggests, a rejection of many of the antichauvinist and nationalist sentiments of the postwar Western Euro-pean democracies.

"Facetta Nera" (Little Black Face): Italian Colonial Images and Racial Policy

> Race constructed as a fear of difference was also a fear of the monstrous
> undead—those presumed dead on arrival to modern age. The living
> dead, ancient forms of nature.
>
> —Brackette Williams, *Women out of Place:*
> *The Gender of Agency and the Race of Nationality*

I had the feeling that I was repeating a cycle. . . . I was haunted by a
galaxy of erosive stereotypes.
                                    —Frantz Fanon, *Black Skin, White Masks*

The Italian invasion of Ethiopia in 1935 was viewed initially as part of
Italy's civilizing mission in Africa. The popular Abyssinian song "Little
Black Face" or "Facetta Nera" was the song that Italian soldiers took
"lighthearted to war" with them, as an admirer of Mussolini, Luis Diel,
a German Nazi observer at the time, noted.[11] The song was very popular
and gave the listener the impression that Ethiopian women would be
part of the "fruits of victory": "[Little] Abyssinian, you will be kissed and
wear the black shirt, even you." In other words, the black shirt of the
Fascist would be worn by the Ethiopian women who would be brought
back to Rome and there could become an Italian subject and object of
desire. The song continues: "Wait and hope for that hour when we draw
near to you, and will give you another Duce and another King." The
Little Black Face is then constructed through a language of sexuality and
domination, one that places the black woman in the role of sexual and
colonial object. The process of colonization is at once cast in images of
sexuality and eroticism, an eroticism that denotes the power and authority of the colonial campaign. Images of black women on picture post-
cards were prominently displayed in the Roman shop windows of the
period (Pankhurst 1969).

Madamism refers to a system of marriage or temporary marriage
practice between Italian men and Ethiopian women, a practice that was
widespread among all social ranks, and very common in Somalia and
Eritrea since the nineteenth century: "Fascist officials complained that
the racial superiority of the Italian conqueror did not exist in Ethiopia
because Italian colonial policy indulged in elevating the Ethiopians,
according them clemency, and tolerating equality between Italian and
Ethiopians" (Sbacchi 1985). After the invasion of Ethiopia in 1935, Fascist
racial policy intensified dramatically, when by 1938 a rigid racial regime
was established by the Fascist Grand Council. The involvement of Italian
men with Ethiopian women, or the institution of *madamismo,* was to become a problem for the Fascist regime of Mussolini.[12] Toward the end of
1935 the policy contradicted the rigid segregation of the colonized from
the colonizer and was thought to detract from the prestige of Italians:

This system of "Marriage" was discussed in 1898 by a French observer,
Paul de Lauribar, who states that it was "considered altogether natural"

for an Italian officer to contract "a marriage the duration of which is
limited to his stay in Africa, or even to his pleasure." Such unions,
which, he claims, gave the woman concerned considerable prestige in
her own society, were effected without any ceremony, the officer having merely to provide the woman thenceforward designated by the
name of "Madame," with the most modest requirements: a tukul, or
traditional hut, an angareb, or bed, one or two wooden stools, and
some clay pots. For maintenance she would receive a sack of grain
every month, as well as a small sum of money, formerly fixed at eight
francs, subsequently somewhat increased as a result of a slight rise in
the requirements of the "madames." (Pankhurst 1969)

According to French observer Paul de Lauribar's *Douze Ans en
Abyssinie* (1898), the women were "abominable flirts, more so even than
Parisian women, if that were possible, and when united with an officer,
their coquetry and ambition knew no bounds" (cited in Pankhurst 1969).
It was therefore the duty of the husband to give the temporary wife many
gifts. The husband gave "presents of silver objects, such as bracelets and
anklets, necklaces and earrings, as well as shirts, shammas, European toilet articles, sheep, and even cattle" (in Pankhurst 1969). This practice of
temporary marriage was not invented for the benefit of Italian soldiers
and others but was no doubt linked to the taking of a servant as a traditional Ethiopian practice.[13] The servant girl *qarad,* who is called a *qallabi*
(who may also prepare the meals) attains the status of wife or *qitir* after a
formal agreement is witnessed before a judge (Walker 1933, 41). The Italian governor of Eritrea in 1898, Ferdinando Martini, blamed the practice
for the loss of "all sense of dignity and decorum" among his troops; government housing encampments were, according to the governor, "being
turned into brothels"; a large part of many of the salaries of the lower
officials were said to be spent on the "madams," and, moreover, "the
natives laugh to see officials thus enraptured by a prostitute" (Pankhurst
1969, 270–71). Martini's concern for the children of the Ethiopian
women and the Italian soldiers also created a potential problem for the
prestige of Italians, these "half-castes or chocolate-coloured children"
could prove a "disgrace for the individual and for the dominant race" if
their maintenance was left unattended by their Italian father. Many of
the Italians provided for the education of their children and, as another
observer notes, most "looked after their 'colonial children.'" In short,
there were those who accorded the "colonial children" a somewhat privileged place in the colonial hierarchy and some of the so-called assimila-

tionists who viewed the "racial intermixing" as an inevitability of the colonial world (Pankhurst 1969, 272). It was in this climate of the temporary marriage structure that the soldiers marched off lightheartedly to Ethiopia in 1935 singing the popular song "Facetta Nera": the lines of the song that say "ti porteremo a Roma" (we will take you to Rome) and "liberata" (liberated by our sun) refer to the widespread practice of the incorporation of "colonial children" and wives into the life of the metropol and that of the colonies.

The first legal basis for discrimination against the half-caste was established in 1933 with the Organic Law for Eritrea and Italian Somaliland, a law that introduced the concept of "physical characteristics" for making distinctions between persons. Paternally recognized children of Italian nations were to be given citizenship automatically, while children of unknown parentage who were assumed through the reading of physical characteristics or other signs to have at least one white parent were entitled to petition for citizenship. The claim had to be made when the child had reached the age of eighteen, had followed a "perfectly Italian education," and committed no crimes requiring the loss of civil liberties. By 1936 the climate had changed and the Italian conquest of empire clearly called for a rigid separation of the races; racist articles began to appear in newspapers. One article read: "Fascism protects the race and tries to keep it pure. The Italian nation possesses qualities which should not be allowed to become general property." The "mixing with the natives" of earlier times was said to injure both "physically and morally, the wonderful race that created Empire." The message was clearly directed at the half-caste children who had returned with their parents to Italy: "We must count ourselves lucky not to see coloured people in the streets, as is the case in other places. . . . In Italy there is only room for us white Italians and our blood must not be mixed" (in Pankhurst 1969, 275). Just a year after the invasion the Italian newspaper *Gazzetta del Popolo* deplored the notion of Italian couples who wished to adopt Abyssinian children and promoted the notion of keeping Italians separated from the "native" population. Further, the paper directly attacked the song "Facetta Nera," suggesting that if the author of the song were to live with Abyssinian people he would see the error in his "romantic state of mind corrupted by affection and vice." "I swear," continues the journalist Paolo Monelli, "two or three hours would be enough in an Abyssinian hut with a black face." Such corrupted and romantic states of mind, Monelli declared, "must be buried under ten metres of earth if we wish . . . to build the empire" (in Pankhurst 1969, 274). According to Mussolini, "Empires are conquered by arms and kept by prestige," and the system of *madamismo* was seen to undercut this prestige. Moreover, Mussolini defined the empire in Fascist doctrine as "not only a territorial, military or mercantile, but also a spiritual and moral expression." By 1937 racial legislation assigned the half-caste to the status of the mother instead of the father, and by 1939 the legally united families of Italians married to "colonial subjects" were forcibly broken up all over Italy (Pankhurst 1969, 284). About 90 percent of Italian men living in Italian East Africa had no European family in Africa. By the time some sort of second-order "special" citizenship or citizenship status equal to that given to the inhabitants of Libya was being considered for the people of Italian East Africa in 1942, it was in effect lost to Italy (Sbacchi 1985).

The Cartoon: The Little Black Face and the Socialist

A Forattini caricature that ran in *La Repubblica* (see fig. 7) depicts former Prime Minister Craxi, the chairman of the Italian Socialist Party, dressed in the regalia of an Italian Fascist circa 1935, chasing the figure of a black woman (Gilbert 1995, 10–11). There is, in fact, the body of a black woman whose face is that of the sponsor of the immigration legislation, Claudio Martelli. The caption reads, "You will ruin all my plans, Little Black Face." The following will be an examination of some of the meanings contained in this caricature (Lumley 1996b).[14]

The cartoon, which appeared in *La Repubblica* on 5 April 1990, was carried on the front page under the title *Il muro di Martelli* (Martelli's wall), contrasting the erection of a wall against peoples of the Third World with the Berlin Wall, which was just coming down. The title places the problem of immigration squarely into the context of an emergent Europe and the turmoil of this process. As the surveillance of the title casts a glance backward to the Europe of the Berlin Wall and the Cold War era, there is a foreshadowing of a parallel "cold war," one against the Third World. Slogans of the papers on subsequent days only further helped to frame this problematic by declaring, "We are not at war with blacks," thus dismissing the use of the armed forces against the "clandestine army" of migrants destined to arrive on Italian shores. This journalistic treatment juxtaposed the great and dramatic historic events of the opening up of Europe, the unification of Germany, and the eminent transformation of the Soviet Union and Eastern Europe on the one hand, and the many problems associated with the new status of Europe on the other. The notion that immigrants from Eastern Europe would come to Italy in greater numbers was something that preoccupied many Italians. Already some Polish and Albanian immigrants had established communities in various cities. These immigrants were seen to be different from those coming from the Third World since the immigrants from Eastern Europe had come from a world of shared European culture and tradition while Third World migrants are viewed as devoid of this cultural similarity.[15]

The Socialist Party and the State: The End of European Socialism

In Forattini's design the caricaturist calls on the great ambiguity of the Socialist Party in the structure of Italian parliamentary power. The role of Socialists in European government, most notably in France and Italy, calls into question the nature of a politics of the Left that becomes a governmental party in the context of Italy with a state dominated by the Christian Democrats. The Socialists have traditionally performed the role of the mediator in Italian politics, while the very constitution of the Italian Communist Party was in theory antithetical to the modern state and thus by definition an extragovernmental party. The Socialists have, as one writer put it, mediated between the Left and the center-right. This role as mediator almost led to the demise of the party in the early 1970s before Craxi's decisive leadership changed the nature of the party.

From about 1978 Craxi began to transform the image of the Socialist Party, attacking the expositions of the Communists and even removing the symbol of the hammer and sickle (this was all a prelude to the name change of the party in the 1990s) and replacing this with that of a red carnation. By the 1980s the notion of a compromise with the Communist Party to bring them into some sort of agreement with the ruling Christian Democrats had vanished. The Socialists moved into the government and began to control important cabinet posts and to participate in the extensive leadership of the state's many enterprises. By the middle of the 1980s the Italian Socialists had become a crucial party in the workings of Italian government; it was virtually impossible to form a cabinet without the participation of this party of the red carnation. It is just this that is problematized in the cartoon by Forattini—this ambiguous relationship of a party of the Left to the trappings of state power.

The Socialists have come to represent for some everything that is wrong with politics. Alberto Cavallari recently argued that the many European Socialists and Communists have reformed themselves over the past century, replacing the society of exploitation with that of "consumption" as its privileged protagonist (Cavallari 1992). Cavallari's caveat notes the preoccupation of these parties with middle sectors of the population deeply involved in the world of consumerism and status seeking. Cavallari continues by noting that the mediation role of the Socialists is in the context of postcommunism no longer necessary; there is no need to make capitalism more social. The resulting configuration of the Socialist Party reveals a reformed anticapitalist party. The integration of Socialists into the new consumer culture of capitalism has meant a loss of prestige and definition of the Socialist role. According to Cavallari, this accounts for the emergence of the many Catholic-inspired groups that call for reform of the "profit motive" of the new capitalism rather than a fluorescence of Left socialistic organizations. The socialism of the European Socialist then resembles a presocialist libertarianism rather than an anticapitalist socialism (Cavallari 1992). There has perhaps been no more close relationship with the state and capitalist development than that which today exists between the Left of the Socialists and the state. Thus the ambiguity of the role of the Socialist may be said to denote the end of "socialism," of a collaboration of the Left with a massive modern state that in the end denies the existence of the former.

The end of socialism was ushered in by the Fascist state and the establishment of corporatism, a unique collaboration of the state with industry. The Socialists seem to founder on the very thing that characterized the Fascist regime. The Socialists in government become, then, just this—a "new regime," one in which the activities of the Left become difficult to distinguish from the repressive measures of the Right. Craxi has often been compared to Mussolini or even to Adolf Hitler for his antidemocratic manner of running the party. This satiric criticism, however, only underscores the play of Socialism in Europe.

Black Woman: Voice and Image

The absence of voice of the black woman parallels the absence of voice of Third World peoples in Italian society. No protest can be mounted that is capable of rejecting the image or characterization of Third World peoples represented by the figure. Even though the critique of the artist is launched against the overtones of right-wing propaganda in the rhetoric of the Left, the images used belie a nonreflexive stance that regards any form of representation of Third World people of color as legitimate. The underlying themes of sexuality and primitiveness evoke in popular imagination the figure of prostitution and the very threat to social order that comes from the alleged primitiveness or alienness of cultural heritage to the West. The unchecked sexuality of the *facetta nera* is then linked to the absence of voice: the little black face can only find expression in the language of sexuality—in the rhythms of the body, the natural world in which the primitive reins. As the large earrings on the black figure in Forattini's drawing highlight the passivity of listening rather than speaking, the subordinate must be master of the auditory, that is, of the anticipation of the wishes of those with the power to speak. And so Martelli must defer to the political designs of Craxi and the overall political long-range demands of the party system. The closed mouth of the figure of the black woman (Martelli) connotes the voicelessness of Africans in their own fate and the sublimation of all proposals on immigration to the will of the party. The lips of the figure may only open sexually, that is, compromised by the dominant dictates of the sociopolitical context.

This metaphor of sexual aperture draws the discussion of the political world into the popular conception of African women as closer to nature and somehow more sexual than Europeans. The image of the African woman has neither the word nor the "use of it" (Sartre 1963). Jean-Paul Sartre, speaking of African decolonization, recognized the new voice of Frantz Fanon, who would turn the relationship of colonizer to colonized on the "use of the word" as giving voice to what had previously been below the level of discussion. Here, however, we see the effect of a voice negated: the images of African women are taken and without their permission or consent reproduced like tokens of a presence that can speak with no other voice. In Turin the photographs of several Somali women would appear in the local paper each time the image of an "immigrant" was required to adorn an article on the topic. The women's remarks in the context in which the photo had been taken were cropped out of the original photograph, which was actually taken in the middle of the eighties although it was passed off as if it were contemporary with the article it adorned. The image relegated to the voiceless archive and brought out for human interest is telling in its subtle consumption of a voiceless "Other." The women represent both a "natural" and "social" silence: the first submerged in a continent that speaks only through its alleged "poverty," through media images of its "struggle to survive" the daily passage of hunger and internal conflict, and the second social silence, in the absence of the voice of African or other Third World women in any official channel. The presence of a black woman presenter on the RAI 2 television program *Non Solo Nero* is confronted by the counterinsurgency of rumors among journalists that "she says just what they tell her to say" and she often "complains of the things she is forced to say." And thus silence is peopled with voices—voices that are never heard and that become trapped in the symbolism of the body.

Bodies, Speech, and Politics

Women have the power to transform men's bodies operating in the political realm—in short, to effeminatize them and therefore to deprive them of the power of speech and of action (Hunt 1991, 108–31). So the effeminatization of Martelli through the introduction of uncontained elements of sexuality and primitiveness threatens to silence the voice of the potential alternate state of politics of Craxi. Within the Italian political world, a world of men primarily, few women have positions of power. The Italian gender asymmetry would relegate African women then to the lowest possible rankings, and so the image of the black woman is shown as body, primarily as an object of erotic and uncontained potentialities, one that could never be empowered: an image that stands so far outside of the world of Italian power that within it, it would have to receive an "exotic status."

Eroticism is in many ways a key concept for understanding the many representations of the immigrant in Italian society, one that is connected to the notions of demography and to the ever recurrent themes of criminality, health, and work. The erotic and its relationship to the body politic at once brings into question the demarcations of the public and private realms, and with them the question of woman's place in the constellation of society. In European traditions women's bodies have often been constructed as sites of control; in short, women's bodies were sites of a kind of naturalness and the corruptive effects of the "flesh" that makes up their bodies. The containment of these disturbing qualities in women's bodies was problematized and made synonymous in many cases with the public good. Montesquieu warned, for instance, of the intrusion of women's sexuality in public affairs (Hunt 1991, 1–12). Similarly, while lauding the honor of masculine virtue, Jean-Jacques Rousseau warned of the corrupting effects of the public display of women. Women in European societies have been represented as somehow dangerous to the process of the smooth functioning of power and thus have provided a site for the representation of contradictions of democratic and antidemocratic undercurrents in such societies.

Women's bodies provide the possibility of representing both "natural" inequalities of gender and the "social" inequalities of class and other distinctions (Frappier-Mazur 1991). The symbolic zoning of women's bodies is capable of epitomizing the contours of the most intimate realms of domestic life and the most distant reaches of the dangerous sectors of society. This is precisely the case with the African woman who calls on a structure of power and representation that opposes the European world of political order and civility with that of an imagined world of African disorder and uncontained sexuality.

The great weight of Others was perhaps made most clear in contemporary thought by the philosophies of Sartre and has resulted in a preoccupation with the presence of the Other, by the mere weight of numbers. The demographic project that exists as a state enterprise is essential to understanding the preoccupation of Europe with the "growth" of populations outside of its borders; a similar preoccupation led Sartre to decide to have no children (Jameson 1990). The logical extension of the counting of persons or "souls" is the intervention of forms of "control," primarily of the bodies of women. The bodies of Third World women can symbolize this "danger," that of the sheer weight of the Third World, which like the dangerous classes of a former Europe threaten to overwhelm with a ubiquitous presence. The African woman may represent a "natural" sexuality that itself contains a danger—both that of an unwanted presence and of a potential presence, thus conflating the potentialities of material presence with a natural potential principle of fecundity.

The association of the black woman with an "unbridled sexuality" is one that has traversed the European consciousness since the late nineteenth century. Cesare Lombroso in his classical studies of delinquent women made this connection altogether clear, associating certain traits of the prostitute and the black women of so-called primitive society. In his *The Female Offender* (1895), written with his son-in-law Guillaume Ferrero, Lombroso attributes to atavism the "virility of the savage woman," presenting portraits of the "Red Indian woman" and the "Negro Woman" as examples. The criminal woman was an atavistic subtype of women who represented the "reversion to the Primitive" and was identified by the two "salient characteristics of primordial women, namely, precocity and minor degree of differentiation from the male." One of these traits, a "peculiar plumpness" of the prostitute, was attributed to both prisoners and the Hottentot by the writer of one of the most widely read books on prostitution in the nineteenth century, A. J. B. Parent-Duchatelet, who in an 1836 study of Paris prostitution provides a detailed study of the physiognomy of prostitutes. Parent-Duchatelet attributed the weight of the prostitute to the great number of baths the women took and to their "lassitude" and low status in the scale of women. Lombroso accepted this notion, stating at one point in his writings: "Hottentot, African, and Abyssinian women when rich and idle grow enormously fat, and the reason for the phenomenon is atavistic"; "the obesity of prostitutes . . . is perhaps of atavistic origin" (Lombroso 1895 [1980]).

In another study that Lombroso published with his son-in-law in 1893 on the prostitute and the normal woman, Lombroso notes the alleged anomalies of the genitalia of the Hottentot and makes the analogy between the Hottentot and the prostitute (Gilman 1986a). Sander Gilman notes that in the nineteenth century the prostitute was viewed as the "essential sexualized female" and that by the end of the nineteenth century through the work of Lombroso, his students, and others such as Parent-Duchatelet "the perception of the prostitute" was merged with that of the "perception of the black" (Gilman 1986a). Lombroso's son-in-law Guillaume Ferrero described the rule of primitive society to be prostitution and constructed a scale of primitive lasciviousness that was correlated to the "poverty of their mental universe." The "primitive or black" was thus given the status of the prostitute and the "essential sexualized female" of the nineteenth century, to use Gilman's expression (Gilman 1986a).

The attribution of primitiveness to Third World women confers the notion of a natural inequality and a predisposition of African women to a more natural sexuality. The motif of the prey-predator privileges the notion of Third World women as victims or prey (Frappier-Mazur 1991). This motif often accompanies the appearance of black women on Italian television programs and commercials. The naturalness that is accorded a sexuality not contained or channeled properly leads to and reinforces the designation of "prostitution," or a misplaced "sexuality" improperly situated in the public domain and dangerous to social order (Nead 1988). The *facetta nera* of the Fascist era was dominated both sexually and socially, the sexual metaphor being a euphemism for colonial conquest. The separation of the colonial subjects was eventually given both a natural and legal justification, which was codified in racial legislation of the period. What is represented in the notion of *madamismo* is a kind of adventurism of the young and robust Italian soldier, a kind of sexual colonialism that was symbolized as a sexual conquest, an ordering of the natural order by the social and political or by the very "civilizing process" of Western imperialism.

The symbolism of eroticism constitutes the manner through which various inequalities are imaged. The body of the African woman is for the state a site of potential social disorder since the state project of accounting or enumerating the population and its control, ordering, and specialization can be disrupted by this new presence. "Why do they emigrate from the South of the World?" asks an *Avvenimenti* article in 1989. The insert to page 17 demonstrates its answer with human figures superimposed on a map of the world in which Latin America, Africa, the Middle East, and the "Orient" are pictured in bright colors while the rest remains in an understated gray. The upper-left corner shows a coffin above which an airplane for the transport of immigrants is drawn. The first insert reads, "The hunger that kills," noting that the equivalent death toll to that lost each day to hunger could be imaged in the form of the daily crashing of three hundred jumbo jets that would disappear without a single survivor: this is the magnitude of the death toll of the many lives that succumb to hunger each year in the Third World (*Avvenimenti* 1989). The great horror of this statement is that it is the plane that brings the magnitude of the tragedy closer to Us: this technological artifact, the plane, mediates the deaths to the reader. This plane transports the significance of distant deaths as it renders understandable the passage of immigrants from lands of death and malnutrition to the

West. Bodies, in short, are accounted for in one of two conditions—
dead in the Third World or living in the First. This is in many ways the
inversion of a public monument: it is that of the creation of a token of a
public tomb that celebrates an antihistory, a place beyond time and progress (Hobsbawm 1983).[16] While the monuments of the great nation-state
placed the solemnity of the state in the public view, this is a way of
according the Third World with the negation of numeration on the
one hand, in the recording of death, and its triumph, in its accounting
for the presence of "unwanted" and yet inevitable "immigrants" on the
other.

The black migrant's body is not marked off as an enclosed space
but, rather, as one open to the exploitation of Italian society. This also
signals an illicit entrance of the "erotic" in the world of politics, a world
of men. Immigrants, in short, are seen to enter into relationships that
are embedded in the world of criminality or on the margins of the
official Italian domains. The world of work is not entered but that of
"off-the-books" illegal work. The world of politics may not be entered
but the world of "influence" and this through the "erotic channels"—in
short, a challenge to the social order. This world of influence is again
associated with a world of criminality.[17]

Clothing, Technology, and Trinkets

The clothed figure of Craxi-Mussolini opposed to the naked image of
the black migrant poses the issue of military fashion. The technology of
the world of the West is opposed to its absence in the Third World and
to the absence of manufactured goods and certain artifacts and therefore
of the means of obtaining them. The image of the Fascist era was wed-
ded not only to a pronounced masculine virtue of militarism but equally
to the notion of technological progress and the expansionist designs of
corporatism. The opposition of the cloth cut by the fashion industry
and the trinkets and grass skirt of the "madam" highlight the conception
of the Third World as a place living off the benefits and technology of
the West—off the trinkets given in honor of an asymmetrical relationship of economies. The allusion is then cut from the cloth of today's
consumerism and the export of a series of "gifts" to the Third World in
the form of subsidies, notably to Morocco and other countries that
attempt to stop the flow of immigrants from their countries.

The importance of fashion and design in Italy is perhaps second only to its role in the symbolism of class and distinction. The attention to fashion is acute, and people often cite it as an index of the preoccupation with status and prestige in large cities. Consumerism is decried especially by some of the new social groups who are associated loosely with the Christian Democrats but who also attempt to remain independent of its bureaucracy. These groups claim that the consumerism is eating away at the values of Italian society, distinctions drawn from the relative success of one's participation in the "utopia of the market" that runs counter to the "traditional" values of "Catholic charity." Many of those who participate in these groups mark their dress with a distinctive, "casual" attire in sharp contrast to the dictates of the world of consumerism. These groups are often organized groups of Catholic volunteers, somewhat to the left of the Christian Democratic Party or young people, generally university students. This may be confined to certain departments: those in political science—and not law, for instance—tend to dress in a more casual manner. This is true for younger members of the lay Left, as it is for those who are unable to afford to keep up with the symbolism of class and status. Some take on an alternate youth style often drawn from the streets of urban North America or elsewhere.

The classical distinction, which some writers have discussed in Italy, between the various worlds of civility of the signori is in many ways reflective of the various manners in which social class is represented. There is still a marked emphasis among those who claim elite status to reenact the world of politeness of the Italian aristocracy. Titles are still used frequently by the descendants of Italian aristocracy; no opportunity will be missed to point out the Italian count who has been a longtime member of Italian Communist leadership. The novelty is not merely gratuitous: the colors of the House of Savoy are still required by law to adorn the houses of Turin, and Turin is the Italian city with the most extensive imperial monumental architecture of any of the Italian cities. Titles, whether those of the aristocratic past or those of the professional or academic fields, are extremely important. The title is a cultural badge that can accord one a little more consideration in the public domain. In lieu of this one may always look "important"—that is to say, deserving of "respect"—in everyday interactions. Just how one fits into the class structure can almost be read on one's sleeve: "If a button moves a fraction of an inch, they know," an Italian fine arts instructor once said. The tremendous pressure to look good, *porta una bella figura,* is considerable; those who are out of step clearly mark themselves. One of the complaints of young people about immigrants is that they "don't know how to dress—they buy the things from the market," and they are said to look and appear poorly.

There is also a division among the youth of Turin who use dress codes to express class: the Barboni, the young people of the periphery, "think that they are dressed well" and yet their clothes, like the immigrant's, are hopelessly out of style; they drive around in their cars with the music playing loud, and yet they do not go to school and basically waste their lives (Bagnasco 1990a). The Barboni are represented as coming from the vast world of the Valette or other urban housing projects on the periphery of the city, as descendants of the southern immigrant, inheritors of 1970s educational reforms that made allowances for the participation of a broader portion of society, although these educational reforms opened up the process to more students from working-class backgrounds formerly in effect blocked from university attendance. And although many students attended classes during the years after these reforms were put into place, few actually graduated. Even today, more than half of the university students never graduate. Little has changed: classes are still overcrowded, and students rarely have the opportunity to participate in class since courses are primarily lectures. An associated problem has been the difficulty of newly graduated university students finding their first employment (see Barbagli 1982).

Although many young people from working-class backgrounds arrive at the gates of the university, few matriculate. The system of preparatory schools in the areas on the periphery are often inadequate to the needs of the students; often parents are not able to manage to offer much assistance to the youth having completed little schooling. The videogame saloons and the corner bars on many of the streets on the periphery are the "schools" for many children in the lower reaches of the working class. While the Piedmontese established working class begins to manage to send their children to the local scientific *liceo*, the world of the periphery remains one in which the legal schooling minimum is attained and often little more. In working-class areas surrounding Turin such as Nichelino, there is not one movie theater, and many of the high school students seldom travel to the downtown center of Turin, although it is only a quarter of an hour away by tram.

The association between the "little black face" and the notion of prostitution, as we have seen, was mentioned by the observers of the colonial system of temporary marriage. In fact, the *facetta nera* was the potential "temporary wife" of the colonialist, a practice that colonial officials were in fact unable to initially control. The loss of prestige of the Italians involved in relationships with Ethiopian women, noted in Martini's comment that "the natives laugh to see officials thus enraptured by a prostitute" (Pankhurst 1969, 270–71), recalls the world of Lombroso, who viewed the Italian as wanting in the exercise of chastity and honor. The unregulated sexuality or the lack of containment of the sexuality of black women is the crucial feature in such a loss of prestige or social honor. The world of respectability and decorum, which is the preserve of the dominant race, is lost through the association with the natural world of sexuality, which clouds the reason and leaves the domain of power and authority of men open to the intervention of "ambitious" women. The prostitute, as Lynda Nead has argued in the case of nineteenth-century British prostitution, is antithetical to the world of respectability and domesticity and therefore threatens the "collapse of identities" of domains and the "leakage" of one category into another (Nead 1988). Nead argues that nineteenth-century prostitution was increasingly codified in law to be associated with "vice" in general, the difficulty being, in spite of its visibility, the spilling over of the practice from the public spaces to "the sites of respectability and domesticity" (Nead 1988, 115).

The "presents of silver objects, such as bracelets and anklets, necklaces and earrings, as well as shirts, shammas, European toilet articles, sheep, and even cattle" (Pankhurst 1969), which mark the status of the madam in contemporary Italian society, are signs of the problem of prostitution in large Italian metropolitan centers like Rome, Turin, and Milan. These objects at once note the women's enclosure in a system of gifts and her dependent status. These articles of adornment are rarely worn by Italian women and thus connote an exotic dimension to women who wear them. The black woman of the caricature by Forattini is a problematic figure implying the ambiguity of boundaries of the domestic and the public and the "inevitability" of keeping the domains separate and distinct in the face of the presence of the "alien" woman.[18] So the predisposition to remove the threat of the immigrant to the world of domesticity is and has been a crucial feature in the propaganda of the racist ideologue, as the Fascist poster in 1944 depicted a black man with a European woman along with the caption, "This could be your wife, your sister . . ." Jean-Marie Le Pen has entered this sentiment only slightly modified into French politics, stating the equation of the 1980s National Front: "Two million immigrant workers = Two million unemployed" (read French citizens), who, Le Pen continues, "want to sleep in my bed, with my wife" (Singer 1991).

7

Desperate Measures: Immigration and the South of the World

> No society . . . has ever been saturated with signs and messages like this one. —Fredric Jameson, *Signatures of the Visible*

The nation is imagined as a kind of community (Chabod 1961; Anderson 1983). Europe, or, rather, an idea of Europe, has traveled in the same orbit of thought as that of the nation/community almost from its inception, just as the emergence of a new European economic and social order seems assured by 1993, with the creation of the "territory of Schengen," a concept derived from an accord between France, Germany, and other nations in 1985 that would ensure a "single area in which people as well as goods, capital and services" might circulate freely (*The Independent* 1990). The notion of the internal circulation of people, goods, capital, and services implied the erection of what has been called the fortress of Europe, closed to the outside through the politics of visas, coordinated policies of entrance and expulsion from its boundaries, and above all measures that could regulate with uniformity "illegal immigration and refugee status." The image of the fortress of Europe stems to a great extent from the preoccupation of such initiatives with police measures. As some observers have noted, repressive measures may be a fine basis for the opening of debate and examination of the problems facing the new Europe; they are, however, an untimely place to signal the outlines of a unified Europe. International migratory trends that bring Third World migrants to Europe in unprecedented numbers and myriad "nationalisms," then, seem to tear at the unity of the imagined whole.

The Foreign Question

In 1986 a report was commissioned by the Italian Ministry of Labor, a small report that except for its peculiar title "Condizione degli Immigrati stranieri in Italia" (The condition of foreign immigrants in Italy) might have gone unnoticed, buried under the constant murmur of statistics, employment figures, and ministerial communications that comprise the daily symbolic documentation of the modern state (Hornziel 1986). This was the first official recognition of the "foreign question," as it was to be called much later—that is, the presence of foreign migrants on Italian soil. The report was commissioned on the basis of another brief note that fell like a meteor into one chapter of another ministerial document in 1985, "Occupational Politics for the Next Decade." This earlier document of the Minister of Work noted the presence of foreign workers in agriculture, domestic work, construction, hotel work, and in the small commerce of the petty street traders. This brief chapter contained a statement that looked forward to the next ten years: "The predictions for the coming years indicate the divergence of paths of growth between underdeveloped countries and countries in high industrialization, creating increasing migratory flows that will enter the various European countries and also into Italy."[1]

A member of parliament, Franco Foschi, wrote the preface to a second report of 1986, which consisted of a body of research conducted to throw light on the predictions of the first. Foschi noted that the presence of the so-called clandestine immigrant, as seen through the lens of the "We," is something that tends to reinforce the "national consciousness" and is thus a necessary phantasm for the bounding of identity—one without a face that consents to maintain the idea of the nonperson, of separation, of precariousness. Discrimination and precariousness are in fact characteristics that are proper to a stranger in another country; from its Latin root, *precarious* (obtained by prayer) suggests the revocability of the promise of the future.

The expansion of European hegemony over labor and labor control may be seen as a process that began with the relaxation of restrictions on foreign labor in the 1950s and 1960s and ended with the protectionism of the European labor market within the EC in the 1970s and 1980s. Massive large-scale labor recruitment across nations in Europe has been followed in the postindustrial context with a very disadvantageous position for labor in many European countries and a severe curtailment of the labor movement in Italy after 1980. Concessions in the Italian context to labor were made late and implemented poorly, leaving the welfare burden largely on the shoulders of working-class contributors. The extension of welfare state benefits to migrants has become a crucial issue in many nations where various aspects of the allegedly "temporary" quality of the migrant and the construction of impediments to their gaining residence serve to place the migrant outside of the welfare system (Wihol de Wenden 1990). As Franco Foschi points out, however, this exclusion of the new migrant from the rights advances of the former European immigrant runs contrary to the postwar struggle for immigrant rights in Italy and elsewhere:

> At first it seems incredible that Italy, a country of a great and not forgotten emigration, should not comprehend that the time has come to apply in our own case the principles that we requested with a great voice of countries that took in Italians—at times, in clandestine conditions. But the truth is that, beyond words, even Italian emigration was the egoistic expulsion of the poor, pushed to the many corners of the world, leaving space for those who remained. In this way, for good reasons we have maintained that the rigid norms and statutes of Switzerland were forms of discrimination, and today we affirm that we are not a country of immigration because we have never requested with specific agreements that anyone come among us, and therefore they can just go away. (Hornziel 1986, 7–8)[2]

At the same time that the EC is opening its borders internally, it is closing down its labor market to non-European members and redefining the boundaries of Europe. The flow of migrants from Eastern Europe is to be stopped by the supply of aid to countries of origin.

Stephen Castles has argued that the political and social isolation of the foreign migrant places the migrant in a particularly vulnerable position for exploitation (Castles 1986). The exclusion of migrants from normal channels of health care and daily social life results in the creation of alternative paths to solve the same problems of everyday life: the charity of the Catholic hospitals for health care, which operate on a humanitarian basis (albeit in violation of state sanctions against the treatment of "clandestine" migrants), or networks of Italian or non-Italian friends and relatives who help to get work and housing. This shadow world of mediation is merely a temporary buffer in the life of the migrant, who even after attaining the required work permits in Italy often finds it nearly impossible to gain access to residence documents or the *carta di sanità* for medical benefits, even when working in compliance with the law and paying the contributions toward health care benefits of Italian citizens and foreign workers alike. One of the most difficult situations is that of the worker who enters the shadow world of *lavoro nero*. Franco Foschi warned of the expansion of this world of work, a "circuit" that predates the arrival of the new migrant, in fact involving work forms particularly evident in the postwar economic expansion of Italy. Unregulated work practices are concentrated in the construction and industrial sectors, yet also to some degree in agriculture, which has been one of the early areas of foreign labor recruitment, especially in the South.

The world of work in Italy resonates for many Italians with a world of organized crime involving many facets of local, national, and international social and political organization. The presence of this world in imagination or in daily practice underscores the inability of the government to impose its will on this arch of criminality; at the same time that immigration becomes a political issue in Italy, the world of criminality and social movements against it (like that of the anti-Mafia movement in Sicily) are coming to maturity. An attack on the practice of *lavoro nero* is in fact an attack on the weak government, a state ruled for forty years by one party, the Christian Democrats, incapable of imposing state authority over the various forms of criminal activity, which have translated into a great loss of annual state revenue. The postponement of action on the foreign question has merely given strength to the growing circle of criminality and fiscal banditry. Clandestine immigration, as Foschi notes, adds fuel to this flame: "Moreover, unregulated clandestine immigration will inevitably end up reinforcing the market of informal work, *lavoro nero*, and the subterranean economy perpetuating and multiplying this circle" (in Hornziel 1986, 9).[3]

By 1992 work had become the primary criterion of the migrant's ability to stay in Italy. For those migrants, like some of the Senegalese working in the African street market as traders or for those forced into work sites of Italian cities without the proper coverage of official employment, it will become more and more difficult to maintain legal residence in Italy. The government has offered a kind of amnesty to workers *in nero* if they will in effect turn in their employer in the underground economy. Many migrants are hired on temporary contracts that last only three to four months. This places the employer—not the government— in the role of guarantor of residence. Yet the replacement of stable employment in the Italian economy to some degree by temporary employment, often managed by the special contract that substantially cuts the worker's benefit package in exchange for short-term higher wages, has been partly responsible for the innovation and vitality of the new economy.

The Power of Monotony

One is reminded of the cultural analysis of Theodor Adorno and Max Horkheimer, and of two statements that indicate their conviction of the power of the culture industry and a profound pessimism at ever escaping it: "Anyone who doubts the power of monotony is a fool," and then the haunting, "The secret of aesthetic sublimation is its representation of fulfillment as a broken promise." The Martelli Bill is somewhat like a promissory note that perpetually promises the migrant various forms of protection including rights to housing, health care benefits, and work. The migrant is, however, never quite granted this promised reality (Ciafaloni 1990). The ideology of happiness in the idiom of the Frankfurt School presents the "promise" as available for consumption; a desired resolution of longing seems to be offered to the consumer. The negation of this promise is, however, a characteristic of late capitalism. "The diner," in short, "must be satisfied with the menu" (Horkheimer and Adorno 1972). The replication of the discourse on immigration in the Italian media and in government reveals an overwhelming monotony of the voices of the powerful, of those capable of defining discourse. The power of what Horkheimer and Adorno called the culture industry consisted first in "repetition" and second, in the "omnipresence of the stereotype" (Horkheimer and Adorno 1972, 136). The voice of the migrant is rarely, if ever, heard, and yet images of the migrant, voiceless and without a name, parade daily in the newspapers, journals, and television screens of the Italian public. The power of the official discourse to classify, name, and stereotype is coupled with the power of vision, the ability to transform the most intimate aspects of the lives of the migrants into the commonplace images available for consumption by the general public. There is a fascination with the inner world of the migrant; the "homes" of the migrants come to reify an imagined "domestic space," a state of disarray that might confirm the dramatically different way of life of the African or Arab migrant. This "omnipresence of the stereotype" receives legitimation through repetition and official pronouncement, in the pages of newspapers and other media. The immigrant becomes a backdrop in a discourse in which he or she appears as merely a variable detached from the context or "co-text" of the argument at hand (Eco 1984). We may say, in a turn of phrase that recalls the Frankfurt School again, that "not migrants are offered but proof that they exist" (Horkheimer and Adorno 1972, 148).[4] Thus the migrant exists in the discourse as a kind of contentless replica of the "immigrant"—now a generic figure that may be replicated endlessly and made to conform to the dictates of circumstance.

"The most mortal of sins is to be an outsider," and the African, Arab, or Asian migrant in Italy is one of the most sharply defined outsiders: the cultural distance that these migrants represent symbolically in Italian society is vast (Horkheimer and Adorno 1972). The distance that a migrant travels to reach Europe from Senegal or Morocco is nothing compared to the historical, cultural, and economic realities that must be traversed in order to come to terms with the contemporary relationship between Europe and this imagined Third World. All arguments that attempt to telescope this relationship to the period of the 1970s' economic crisis and the subsequent economic upswing of the Italian economy ignore the historical depth of the phenomenon of European and Third World relationships. We must look, rather, at the elaborate menu of European colonialism and postcolonialism, which has given adequate encouragement to the Third World diner to join the meal, alone with the endless parade of styles, consumer goods, and the rhythms of International monetary fluctuations that have perhaps more than other elements provided the atmosphere of the imminent feast.

The Martelli Bill: The Italian State and the Discourse on Immigration

> Our freedom is always determined; our freedom is determined by the outside and the inside.
> —Madan Sarup, *Identity, Culture and the Postmodern World*

"It is not a law for foreigners—it is a law against foreigners. I see the problems here everyday. There are people sleeping in the train cars at night and those who are living in the parks.

> —Tahar, a Tunisian migrant in Turin for
> more than twenty years, of the Martelli Bill

Si afferma, fra L'altro, che Governo, forze politiche, paese intero annettono il massimo rilievo e riconoscono la delicatezza estrema della questione stranieri rilevando che un'equa ed efficace soluzione sia ormai indifferiblile, sia per il verificarsi di manifestazioni di insofferenza, e a volte di vera e propria intolleranza, che hanno suscitato il piu' vivo allarme (This is an affirmation that the government and the political forces of the entire country must join together in the greatest effort to recognize the extremely delicate situation concerning the foreign question, that an impartial and effective solution to the problem is not deferrable. This has been verified by various forms of impatience, and at times intolerance, which has sounded the most sharp alarm).

The discussion above accompanies the Martelli Bill. The statement continues maintaining that the Italian government will refuse to accept values and moral positions "that might be foreign to those of Italian society or to its customs" (estranea ai valori della morale, della cultura e della civiltà del nostro Paese). What are the cultural frontiers that define the boundaries of the *acceptable Other*? Immigration legislation often rests on unexplored ideas about the nature of modernity, identity, and Otherness.

The principal focus of the governmental debate was on the regulative state apparatus that would control the flow of the new Third World immigration into Italy. There was an attempt to assess the scope of the phenomenon, given the early lack of statistical information. Initially, little was known about the numbers of migrants or anything about the migrant communities, for that matter. The steady murmurs of statistics, medical and criminal records, work histories and marriages only began to take shape after and through the registration of migrants for residence in Italian communities after the *sanatoria,* an amnesty for immigrants resident in Italy since 1989 (Anderson 1983; Zanchetta 1991). Italy, the country of emigration that ushered some twenty-six million migrant workers into the world labor market, is today a nation of immigration. The transformation has been so rapid that the first comprehensive legislation dealing with immigration in almost sixty years, the Martelli Bill, was passed into law in February 1990.[5] The passage of the Martelli Bill marked the beginning of a new era in Italian contemporary history, granting the right to housing, work, education, and health care to immigrants. The law called for a *sanatoria*, the rapid and immediate registration of foreigners living in Italy since December 1989, granting periods of stay of up to two years for study or work and political refugee status to those applicants from outside of the European Community (Martelli 1990).

The "foreign question," as it was called in the legislation, was "verified by various forms of impatience, and at times intolerance, which has sounded the most sharp alarm." In fact, for the first time in Italy's postwar history the issue of race was brought to the forefront of social and political discussions as acts of intolerance, specifically the killing of a young South African migrant recognized by the United Nations as a political refugee and the spontaneous demonstrations of "clandestine" immigrants calling for the end of "racism," brought the Italian state to confront this problem.

The Martelli Bill continues in many ways to construct the immigrant as an "economic refugee." One must not be deceived into believing for a moment, according to the bill, that "our country alone could take upon its shoulders all the pains and all of the desperation of the influx of immigration coming from the south of the world" (Che nessuno deve illudere o puo illudersi di poter caricare sulle spalle del nostro solo Paese tutto il dolore e tutta la disperazione propri dei flussi di immigrazione provenienti dal sud del mondo). This imagined continent of pain and desperation is a prevalent trope in the figure of the migrant in Italian society—just as once the *Mezzogiorno* was an image of the southern Italian land of the midday sun, of poverty, misery, and illiteracy and, in fact, is so viewed today by the right-wing leagues who wish to separate the industrial North, where they are based, from the impoverished South. The image of an uncharted south of the world, *sud del mondo,* against which the European forces must join together to regulate is one communicated throughout popular ideology and the media through representations of the increasing African population and through the Italian right-wing leagues that focus on "regulative measures."[6] As Umberto Eco, in a play of images addressing the underlying fear of such proposals, writes, "We must simply prepare ourselves to live in another season of culture, Afro-Europe" (Eco 1990).

A World of Pain and Desperation

In fact, the Martelli Bill was ushered in by the manifestations of wide-spread intolerance and at once sounds the alarm within Italian society of not only the need for a preliminary curative legislation that might serve to regulate the flow of migrants, but also for a clear and definitive anti-racist statement from the government. This bill is indeed not a law for foreigners. As one Ivory Coast student said: "Italy wants to open and close the door at the same time. All the other European countries have been dealing with the problem of immigration for years. There are thousands of immigrants in France, in Germany, and all over Europe, but without really taking on its responsibility, Italy wants to stop it all at once." Measures for the closure of Italian borders to immigration have been especially severe for such countries as Tunisia, Morocco, and Senegal, which according to Italian authorities pose particular problems due to the imagined numbers of potential migrants. A system requiring visas for people from these nations has been instituted. The notion of the south of the world, which is the home of the problem of immigration, contains a certain Western arrogance along with a series of distinctions—a kind of global taxonomy, with wealth and development at one end and people and cultures that exist in the south of the world at another. The desperation and pain of the south of the world is not merely a figment of the Western imagination but, rather, a product of a historical relationship with what has come to be called the Third World.

It is telling that this notion of the south of the world appears in the comment that accompanies the Martelli Bill. A world of pain and desperation is the image in which the other world, the home of the migrant, is painted, and from this world nothing is born but misery and need. The Martelli Bill is a curative measure in a double sense: it relieves the situation of intolerance and alarm within Italy by presenting formal permission to exist within the Italian territory, and it seeks to erect barriers in the same moment against a world of pain and desperation—just to the south of the known world.

8
Closing the Circle:
On Sounding Difference

He said: "It is all useless, if the last landing place can only be the in-
fernal city, and it is there that, in ever narrowing circles, the current is
drawing us."

And Polo said: "The inferno of the living is not something that will
be; if there is one, it is what is already here, the inferno where we live
every day, that we form by being together. There are two ways to
escape suffering it. The first is easy for many: accept the inferno and
become such a part of it that you can no longer see it. The second is
risky and demands constant vigilance and apprehension: seek and
learn to recognize who and what, in the midst of the inferno, are not
inferno, then make them endure, give them space."
—Italo Calvino, *Invisible Cities*

Euro-Africa and Afro-Europe

Culture was perhaps the greatest form of fetishism of the nineteenth and
part of the twentieth centuries, which "when treated as an immutable
identity" helped to transform people's identities into points of contrast
and "invention" (Derrida 1985). This discussion has taken the challenge
of the wide gaze of the European social formation and attempted, through

analysis of the processes on the articulation of state and popular ideologies in one locality, to give some indication of much wider problems in the nature of European societies and the increasing heterogeneity of various populations. From a host of possible approaches to the phenomena, I have chosen to focus on the anthropology of the contemporary nation-state and the play of difference in this unique context of tremendous shifts in global relations and contemporary migrations. The greater social and cultural heterogeneity of Europe poses serious questions about failing state welfare structures throughout Europe,[1] many forced in recent years to curtail the extension of benefits and to reconsider the costs of an increasingly expansive welfare structure on a diminishing productive base. The national collectivity or identity has been popularly posed against the appearance of alleged outsiders and strangers; membership in an imagined community has been put forward in a context in which the conjuncture of economic crisis and racism amplifies and alters the significance of the mere comings and goings of people. Racism is not merely becoming more "visible," as Etienne Balibar suggests: it is becoming critical for an articulation of an institutionalization of exclusion and often a reaction of middle classes to the present crisis (Balibar 1991).

The emergent Europe, which will unify under the Maastricht Treaty, will bring into existence that which has been conceived of cloudily for some time—as a kind of European universe, one of the world's most extensive markets. And yet the very conception of Europe is challenged by its increasing heterogeneity. Anthropology must face the challenge of the increasing blurring of genres that the attention to such phenomena involve. The contours of this work have been set by the issues at hand and have therefore taken liberty in the examination of issues of state routine, urban planning, and the memory of a social world created by the interchange of industrial expansion and local attempts of workers in the arch of their lives from the factory to the polling place. The New Europe is not a single universe that exalts some immutable identity of either the economy or society of the West but is, rather, a multiuniverse with worlds of meanings that cascade upon this new entity with every newcomer. It is this new reticulation of worlds and possible worlds that must guide our gaze. This brings us to the insight of the Gramscian conviction that "every relationship of hegemony is necessarily an educative relationship"—here, the emergent Europe is the school of the state. As those interested in the working class once sought to inform themselves in Turin, the home of Europe's largest working class, we must draw our gaze to the European social formation and understand what the contours of this new state system are to be, and just what relationship this is to have with the "hegemony" of Europe or its loss (Tilly 1990).

Prime Minister Francesco Crispi (1819–1901) overrode objections to the Italian colonial party of the 1890s in the face of parliamentarians who complained that an African adventure would deplete even further a poor treasury that could not sustain an "ambitious colonial policy" in a "far too inhospitable climate." The prime minister, however, and the Italian king, Umberto I (1844–1900), prevailed in their attempts to create an imperial Italy with instructions sent secretly to the army to invade "Asmara in the highlands of the interior." "Imperial Italy needed air for her lungs," explained the prime minister. This colonial adventure was to end in one of the greatest military defeats in Italy's young history: its untrained soldiers and inadequate maps were to come face to face with one of the best trained armies in Africa (Smith 1989). The Italian defeat marked a loss of prestige "for the honor of Italy and the monarchy." Already the idea of reclaiming the "imperial traditions of ancient Rome" had influenced Italian interests in 1869–70 in North Africa when a government-backed private company established a trading post in Assab in the Red Sea. Although Italy's right to a claim in Tunisia was recognized by other European powers, the Republican government in Paris after 1870, according to Denis Mack Smith, made it clear that North Africa was to be a French region of influence and that Italian claims to colonies should instead look to Albania or Libya (Smith 1989). After King Umberto I and his prime minister, Benedetto Cairoli, expressed interest in North Africa, the French occupation of Tunis in 1881 came as a response. The failure of Italy to annex Tunisia, where a substantial Italian community was already established, led to a great loss of prestige in the international context; Crispi, as envoy to Bismarck in 1877, had even suggested that Italy might annex the French territory formerly known as the Italian Savoy. This loss of prestige, and in later years the demographic conditions of a large impoverished cultivator population in southern Italy, contributed to the Fascist's capture of Ethiopia, when Mussolini's efforts to recapture the grandeur of imperial Rome led to the colonial venture of 1935 and to the invasion of Ethiopia that would effectively consolidate Italian Empire in Somalia, Eritrea, and Ethiopia.[2] In the absence of any serious land reform in the South of Italy, "land for Italians" was a liberating message for many Italians, and the prestige gained through the creation of an empire was foremost in placing Italians on equal footing with other European nations.

Cesare Lombroso, in his 1868 and 1870 lectures, titled "L'Uomo Bianco e L'Uomo di Colore" (The white man and the colored man), pointed out the existence among human races of "profound inequalities, which are manifest in their origin and which persist immutable through the variations of time and climate, remaining in history and destiny of the people as their eternal coinage" (Lombroso 1871). Difference was inscribed in language, art, the triumphs of Western architecture, and, finally and most definitively, in the body and brain. Armed with scientific theory, Lombroso wished to purify the nation and to set humanity on its true path to greater perfection and even greater achievement. In the conclusion to this series of lectures, Lombroso sets out in terms, later replicated in Fascist ideology and in commonsense racialist views in Italy, the placement of whites in the unfolding of history. This taxonomy held blacks to be the most imperfect and excluded those whites such as the "southerner," who were deemed closer to the atavistic elements of "backward societies" than to the perfection of the European. The exotic marked the realm of domination and control of the superior in the natural ideology based on scientific rationale—a cultural logic that not only seemed just, but seemed the only possible outcome of "eternal" inequality, that is to say, imperfection of the Other:

> Only we whites have touched the most perfect symmetry of the form of the body. And only we, with alphabetic writing and extensive language, have provided thought with a more comfortable and ample vestment that we may diffuse and immortalize it in monuments, in books, and in the press. Only we possess true musical art. Only we have, through the mouths of Christ and Buddha, proclaimed the liberty of slaves, the rights of man and respect for the aged, women, the weak, and pardon for enemies. And only we have, with Washington and Franklin and Mirabeau, proclaimed the concept of the true nation. Only we, finally, with Lutero and Galileo, Epicurus and Spinoza, Lucrezio and Voltaire, have brought forward the liberty of thought with which you, dear listeners, offer an example, assisting without disgust, to the development of themes somewhat unorthodox. (Lombroso 1871, 219–23)

This passage is truly extraordinary as Lombroso uses the trope of turning to the "listener" who "assists" in the development, telling, or unwinding of the tale (Svolgersi di temi si poco ortodossi)—in the unwinding of somewhat unorthodox themes, thus drawing the listener into the greater community of "white" members of society as opposed to the "colored" realm that includes Asian and African communities. That the reader listens "senza ribetzzo" (without disgust) is significant since this demonstrates the listener's complicity in the "true" of the scientific reality of the immutable and the unequal constitution of humanity into separate and wholly incommensurate divisions. Lombroso seems to follow Giambattista Vico in his emphasis on the meaning of the "true," a kind of eternal and unchanging category of thought that may be reached through the knowledge of human society. For Lombroso, however, the poetic voyage of Vico's various ages of the world are reified into the unchanging structures of a global taxonomy, which we may appreciate, if at all, by using what Vico considered the greatest of the tropes, irony. It is indeed ironic that the ideas that were so diligently unfolded by such thinkers as Lombroso—who sought the highest good in a kind of enthusiastic model of a nation-state purified through the reason of scientific method and order—should lead to notions so antithetical to democratic and humanistic ideals. This is what Vico called the conceit of scholars "who will have it that what they know is as old as the world"; the attempt of scientific imagination to temporalize Western supremacy may be seen in this light. Such knowledge of the scholar's soon became a popular common sense and was diffused as widely as Lombroso suggests, and through just the mediums that he acknowledges as the carriers of "reason," from literature to monumental architecture to music. As Vico points out and as Gramsci later follows, "Common sense is judgment without reflection, shared by an entire class, an entire people, an entire nation, or the entire human race" (Vico 1988 [1744]). It is human choice, Vico continues, that is made "certain" by the "commonsense" judgment. Such notions as "nation," "community," and "progress" took on, particularly during the nineteenth century, such seemingly transformative powers that underlying premises were hardly questioned. The invasion by civilized people of backward and inhospitable places like the highlands of Asmara or those of southern Italy was perfectly in keeping with the rational process of state formation or the articulation of an imperial empire like that of ancient Rome.

Memories of Underdevelopment

> Dialects are like dreams . . . remote and revealing.
> —Federico Fellini

In many ways Italian history has been plagued by the problem of trying to find something other than itself (the nation-state) by which to define itself; regionalism and a cosmopolitan elite contributed to a fragmented and contested Italian reality.[3] In the film *Padre Padrone* a young man from the island of Sardinia enters the Italian army and realizes for the first time that he has been speaking a dialect, and not Italian, all his life. It is difficult to convey how fragile the conception of national unity and culture is and has been in Italy. It is important to understand, however, the great force and attractiveness of the local: for example, the anti-Mafia movement in the South of the country clearly poses a local elite against the hegemony of the state in this region. Like the fragments of a recurrent dream, the local structures, languages, and social practices seem to plague the construction of national "totality." There are, moreover, many examples of the inability of the state to enforce hegemonic powers, as in the realm of the *economia sommersa*, which represents a tremendous loss of revenue to the state, a practice that is diffuse throughout the country.

It is only recently that some sense of well-being has begun to pervade daily Italian life; the reconstruction in intensive worker and union struggles characterized much of the postwar period and the "years of lead," during which various forms of antigovernment terrorism or liberation struggles took a heavy toll on social and political life. Consumerism has been one of the signs of this new feeling of well-being, although prosperity has been somewhat short-lived as the decline of the Fordist era was brought in abruptly with the reorganization of large industry and the shifts of labor markets to concentrations of highly skilled labor in an arch of the north from Turin to Ivrea and back to Milan. In fact, just as the newfound sense of well-being was beginning to be felt by many, a new period of economic uncertainty was ushered in with the unforeseeable changes in the sociopolitical landscape of the new European social formation. Not only have migratory trends from the Third World entered into the balance of contemporary problems of Europe, but now Eastern Europe has added its economic deficits, migrants, and political crisis to the new face of Europe.

There is no ready construct with which to classify these newcomers.

Europe has not been conceived of as a community of pluralities but, rather, as diverse communities, each with its own orbit surrounded by its own spheres of influence, economic dependents, and historical relations. Today, the phantasmagoria of difference unaccompanied by its colonial counterpart has presented itself in the garden of Europe, bringing the problems of race, ethnicity, and class into this previously "tranquil" space. In Italy, where no migrant construct existed—the phenomenon is new—some effort has been made to borrow tropes from the North American ethnic myth of the melting pot and to combine this with the construct of the southern Italian migrant to northern Italy. The trope of the southern Italian migrant remains, however, the most resonant with the weight of Italian constructions of "internal Otherness"—a world of difference of an order that draws on the social life of the Italian southern peasant of the past and that is sedimented with meanings of the urban industrial worker, a southern migrant in the northern cities of Turin, Milan, and Genoa. This image is fixed in a discourse of state instability and social order, which extends from the highland retreats of the southern brigand to the many ways of evading the authority of the state and the centralizing powers, which, posed against the local, fade in importance. There is a strong critique of the hegemony of the Christian Democratic rule of the country in the postwar period; the problems of the new immigrants recall the many unresolved difficulties of the former generation of disadvantaged citizens and poor migrants from largely southern regions seeking a life in the north of Italy, Europe, the United States, or elsewhere.

Some Italian emigrants established a community of Italians in Dakar, joining the ranks of the *petit blanc* and even publishing a newspaper of their own (R. Cruise O'Brien 1972). Indeed, the community of Italians abroad has given a global dimension to an Italian society extended through expatriate communities all over the world. The many Little Italies are an important part of North American immigrant ideology in the United States and Canada. And yet this image of the Italian migrant has been riddled with anti-Italian stereotypes that depict Italian migrants as semiliterate, unskilled workers from rural worlds. In fact, until quite recently Italy was thought of as a poor nation, and it is only since the late 1970s that this notion of Italy's backward economy has faded to some degree. In other words, Italy has been from the perspective of a commonsense view of Europe a backward country with a backward economy and an unstable political system. In short, Italy has been—

along with perhaps Spain, Portugal, and Greece—Europe's Other (Papagaroufali and Georges 1993).

The European construct of the foreign worker has often been that of the foreign Italian worker, still a favorite for British humorists. The film *Bread and Chocolate*, for example, depicts the life of an Italian migrant in Switzerland, where conditions for migrants are very poor. The protagonist of the film is often taken by a vision of the Northern European residents of this new country. Hierarchy within the European Community has now only been reinforced by the entrance of Eastern European nations that will become the new dependents and labor providers to the more wealthy countries. The closure of the European Community against non-European Community members thus becomes more urgent. The responsibility of the European Community for the greater global impoverishment of those nations, which through colonial and postcolonial relations contribute and have contributed to the expansion of one of the world's largest markets, must be accounted for in a manner other than the exclusion of workers who hail from destinations outside of the European Community.

Without the historical backdrop of the long and intensive relationship between Africa and the West, the voyage of the contemporary Third World migrant remains unintelligible and seems an abrupt disjunction in an otherwise continuous historical process. Viewed from the perspective of a relationship that began through the interchange of markets, human labor, and raw materials—starting at the crucial period of state formation in the European social formation and not yet ended— the new international migration appears as an outgrowth of historical continuities between Africa and the West.

In this study, an attempt has been made to present the continuities between past forms of racism and contemporary European society. Many forms of difference constructed in this process are articulated by new technologies of the scientific arts developed from the latter part of the eighteenth century and incorporated into the colonial adventures of European imperialism in the nineteenth. Contemporary media representations have been examined as these portray the stereotypes and commonsense notions about the newcomer.

In Italy, the absence of a coherent "immigrant" construct due to the newness of the phenomenon has led to the adoption of the model of the "southern migrant" who populated Northern European and Italian industrial cities during the postwar period, creating one of the largest

working-class concentrations in all of Europe, in Turin. The comparison
of the new migrant to this historical figure of the southerner at once
calls into question the ideology of difference that has separated Italy
since its unification through a deeply resonant system of regional differences. Many of the problems of the modern Italian state revolve around
the complex of issues concerning the economic, social, and political
cleavages of North and South. A great deal of the uneasiness about the
new arrivals stems from the fact that serious issues concerning health
care, housing, and work have never been satisfactorily resolved for this
first wave of Italian immigrants; in short, many Italians do not yet view
Italy as a receiver nation capable of incorporating a permanent migrant
community. The issue of race has complicated matters even further; a
new racism has emerged that targets persons of color and yet also contains a strong anti-Moslem component. In fact, there are many kinds of
racisms directed at the Italian southerner, the black, the Albanian, and
others—all of whom encroach or potentially encroach on Italian soil.
The generalized atmosphere of racialist reactions has revived the Far
Right, which now articulates "small nationalisms" in the form of separatist programs such as that of the Northern Leagues, which are strongly
anti-immigrant and anti-southern-Italian and which advocate speaking
local dialects and withholding state revenue from the South.

In this study, some attempt has also been made to give an indication
of the rich diversity of that entity called the nation-state that appears to
be a tenuous veneer of a multiple reality, one that daily becomes more
difficult to define. The problem of boundaries in anthropological study
is here viewed as an open question rather than a beginning. Indeed,
what are the boundaries of the Mourid Brotherhood or of the Senegalese
state or of the Italian state? And what, if any, can be the closure attained
by the new European social formation on a process of interchange, exchange, and social change that it began with Africa in the fifteenth century or before?

The first black woman to join the Italian police in Palermo, Dacia
Valent, once noted that the mood of contemporary Italy resembles
the climate of medieval Europe: "Back then they said the Jews carried
the plague. Now they say black people bring AIDS and drug addiction.
For immigrants, Italy is a closed circle" (cited in Colby 1989). Medieval
Europe, an imagined community, gave rise to the idea of the nation and
of Europe, of people joined by language and traditions that could distinguish their world among others. Now, in the contemporary world, the

idea of a unified Europe detailed in the Maastricht Treaty seems to be strangling the very humanist traditions by which the idea of Europe was once said to be guided. Benedict Anderson once wrote that we might call "the Beauty of Gemeinschaft" the capacity of the notion of community to seem so natural in its "halo of disinterestedness" (Anderson 1983, 143). Racism, however, cuts into the mythic community writ large, the nation-state, and mutilates the possibility of some gaining the "naturalized" status without receiving the stigma of impurity and the ideological designation as a counterfeit citizen. As Anderson points out, ideologies of racism clearly derive their justification from the legitimation of domination and repression in the colonial party of Europeans: "Racism dreams of eternal contaminations, transmitted from the origins of time" (Anderson 1983, 143). The nation is no longer free from this interplay of community and society. The introduction of race into the play of state, community, and Europe has inextricably bound these notions together in the free fall of historical destinies. The recent eruption of anti-immigrant violence throughout the European social formation, and particularly that in the newly unified Germany, calls into question what is to be the nature of the heterogeneity of European society. Such slogans as "Germany to the Germans" strike us oddly in the present context: who in fact are the Germans or the Italians?[4]

The Breakup of a Historic Bloc

> It is not the voice that commands the story: it is the ear.
> —Italo Calvino, *Invisible Cities*

In the pages of *La Repubblica,* the Italian cartoonist Giorgio Forattini in the 1970s depicted the Italian state as a giant caterpillar; each segment of the creature had the upper body and face of Giulio Andreotti and carried a little black suitcase symbolizing the Christian Democrat's control of all of the most important portfolios in each government. Indeed, Andreotti, who began his ministerial career in 1947 and participated in fifty-two postwar governments, has simply been one of the faces of Christian Democratic postwar hegemony. Italy, often depicted as a fragile state having had so many governments since the war, has not been fragile at all: until the current crisis, no other European nation has had the same party in power since the war. Recent political shifts have completely changed this situation; the rise of right-wing parties and the collapse of the popular bases of both the former Communist Party and the Christian Democratic Party have radically transformed the situation. The absence of the Communist threat has shattered hegemonic politics all over Europe. The absence of Giulio Andreotti in the current cabinet and of any Italian first-tier political player marks dramatically the transformation of Italian politics. The current scandals of kickbacks in which all of the major parties were involved have only weakened further the power of the old party system, although as Bettino Craxi, the head of the Socialist Party pointed out recently, the losses of the old party system are the gains of the right-wing fringe.

The 1990s have changed everything. The collapse of the Soviet Union and the opening up of Eastern Europe have created one further difficulty for the closing of the circle on European unity: the new migratory trends of Eastern Europeans seeking a new life in Western Europe have given rise to a new xenophobia toward this new category of "Europeans." There is an official collection of articles in the Italian and foreign press that treat the phenomenon of immigration. A document that represents the president of the Council of Ministers, prepared by the department of information and distributed in early 1990 in Rome at one of the first national conferences on immigration, contains a section in the foreign press collection on the boat people who were turned away by Britain in Hong Kong, as these Vietnamese citizens sought refuge from a failing economy and runaway unemployment. These discussions seem to say: "This is the way things shall go in Europe, and we intend to follow in turn; closure of the borders is only a first step. Vigilance and control must complete the circle." Although migration has often been seen as merely a phenomenon of Western Europe, during the 1990s the position of thousands of Vietnamese in East Germany, Poland, Bulgaria, and Czechoslovakia has become very tenuous, and relations within socialist nations are increasingly hostile to the category of foreign worker. The anti-immigrant call has not only been restricted to Eastern Europe, as is now clearly seen in the context of the unified Germany in which former East and West Germans call for the repatriation of foreign workers. Such euphemisms as "boat people" and "clandestine" attempts to make open state forms of coercion seem necessary and justified or legitimate. Forced repatriation has been used in the United States in the case of Haitian migrants and in Italy with Albanian migrants. The expulsion of thousands of Albanian political refugees represented a postwar voyage of the national Italian collectivity into the abyss of xenophobia: "Almost everyone in Italy wanted them shipped home at once, although some accompanied their cries of 'good riddance' with murmurs of regret" (Kopkind 1991). These problems of localism and xenophobic sentiment create a difficult political and social climate in Italy, which today faces its first encounter with immigration (see fig. 5).

In the Italian fragmentary and unfinished process of nation building enter the neofascists and other right-wing components as the political party system has imploded through the disclosure of its interlinking accomplices, in much the same way that terrorist networks are allegedly discovered in the Bernardo Bertolucci film *Secrets,* in which each member of a former underground cell seems almost relieved to reveal all about the clandestine organization. Clearly, the political system of the postwar years is undergoing a transformation. In the space of a few years almost every politician in Italy who participated in the postwar era has vanished from the political scene, is under investigation for wrongdoing, or has voluntarily chosen to exit the political arena. The vision of the rest of Europe is similar: the postwar generation has all but vanished from the European political scene. With the disappearance of the postwar favored enemy, communism, new preoccupations, in some cases new political subjects, now plague the European social formation as issues of cultural diversity, migration, and a recasting of the social imaginary of the nation-state now become concerns of a new generation and another political culture.

In the larger framework one may ask: what is to be the fate of the European social formation, in light of its growing internal diversity, economic crisis, and massive geopolitical reformulations, and of the breakup of the former Soviet Union and the unleashing of Eastern Europe back into the European Community? The recent rise in forms of xenophobia and racism has been translated into political advantage in many contexts with the formation of political parties with open anti-immigrant stances in Belgium, Germany, France, and Italy. The issue of immigration is crucial to the formation of a united Europe and the consolidation of the benefits of Maastricht and the plan of a unity of European Community partners. Yet violence against foreigners in Italy, France, and Germany has been on the rise along with the spread of an antidemocratic, openly racialist popular localism.[5] The French Le Pen National Front and the Italian *leghe,* the latter now consolidated into a kind of northern federation calling themselves the Northern League, hold in common a grassroots support built in many ways on the failure of postwar official poli-

tics that were unable to halt the growth of urban poverty or the decline
of the benefits of the massive apparatus of the welfare state. The tolerance of the "uncontrolled immigration" in France began to change during the early 1970s when the inflow of immigration began to be called
"illegal immigration" and when stricter regulations concerning the arrival of African, Iberian, and other migrants were introduced (Wihol de
Wenden 1990a). Particularly after 1973, the world economic crisis translated the increasing closure of European borders to immigration. Yet
racism is not only a phenomenon of crisis; both ideologies of xenophobia and racism have been integral parts of the immigrant complex as a
whole, including that of inter-European migrants during the postwar period. The rise in forms of xenophobia and racism in the 1980s, however,
cannot be denied. The house in which many of the Senegalese resided
when I spoke with them and participated in their communal events has
now been destroyed by a bombing and fire, and the community has dispersed (see fig. 5). As anthropologist Vanessa Maher has recently pointed
out, for some of the neighborhoods of Turin the license to commit violence against immigrants among Italian youth is often reflected in the
sentiments of the larger community: "While many Italians of these and
other neighborhoods pay lip-service to the condemnation of racism,
they nevertheless condone violence against immigrants" (Maher 1996).
In their classic study of immigrant workers in Europe, first published in
1973, *Immigrant Workers and Class Structure in Western Europe,* Stephen
Castles and Godula Kosack cite in the postscript to the second edition
of 1985 a World Council of Churches report that notes an "escalation of
racism" throughout Western Europe in the 1980s. During this period
racially motivated attacks against migrants had already become a frequent phenomenon:

> The resurgence of extreme right parties and Neo-Nazi terrorist organi-
> zations in the seventies and early eighties has been based almost entirely
> on anti-immigrant campaigns. Attitude surveys show growing accep-
> tance of policies of increased policing and control of blacks and for-
> eigners, and support for policies of repatriation. Large proportions of
> the population seem to believe that immigrants are somehow respon-
> sible for the crisis and that repatriation would solve the problems of
> unemployment and lack of social amenities. (Castles and Kosack 1985)

During the 1970s, the New Toryism in Britain was said to incorporate elements of a racialist ideology, a "new racism" that was articulated

to "make sense" of the global economic crisis (Lawrence 1982). The traces of this crisis are still felt today, and yet the present crisis that presents the daily fluctuation of currencies and the shifting of fortunes across national borders at an unprecedented rate, in preparation for the New Europe, seems more profound and disturbing. We can only hope that the New Europe may come to treasure diversity, as it approaches this idiomatic and haunting old dream—at once, remote and revealing—called Europe.

Of Nations and Nationalism

> Collective identities are funny fictions.
> —Virginia R. Domínguez,
> *People as Subject, People as Object*

> The fiction of the census is that everyone is in it, and that everyone has one—and only one—extremely clear place. No fractions.
> —Benedict Anderson, *Imagined Communities*

Alterity seems to take its revenge on notions of cultural homogeneity in countless ways in the peculiar interplay between localism and difference in contemporary Europe. An articulation of right-wing ideologies and efforts at closure of national boundaries confounds the myth of the nation. In the current situation, with a movement to the Right in Europe, what was once a taken-for-granted reality of the legacy of humanism, is now clouded and uncertain in the emergence of the New Europe. The myth of the nation, the idea of an overarching cultural unity, has given way to a kind of politics of identification masquerading as reform in which localisms use the language of nationalism in order to gain respectability for programs of exclusion. Although the process of the incorporation of transmigrants into European centers is often viewed through an assimilationist lens, the current situation leads us to seek other manners of evaluating the nature of the newcomers in national discourse and in relation to the various issues of inclusion and exclusion that are prefigured in them. Some have suggested that various forms of incorporation act in a neutral manner, granting the benefits of European societies to those with access to education and entrance into the system, and yet neither the form of education nor the skill package one attains through them is value free: there is no "neutral technical instrument," as

Ernest Gellner suggests (cited in Maher 1986).The current situation has seen the rise of forms of closure and rejection often articulated through localist and essentialist constructs now challenged by the call for tolerance and acknowledgment of cultural diversity. The increasing heterogeneity of Italian and other Western nation-states seems posed to bring about what Stuart Hall has called "the decentering of the West and the end of the 'imagined community' of the pure" (Hall 1994, 5). And in this process these nations must come to terms with systems of privileged representation, classification, and Othering built into the national myth structure. This new self-image must account for a circumstance in which Western nation-states are, in Hall's phrase, "hybridized beyond repair" (Hall 1994, 3). Both the claims and the modes of representation of the nation-state must also shift to include what Homi K. Bhabha has referred to as the "desolate silences of wandering people," a silence peopled with the voices of new and potential subjects whose displacement often enters into national and international discourse (Bhabha 1994).

As the film by Cuban film director Tomas Gutierrez Alea *Memories of Underdevelopment* suggests, the very process of one's inclusion in a certain class, in a certain circle of friends, and in the vague and illusive image of the nation situates, classifies, and may cast, as in the life of the protagonist, an invisible curtain that makes it impossible to leave, as some do, the nation. This bond, this invisible curtain, is the thin veneer of power in the film. The differential of positions present in the notion of "intellectuals," as a category controlled by those located in the heart of dominant countries in Europe and in the United States, was impossible for the protagonist of the film to throw off. The image of underdevelopment is a kind of totalizing social fact that encompasses as it subordinates. This is part of the process that Fredric Jameson has referred to as "cultural imperialism," for which postmodernism is a "synonym" (Jameson and Hall 1990, 29). In this same manner, when we enter into the discussions of immigration in Europe and touch such issues as health care, housing, and population, this invisible ideological curtain is always coming into play, framing the dramatic action, defining the unseen boundaries of certain discourses, while precluding others. As Virginia R. Domínguez suggests, the Other may participate in a number of discursive constructions, simultaneously being not only cast as an oppositional element of the "national" or naturalized conception of the citizen but perhaps "internalized," "Otherized," incorporated, and appropriated" (Domínguez 1989, 188).

The image of the immigrant in Italy has been appropriated to that of the internal southern migrant of the 1950s and earlier in part to raise issues never fully resolved about the nature of Italian society and the disequilibrium between various sectors of its population. The so-called southern question is an issue that cuts to the heart of what Italy's position has been historically in a system of states and other formations out of which the notion of Italy has been carved. The discursive construction of Italian society, complicated from the very beginning of the Italian enterprise of nationhood, has been largely mediated through other voices. The most recent voices have been those that have cast Italy as the relatively poor society of the postwar era, sending out immigrants to Europe and elsewhere to participate in the great labor force of core European centers. At the same time that this out-migration and internal migration created a new Italy, populating the ranks of a European industrial proletariat while drawing distant regions into urban centers that contained increasingly diverse populations, the sun was setting on the mass form of production. The wake left in this post-Fordist world reveals the traces of increasing globalization of culture and economies, along with a multiplicity of linkages of population movements and the gravity of various forms of crisis—economic, political, and religious—in other yet interconnected parts of the world.

The myth of the nation provides a channel of collective imagining through which the multiplicity of a kind of ethnographic vision is precluded in preference to a transcendent fiction in which exclusions, historical and emergent, may be forgotten. Vanessa Maher has noted that often internal boundaries define the nation, particularly the "creation of persons without access," such as women and other Others in the nation-state. During a period of intensive Italian nationalist propaganda in Europe near the turn of this century, images of ethnic purity gave rise to the appropriation of the national for certain segments of the population, so that women of the more cultivated class (*classi colte*) might contribute to the growth of the nation stemming the tide of the *i poveri, stupidi e ignoranti in patria*, thereby excluding certain groups from the nation (Maher 1986, 229). This process is a fluid and ever-changing making and unmaking of the nation, and its expansive idea and image-scape are part of a perpetual remembering and forgetting.

This perhaps leads us to consider "routes" of cultural identification that may attain a political force in the new configuration of Europe. Where are the ruptures, the points that allow the possibility of cultural, political, and other forms of contestation? The points at which other collective imaginings may coexist side by side with preexistent identifications? Homi K. Bhabha has noted in a Gramscian language the possibility of cultural innovation through the play of difference:

> The very possibility of cultural contestation, the ability to shift the ground of knowledges, or to engage in the "war of position," marks the establishment of new forms of meaning, and strategies of identification. Designations of cultural difference interpellate forms of identity which, because of their continual implication in other symbolic systems, are always "incomplete" or open to cultural translation. (Bhabha 1994, 162)

For Gramsci the logic and power of the industrializing process made particular forms of identification less important; such identifications as his own regional or local origins might fade in significance. Yet the post-Fordist world in the misty terrain of the emergent Europe seems to have rendered heterogeneity and the multiplicity of identifications possible—within its confines, the frontiers of a new state of play. We may now consider constitutive of this emergent social formation that which we have held to be peripheral, fragmentary, and at times inconsequential, cast in classificatory nets of other economies, territories, and politics; entire historical processes, the movement of people, and the collision of the worlds in which they live may be and may have always been integral to processes constituting a new state of Europe, new states of grace.

Notes

Preface

1. The idea of the desert as a tropic terrain refers to the operation of discursive composition that constitutes the Other, or the process of Othering, often in an effort to define boundaries or classificatory schemes that fix the term, as in cosmologies or ethnosociologies.

1. Desert Crossings

1. As James L. A. Webb Jr. points out, the notion of the "desert ethnicity," often imported with the idea of Arabization in West Africa, "glosses over a complex process of cultural selection from Black African, Berber, and Arab sources," so that the image that has crystallized in myth itself contains a myth (Webb 1995). The notion of a transparent landscape comes into some difficulty when confronted by divergent apprehensions of cultural landscapes; the notion of "reading" the desert as a kind of map of a society implicit in Western mythology often contains also culturally specific renderings of proprietary designations and ecological expectations. The mapping relationships may be more significant to the inhabitants of a given space than the predictable patternings of coordinates along grids and other landmarks—in short, such images may completely misfire across cultural understandings. See Layton 1995.

2. On the role of the Senegalese political class and its consolidation through state means of various economic, political, and personal resources, see Boone 1990.

3. Such cities as Dakar, however, have less and less to offer the rural migrants, who are often displaced to make more room for the administrative residents. See Brokerhoff 1990.

4. I thank Philip D. Curtin for introducing me to the work of François Manchuelle, who has recently written a detailed history of this process for Soninke in France. His work confirms a widespread intercontinental migration that often precedes an extension of the migration to Europe. In addition, Manchuelle points to a growing population of migrants arriving from Black Africa to European destinations of which the Soninke and Wolof are only a small part (Manchuelle 1994). I would like to thank the late Dr. Manchuelle for sharing many of his insights on migration with me.

5. There is an extensive body of literature that treats the problem of rural-urban migration and urbanization in colonial and postcolonial African cities; my study will particularly focus on the issue of West African agricultural and economic "crisis," which contributes to rural flight. The international migration to European countries that began in earnest in the Senegal River area in the 1950s, initially among former soldiers who fought for France in the Second World War, has continued and extended to other regions. Many of the Senegalese migrants in this study come from Louga and other areas hardest hit by soil deterioration, prolonged drought, and inadequate state planning and intervention. In short, I see a continuity with many of the intellectual issues of the work of Kenneth Little (1965), Max Gluckman (1961), Hilda Kuper (1965), Ellen Hellmann (1948), Michael Banton (1955), Clyde Mitchell (1956), Isaac Schapera (1947), St. Clair Drake and Horace R. Cayton (1962), and Monica Hunter (1961).

6. Neapolitan, considered a southern dialect, is a language with an extensive literary tradition.

7. It is curious that while other Italian cities retain much more of the flavor of their history, Turin has very little of the character of the House of Savoy. In spite of the fact that the city still has a small yet significant aristocratic group of residents, some of whom may have exclusive clubs and titles, Turin is viewed as an industrial center. While in Aosta a real nostalgia remains for the relatives and members of the House of Savoy, the association of this house with Fascism seems to have greatly diminished this aspect of Turin. In short, Turin has become in Italian folklore the town of the captains of industry like the Agnellis and the workers.

8. Europeans arrived in the Senegambia at the end of the fifteenth century and continued to extend their trading posts through the seventeenth century. European bases along the coasts traded in slaves, gum arabic, leather, gold, and ivory. Europeans merely redirected trade that had previously been directed to the transsaharan trade toward the ocean. In the Senegal River basin, barter was conducted for products from the Maghreb, slaves for horses and salt carried by camel caravans. Integration into the cash economy was accomplished through the conquest of the oceans by the mercantile capitalism of France, Portugal, England, Holland, and the Atlantic slave trade that dominated Senegambian

societies (Barry 1981). Thus the convergence of the Mediterranean world, Islam, the Sudan, and the Senegambia was accomplished during the crucial period of European state formations. The Saharan front of Islam, however, was felt into the Senegambia from about the eighth century, and the only distance-trade circuits of the Sudan in the fifteenth century (Barry 1981).

The semiautonomous trading communities of Moslems were operating in long-distance trade and coming into frequent contact with societies of the Wolof, Serer, Fulbe, and Mandinka. Some of these societies such as the Wolof were rigidly hierarchical containing endogamous occupational castes and a ranking system that distinguished between free-born and nonfree classes. The Laobe wood-carvers who set up their street shops throughout Europe today are the descendants of this subcaste of the Wolof. Such trade items as kola and textiles from Mali have had a fascinating circuit changing as in the case of kola trade, which was taken from the Akou by the Lebanese who began to come to Senegal after the First World War, assisted by the declaration of the French mandate in the Levant. After the Second World War this trade gradually returned to Senegalese traders in collaboration with Ivory Coast firms and producers. Textiles are traded by Senegalese women who make their way from Mali to Paris and Holland, where a very fine quality cloth is also manufactured that may be utilized in the making of clothing and other products among the African communities in Europe.

The Senegambia, which until the fifteenth century had been a kind of cul-de-sac of the transsaharan trade and the many *caravansérai,* became as a region and later as an individual nation-state among the earliest and mostly fully integrated African economies in the world market (Amin 1981). The slave trade, which was the cornerstone of the colonial mercantile structure, became the principal activity of the eighteenth century. Already in the seventeenth century, European products such as French jewelry, iron bars, firearms, and textiles mainly destined for elites were making their way into the Senegambia. The consequences of the demographic drain and the economy based on "human hunting" can only partially be seen in the region's instability and the impossibility of establishing any stable productive activities (Barry 1981). The abolition of the slave trade in the nineteenth century led directly to the beginning of the colonial moment of African and European relations, as commercial mercantilism was eclipsed by an emergent industrial capitalism. French colonial expansion in Senegal was predicated on the shift from the transporting of human labor overseas to the deployment of agricultural labor and, much later, to the forced incorporation into the capitalist economy of peripheral workers through taxation, labor recruitment, and the establishment of commercial monopolies (Colvin et al. 1981, 4).

9. Nader Saiedi (1987) has argued that Simmel constructs a multidimensional, perspectivist, and relativistic ontology in his work. Simmel's forms have

given rise to different types of knowledge and different, equally valid worlds among which the stranger's is one.

2. Turin: Work and Its Shadow in a Post-Fordist City

1. "Bisogna però cercare di non bruciarsi, con il gioco delle lunghe durate" (Bagnasco 1986, 80).

2. In an inquiry to document the housing emergency in the Senegalese community in Turin, in a group of 106 respondents, 75 were married, many have children, and 30 were unmarried, with one divorced with children. When many of the Senegalese speak of dependents in Senegal, they identify dependents laterally, including cousins and siblings and also other generations. A typical listing would include the mother, father, siblings, children, and spouse. Some may consider as many as ten to twenty-five persons as depending in some way on the wages they have earned and sent home.

3. See, e.g., the article "Anche i vu' cumprà dicono no, i partiti di governo spiazzati dal blitz del ministro del Lavoro" (*Il Giornale,* December 16, 1989), in which the immigrant is drawn into parliamentary politics through this ritual presence in the discussion of political parties. The article notes the sending of a telex by the Minister of Labor, the late Carlo Donat-Cattin, one of the Piedmontese leaders of a Christian Democrat faction. The telex sent to the provinces and local governments made it possible for employers to hire non-European community workers. Extracommunitary workers could be hired with only the permit to stay in Italy, even if this document were obtained for the purposes of tourism. The worker would have to verify his or her presence in Italy as of December 1, 1989. This legislation by decree was typical of state policy prior to the passage of the Martelli Bill, which was referred to in December 1989 as a package that was to be worked out in detail. The interim period was to be administered by ministerial decree.

4. Although in many contexts the function of racism was to "delay class consciousness by opposing immigrants to the indigenous workers or against other immigrants on the basis of their ethnic differences or national identity to which they are referred for self-recognitions, identity and organization," as Meillassoux describes it, this was not the case in Italy. Although popular ideology among many of the construction trade had it that Senegalese workers were more diligent and hardworking than Moroccan workers and that the latter, being tied to Islam, were rigid in their social and cultural practices, these ideologies had little effect on the relationships between Senegalese and Moroccans or, for that matter, other North African populations. Having the common bond of a Moslem culture, many Senegalese and Moroccan workers saw each other in much the same conditions and often as in worse conditions since there is a long tradition of exclusion of these Islamic cultures from the Western

Catholic world. Popularly, however, Senegalese were not perceived as being Moslem and thus were not thought of as being a religious Other. The primary distinction used in the case of Senegalese was that of race. Both sets of migrants, once having attained the requisite documents, were opened to an identification with the benefit structure corresponding to their work category. Some Italian trade unions, however, worked to "delay class consciousness" through the practice, fairly widespread in some sectors, of identifying migrants who had called on the union's foreign office for information as being trade union members. A list of these persons was then sent to the employer, and many of those named were in turn asked to pay union membership dues (a cost many migrants thought exploitative since the benefit of union membership to the foreign worker is all but clear). The employers often proceeded to give these workers a hard time and to threaten to fire them, which, although illegal, served to intimidate many nonetheless.

I was involved in the organization of many informal meetings at which migrants could hear presentations on Italian work-related legislations protecting workers' rights, and there was widespread interest among all migrants. Senegalese often asked for clarification of work practices. All of the major trade unions in Turin had instituted a foreign office or representative structure, although during the period between 1990 and 1992 there was no trade union representative who spoke Wolof, primarily the language of Senegalese nonliterate workers.

5. Stendhal's Italian travelogue cast Italy in one of its most romantic lights. As Richard N. Coe points out, Stendhal's vision, not unlike more contemporary views, paints a portrait of a contradictory Italy where art and passion arise from the dynamic tensions within the society: "[Italy] is a land of informality, and yet of natural grace and manners; of rational cynicism, and yet of decent respect towards the established superstitions; of an ignorant and vicious despotism which itself breeds heroes out of slaves and conjures up painters, sculptors and musicians by the very restraint which it imposes upon all more direct and forceful means of expression." In short, Italy for Stendhal is a kind of utopia (in Stendhal [1826] 1959).

6. A. Portelli argues that the problem of racism in Italy in popular conceptions is that there is not a clear opposition between black and white as, for example, in the United States; rather, there is an opposition between Italian and non-Italian. Portelli explains: "Gli italiani invece tendono a percepire il mondo come diviso in termini marcati e termini non marcati. I termini 'non marcati' sono le persone normali, e i termini marcati sono e 'negri'—o gli ebrei . . . nel discorso del colonialismo l'italiano l'opposizione non è mai fra il bianco e il nero, ma fra l'Italiano e il negro" (Italians instead tend to view the world divided into marked terms and unmarked terms. The unmarked terms are the "normal" persons, and the marked are "Blacks" or "Jews." In the Italian colonial

discourse, the opposition is never between Whites and Blacks, but between the Italian and the Black.) The color of the skin, says Portelli, is something extra added to the original distinction of marked and unmarked categories (1989).

7. I thank Vanessa Maher for pointing out the importance of language and gesture in relations between migrants and Italians in the context of contemporary immigration in Italy. The work of David Efron in *Gesture, Race and Culture* (1972) suggests a methodology for the investigation of various patterns of gesture that distinguish two social groups in New York. Taking the notion of gesture in a very broad sense similar to that of the concept of "habitus," a set of generative schemes that agents employ in social practice, it may be possible to begin to talk about distinctions in the use of space, types of gesture, and patterns of gesture that are used to communicate in situations in which the possibility of verbal mastery is significantly reduced for both parties.

3. Mouridism Touba Turin

I would like to thank Heather Merrill-Carter for all translations from the French in this chapter.

1. There have been both Tidjan and Mourid Da'ira in Turin since 1982. Both the Tidjan and the Mourid represent substantial portions of the population of Senegalese in Turin. This discussion will treat primarily the Mourid. The Tidjan have also made use of some of the relations made for the Mourid for the use of space in which to pray and hold ceremonies. Until recently, the leaders of both religious communities lived in the same house in Turin, one of the oldest houses of Senegalese in Turin. This house was founded, in fact, by a Tidjan, and Senegalese Christians also live in the house.

2. There are many basic inequalities of knowledge within the orders. Many of the followers have a minimal knowledge of the Koran and in many cases know only the few essential chants and prayers or *Dhikr*, prayers of the founder of the order. Religious specialists organize and maintain the regular practice of the order.

3. This period is referred to as the *hijira* or exile of Amadu Bamba.

4. The trading post of the French at Saint-Louis, at the mouth of the Senegal River, and Gorèe, which faces what is now Dakar harbor, operated with no real presence of the mainland in the 1850s. "The lowly peanut transformed the situation," writes Martin Klein (1979). British trade based in palm oil used for making soap was one of the components of this transformation. The French refused to buy the "yellow soap"; in the 1830s a Marseilles firm mixed peanut oil with olive oil and created a soap that seemed more attractive to the French consumer. Beginning actually in the Gambia in the 1830s, the peanut trade increased rapidly. "The French traded to colonize the peanut-exporting areas," according to Klein (1979).

5. François Manchuelle (1994) has pointed out this feature of the diaspora communities of Soninke in the precolonial period: "the crossing of classes" and the important influences, since all classes in precolonial trade migration of various groups had the impact of unifying the many strands of Soninke migration. Further relations of Maraboutic networks across familial and clan linkages make it possible to speak of a more or less unified Soninke migration built out of the negotiation of historical diversity. From this perspective it might be useful to look at the Wolof as a more complexly variegated cultural inclusion, and at times exclusion, rather than as an uncontested social fact.

6. *Serin* is used to designate a Marabout in Wolof.

7. "The holy city of Touba, the equivalent of the celebrated *Sanusi* 'university *zawiya*' of Jaghbub, serves as a place of pilgrimage, a centre for Quran studies and as residence for the *Khalifa* General of the Order, his collateral relatives and descendants, and the great Marabouts. The *tariqa* pioneers sedentarization and land reclamation, and, in a country where the economy depends in large measure on the ground-nut crop, the *Muridiya* communities produce a little more than half of the total harvest according to Monteil" (Gilsenan 1973).

8. The mosque of Touba, the spiritual center, situated on the spot where Amadou Bamba received the revelation of his mission, is one of the largest in Africa. Great stress is placed on the sanctity of the founder and his successors, for this redeems the sins of affiliates, provided they submit themselves, abandon their personal spiritual life, and are ready to undertake the temporal tasks assigned to them. A formula forever on their lips is: "The prayer of the Master obliterates the sins of the *murid*." The order has deeply influenced social structure to the service of God and His Chaikh and a system of collective farms has been developed (Trimingham 1959, 94–95).

9. See also Tapper 1990; Mandel 1990; Eickelman and Piscatori 1990a, 1990b, 1990c.

10. In his examination of the concept of *hijira* in Islamic law, Masud points to a change in the concept in the nineteenth century when the interchange of travelers for various reasons changed: "Moslems traveled to non-Muslim lands and stayed there for longer periods. In some cases they migrated in order to settle. This was altogether a new type of *hijira*." In one text examined by Masud, the issue of travel by Moslem students is addressed: "Education and training in modern science and technology are obligatory for the progress of Muslim societies, since otherwise they would remain dependent on developed countries" (Masud 1990).

11. E. E. Evans-Pritchard points out that the emergent role of the Sanusi in the coalescence of national sentiments in the face of various "government administrations" and the opposition of tribal conflicts in the face of Turkish administration gave the order a privileged space in which to form the rudiments of an imagined community distinctive from former systems of distinction, a

"protostate." As Evans-Pritchard puts it, "They were all 'Sanusi' vis-à-vis the Administration." The tendency of the Mourid is to identify anticolonial activity with Mouridism, as is the case for Wolof, and to think of themselves (partly resulting from the prolonged contact of the Wolof with foreign presence in the Wolof periphery) as somewhat more "Senegalese" than other groups (Evans-Pritchard 1949, 71).

12. This incident is mentioned in the book of Omar Ba, *Ahmadu Bamba in France,* which has been translated under the direction of Djilly Fall Mamour by Maria Nicola and Anna Pidello for diffusion of Mourid ideology in Italy for the Cheikh Amadu Bamba Week celebration in Turin, Italy, April 4–7, 1991 (*Mom Sa Bob* in Wolof, *Avere se stessi* in Italian, and self-definition or self-possession in English.) This was the first celebration of Cheikh Amadu Bamba Week sponsored in part by regional and local official agencies in collaboration with the Senegalese association in Piedmont, in Turin, and in fact in Italy. One line from the text says, "not only did the masses run to him [Bamba] but he founded the city of Touba in order to better serve with them the cause of God."

13. Solidarity with a community of faith is one of the fundamental precepts of Mouridism.

14. In modern times the economic-religious movement of the Mourids in Senegal has been a powerful proselytizing force (Trimingham 1959, 28).

15. It is often said that things (visions) come to the mystic through dreams.

16. The support of the Mourid was sustained by Senghor's Bloc Démocratique Sénégalais over that of Lamine Gueéye's Section Française de l'Internationale Ouvrière, which the Mourid had supported before the election of the Christian, Léopold Senghor who maintained a close relationship with the leaders of the order throughout his political career (Trimingham 1980).

17. The Jinn in the Mourid system, I suggest, have a very similar quality to the "lineage" guardian spirits of Wolof and Lebou societies. These ancestral spirits such as the "*Tuur* are water spirits and spirits of uncultivated land," which are transmitted from generation to generation through the lineage of the founding ancestor (Zempleni 1977).The ancestral spirits became the guardians of the lineage in much the way that the Jinns seem in the Mourid system to be guardians of the process of accumulation of the saint, providing the container that is never empty, a source of continual wealth, both spiritual and material. The money placed in the suitcases is at once purified and fixed in the process of "travel"; in fact, the money travels in the direction of the community of believers and from the sources of non-Moslems.

18. "The Mourids have adapted the spirits and divinities of traditional religion to the jinn and angels of Islam, and with the inter-play of powerful unseen forces the protection of a Shaikh is much sought" (Cruise O'Brien 1971).

19. Abbé David Boilat (1814–1901), in *Esquisses Sénégalaises,* notes: "Ce grands Marabouts ne portent point de grigis et n'en font point, ils se contentent

de prier pour ceux qui se recommandent à eux, et de leur imposer les mains en jetant un peu de salive sur leur tete ou sur leurs mains. Lorsqu'ils joignent à ce prestige un âge avancé, alors les Wolofs les regardant comme des représentants de la Divinité, ils leur touchent les cheveux blancs et se frottent ensuite la figure avec les mains qui les ont touchés, afin d'obtenir de Dieu la grace de vivre longtemps, comme ces saints personages" (Important Marabouts do not wear gris-gris and do not use them. They are content to pray for those who seek their guidance and to lay on hands, letting out a bit of spittle on their head and hands. When they combine this with an advanced age, the Wolof regard them as representatives of divinity. They touch their white hair and rub their faces with their hands in order to obtain from God the grace to live a long time, like those saintly people; Boilat 1853 [1984]).

20. Demons and Jinn of course populate the tales of the *Arabian Nights* of India, Persia, and Arabic origin. Many of the Victorian translators of the *Nights,* through compendious notes, claimed to introduce the reader to various aspects of Arab culture, social customs, religion, and myth (Haddawy 1990). Although many of the translations of Sir Richard F. Burton and Payne contained a style and invented colloquial tone absent in the Arabic original texts, the works demonstrated a "Victorian tendency to archaize and make more colorful the 'rude' works of primitive times and places" (Haddawy 1990). The *Nights* have actually been constructed through a very complex historical exchange of popular stories, and more formal versions of such tales as "The Story of Aladdin and the Magic Lamp," in fact, seem to have entered the story cycle as late as 1787 (in the Arabic text). Not being part of the original eleven basic stories, this story seems actually to have been a forgery that was translated from French and then to Arabic in order to give the story its authenticity in the eyes of scholars. This of course merely demonstrates the great state of play in the construction and power of a compelling story. The many images of the Other, however, when taken for the actual contours of Arab society, have merely lead to misunderstanding and misconception. The tales are perhaps one of the best examples of a kind of "Victorian Orientalism" translated from scholarly practices to commonsense images in a very short space of time (Haddawy 1990).

21. See also Doughty 1926: "They [the Jinn] inhabit seven stages."

22. Crapanzano says of the holy places that "sacred springs and grottoes, trees, stones and animals believed to contain baraka, and spots to which the jinn, or devils, are said to gravitate, are found near the tombs." This gives the tomb the totemic quality that links the practitioner with the fixity of the *Baraka* in a certain center or locality (Crapanzano 1973). Edward Westermarck also noted that mosques and other holy places are said to be haunted by Moslem jinn who may strike those entering in various states of "uncleanness or drunkenness" (Westermarck 1968).

23. Some of the Jinn in the Koran say, "We have heard a wonderful dis-

course giving guidance to the right path." These Moslem Jinn are divided off from others who follow different religious paths: "We follow different ways." See Dawood 1956; Westermarck 1968, 264.

24. "He who works in his own interest, his toil shall be entirely wasted. He must work in the service of the one [the *talibé*] whose good pleasure can protect from that which he fears in this world and in the next" (cited in A.-B. Diop 1981). For a discussion of the notion of exploitation in the work practices of the Mourid in the agricultural domain, see A.-B. Diop 1981; Copans 1988.

25. "La doctrine (*murid*) pose le principle de la sanctification par le travail. Le mouridisme et le protestantisme sont ainsi les deux seules religions qui définissent une telle attitude à l'égard de l'économie" (cited in A.-B. Diop 1981).

26. There is a very well-organized Da'ira in New York and groups of followers have organized into informal groups in Atlanta, Los Angeles, and New Jersey. In Senegal there are Da'ira all over the country in Diourbel, Koalack, Louga, Casamance, and many in Dakar. There is a magazine published in French and Wolof, a publication that many of the Mourid Da'ira internationally receive called *Ndigël,* under the direction of Serigne Sarr Diop and distributed in more than fifteen countries. The publication is organized by the Movement Islamique des Mourides d'Europe (MIME). A. Moustapha Diop writes of this organization: "Ce mouvement, composé d'intellectuels, ne se cantonne pas seulement à organiser des soirées hebdomadaires religieuses; il tente aussi de diffuser hors du cercle murid la pensée du fondateur de la confrérie, et aussi de servir de trait d'union entre les adepres essaimés au autre coins du monde par le biais d'un journal" (Diop 1985; Xadim 1990).

27. Pap Khouma wrote a book in collaboration with the journalist Oreste Pivetta, *Io venditore di elefanti* (1990). The Milan group had conducted a demonstration against housing conditions in Milan. Many of the Senegalese there were thrown out of a housing complex and in protest marched through the streets and mounted a campaign against apartheid in Milan, with the slogan "Stop Apartheid." When an event like this occurs, often Senegalese from other cities come to support the event; many of the Senegalese in Turin, for example, had the "Stop Apartheid" T-shirts.

28. The first disciple and supporter of Cheikh Amadu Bamba was Cheikh Ibra Fall, who was also the first to establish an urban settlement of Mourid in Senegal. The Fall of this lineage are Baye Fall, a group of followers of Mouridism who consider themselves the "true Mourid" and who are very enthusiastic about their practice of Mouridism (Cruise O'Brien 1971).

29. The reggae music is part of a Pan-Africanism, an appreciation for things African. One of the reggae musicians, Jimmy Cliff, is said to have converted to Mouridism during a visit to Africa. Some musicians are said to exchange the name of Jah for that of Bamba in their lyrics. The musician of choice is Bob Marley.

30. "Le problème fondamental de la vulgarisation du mouridisme est intrinséquement lié à la désénegalisation de la pensée de Cheikh Ahmadou Bamba, en lui redonnant sa splendeur d'avant, tel que le Cheikh l'avait tiré du Koran et de la Sunnah du Prophète. A partir de ce moment le mouridisme aura droit de cité partout dans le monde." The Mourid founder is credited with having said that he would send out a call of this message to all peoples so that his disciples might come from all peoples and civilizations.

31. "La progresson du mouridisme ne se fera qu'avec l'adésion toujours croissante de personnes venues d'horizons très divers."

32. "Le premier travail d'un vulgarisateur est de décourvrir les us et coutumes des pays hotes. Si la pay est médiatisé il se doit d'utiliser ses mass-médiats pour faire passer son message. Si la pay est une pay de reflexion, il dit priviléger la discussion."

33. Le problème primordial est celui de la formation et de l'education. Il faut de presser ces deux blocages pour arriver à vulgariser la pensée de Serigne Touba (C. Amadu Bomba). On ne doit pas s'arrêter aux manifestations culturelles, mais s'investir activement. Ce n'est que de cette façon qu'on arrivera à faire progresser le mouridisme dans le monde. Cette progression n'est réalisable qu'avec l'ouverture vers d'autres horizons. Mais si on arrive à sonner la formation et l'education nécessaire, les facilités et vertus permettront aux furturs vulgarisateurs de venir au niveau des universités, de connaître la sociologie du pays où ils vont délivrer leur message, tout en respectant leur réalités culturelles ainsi que leur vision du monde."

34. *Khidma* actually means service or work as service. I thank Richard Randolph for pointing this out.

35. I thank Vanessa Maher for first pointing out to me the precarious nature of this class among all migrants in Turin.

36. Turin had a very important Somalian and Eritrean community. Both communities had very highly educated and influential intellectuals, many trained in Italian universities. Both groups figured in establishing the array of associations that are still active in Turin.

37. The *dhikr* is a prayer formula or phrase. Often the Sufi order has a prayer of the founder that is taught to each new member of the order during the prayer circles of the Da'ira in the procession around a prayer circle. People usually recite the *Shahada* ("There is no god but God and Muhammad is his Prophet") and other devotional activities such as the reading of the Koran. While non-Mourids would attend the religious services, often commanded to do so by the Marabout, they did not take part in the singing of the *Shahada*. One Senegalese said, "I am from the city and this is not my culture. Many of these boys are from the country and they know how to do this singing. In the country they sing and they become dizzy, and they will move all around and never hurt themselves." The young spiritual guide told me shortly after one

prayer session that ten of the boys had been filled with so much spirit that they left the circle and beat their heads against the walls and remained unharmed (Cruise O'Brien 1971, 49).

38. Religious compounds for the sons of the most privileged Mourid Marabout are conducted in Gassane and Cocci Senegal. The students are inducted into the schools around the age of seven, and a complete religious training could last until the student reaches the age of seventeen or even later. Instruction may include Tassafoufe, Fikne Islam, Tanshide, a knowledge of Islamic law, studies of the knowledge of God, and knowledge of the application of the path of Islam. In addition to this the students study the texts of the founder and may learn the "secret" writings of the founder, written with characters created by him that hold special "mystical" significance. The closer the Mourid's attention is to the spiritual world of the teaching, the greater the prestige and possibility of advance in the hierarchy of the order on the spiritual side, as opposed to the more secular and mundane affairs of the order. Some of the great Mourid Marabout are known for their great spiritual accomplishments, and several have attained the title of Moufti amd Soufiou of the order due to their great knowledge, training, and spiritual powers, including Cheikh Mbacké Madina, Mortada Mbacké, Moustapha Mbacké, Mountakha Mbacké, Abdou Akime Mbacké, and the Khalifa-General (personal communication, Djilly Fall Mamour).

39. So much of the authority and power of the Marabout comes from the fear of supernatural sanction and the systems of belief behind a tradition of mystical actors that the notion of *Baraka* is not sufficient or adequate to the understanding of the Marabout power.

40. "Le personage du Marabout est une donnée incontournable dans l'imagerie religieuse des populations sahéliennes; c'est un personage vénére, craint, mais c'est aussi un personage parfois tourné en dérision sous les traits de charlatan ou de faux dévout."

41. "Cette catégorie, issue de families maraboutiques ou anciens étudiants en sciences théologiques, fait office de conseilier, gestionnaire, secrétaire, parce que disposant de l'efficace de l'ecriture, et d'homme de Dieu en relation avec le monde de l'invisible."

4. The Art of the State: Difference and Other Abstractions

I would like to thank Philip Corrigan for his encouragement and early reading of other versions of this chapter; and Daniel Nugent for his editorial support on an earlier version for the *Journal of Historical Sociology*.

1. For a discussion of anthropological discourse and history, see Cohn and Dirks 1988; Cohn 1980, 1983, 1985.

2. This is particularly the case with such right-wing groups as the Movi-

mento Sociale Italiano (MSI), and other Right-fringe organizations. The post–World War II right wing was split between the strategies of accommodation with the government and parliamentary politics and the direct action of militant groups who sought to destabilize the state through attacks on democratic institutions. In 1964 a plan was drawn up by a general of the *Carabinieri*, the Italian police force that called for the suspension of political parties and trade union activity in the event of a threat to the integrity of the state from the Left. The plan, an outright coup scenario, revealed the attempt of right-wing elements to take full control of the state and isolate democratic forces. During the next decade the MSI, led by Giorgio Almirante, attempted to turn itself into a respectable right-wing party along the lines of other fringe parties in Europe. This strategy, however, failed. The MSI, from the early period after World War II until quite recently, has had trouble discarding the stigma of Fascism; never able to reconstitute fascist elements in a new form, the party drifted away from the central ruling powers of the country. In the 1980s this began to change again: the MSI was consulted by Bettino Craxi during the formation of his new government. This was a decisive move in the transformation of the isolation of the MSI. With the election of the granddaughter of Benito Mussolini the party has given new life to fascist ideas and brought in the monarchist fringe once again, as the Mussolini family is related to a very ancient aristocratic tradition. This has, of course, all changed with the recent rise of the national right-wing coalition lead by Silvio Berlusconi and the rise to prominence of the anti-immigrant platform of such groups. See Chiarini 1991; and Cheles 1991.

3. Much of this new voting revolt has occurred around the emergence of a new Right in Italy and elsewhere in Europe, particularly in France and Germany. The recent election of Mussolini's granddaughter only underscores the uneasy displacement of the five-party ruling coalition in Italy headed by the Christian Democrats. The neo-Fascists have been gaining strength in Italy since the mid-1970s. Alessandra Mussolini will place the family name back in parliament for the first time in more than forty years under the banner of the neo-Fascist party, the MSI (Cheles et al. 1991).

4. The Ciampi government is, of course, the latest in this line of new technical governments, run by the former president of one of the most powerful banking concerns in Italy, the Italian Central Bank. Carlo Azeglio Ciampi is one of the technocrats of the powerful hidden government in Italy, its so-called *sottogoverno*. For such a figure to emerge into the rough-and-tumble of politics at once marks the serious nature of the political crisis and Italy's resilience in the face of adversity. One of Ciampi's government's first tasks was to sweep away some of the charges against former Socialist Party leader Bettino Craxi. This so angered members of the young government that all of the Communist ministers and many others resigned on the first day of the new government's tenure. Craxi will be tried on lesser charges and the reluctant ministers (the first Com-

munists to hold such posts since 1946) may rejoin the dance, until elections may be held. What is clear is that an era has ended and a new, more uncertain one is about to begin, in which European concerns will become the all-important cry of the day. When bankers become temporary politicians in order to placate market fears, political security may be read in the lines and graphs of the international market. Perhaps here the prototype of the new-era document may take shape.

5. This may include both scientific fact-finding investigations and a whole host of investigative practices that developed throughout the eighteenth and nineteenth centuries.

6. Spontaneity for Gramsci is the character of social, political, and economic life after the assertion and capture of the state by the subaltern masses and their representatives. This process would create a state with a true state character as the direct expression of the subaltern.

7. Shortly after the proclamation of the new nation, Prime Minister Camillo di Cavour's dying words were to turn to the problem of the two Italies: "North Italy has been established. There are no longer Lombards, Piedmontese, Tuscans, Romagnese, we are all Italians, but there are still the Neapolitans"; at this time to speak of the Neapolitans was shorthand for southern Italy generally. Quoted in Barzini 1964. See also Barzini 1971, 1983.

8. The dangerous classes "formed from all individuals who, being destitute of the necessary means of subsistence, live in idleness and vagabondage at the expense of other citizens," as defined by Giovanni Bolis, a writer of the 1870s in his *La polizia e le classi pericolose della società* (cited in Gibson 1986). The prostitute, according to Bolis, was the most common figure of an emergent lumpen proletariat. Prostitution was regulated by the government in tolerated locations from the 1860s in Italy until 1958, with the passage of the Merlin Law, sponsored and named for Lina Merlin, a Socialist parliamentarian. Major urban centers like Turin, Rome, and Milan between 1811 and 1911 increased growth in populations at unprecedented rates, more than doubling in size from unification to World War I. The life of a prostitute was said to lack routine, discipline, and order, according to commentators like Bolis. These single women who filled the ranks of the new poor swept into the urban centers of Italy in the nineteenth century and were seen as the victims of the absence of "all moral sense" by the contemporaries of Bolis. This absence of a moral center, key in the regulation of moral issues by the state, marked the prostitute as a participant in a marginal world in which the very moral core of the rest of society was effaced. In the contemporary context prostitution among Third World women is seen in Italy as a moral and health issue, not as a labor problem of the closure or lack of labor markets to newcomers in periods of rapid transition. See Gibson 1986.

9. Aihwa Ong notes the manner in which in the ambiguous spaces between citizenship and other categories of citizenship may be glossed in terms of

certain preferred "biotypical criteria" for particular populations who are in effect differentially "racialized" and accorded specific ideological spaces in a transnational formation of race. See Ong 1993.

10. Massimo Pastore has noted that the close of such countries as Greece, Italy, Spain, and Portugal with very stringent immigration legislation in comparison to the rest of Europe marks a shift away from the "shared shores of the Mediterranean" to the fortress of Europe. Rather, European borders begin in these countries, although they are no longer merely national borders but those of Europe as a whole. Intergovernmental agencies that monitor the transition to the new Europe place the concerns of security, drug traffic, crime, terrorism, and immigration on the same agenda; all represent threats to the security and policing of the new Europe (Pastore, personal communication). For a more detailed discussion of the problem, see Carter 1992.

11. Cesare Lombroso, the inventor of modern criminology, conducted his first studies while in Calabria as a young man, and these early notes on the nature of Calabria have the quality of a classical topography or state study (that is similar to Bertolotti's study of Turin. Lombroso's work was republished in 1898. This time the publication was accompanied by commentary from Giuseppe Pelaggi, a very "cultivated" Calabrese who added notes on the statistics of the population, emigration, and education. One area of interest and analysis of the work *In Calabria (1862–1897)* is the second chapter, which notes the presence of communities of Piedmontese and Greek and documents the traces of ancient Greek songs. The third and fourth chapters contain notes on the Albanian community and on the Calabrians themselves. Later chapters treat popular literature; fecundity, morality, and criminality; public hygiene; schools, emigration, food, and customs; medical and pathological conditions; and hygiene and beneficent societies (Lombroso 1898).

12. See Wetergaard 1932 for a detailed history of the development of the conception of statistical works in the field.

13. Speaking of collective landholding practice in the new Italian state, Cattaneo, with a cultural signature that characterized his studies, wrote, "These are not abuses, they are not privileges, they are not usurpations: it is another way of possessing, another system of legislation, another social order, which unobserved, has descended to us from centuries past" (cited in Grossi 1981).

14. Positivist ideology in its "confrontation with the problem of Man" was to come to use the new methods developed in statistics and aided by the errors of observation elaborated by Frédéric La Play and Carl Friedrich Gauss; these rigorous numerical methods seemed to promise regularities that could then be transformed into laws. The quantitative methods of statistics that could provide "average values" seemed to establish a secure method for attaining information about the world through quantification, "analogy and homogeneity" and through the variation between normalcy and pathology. See Pazzagli 1980.

15. Using the metaphor of an archer, Adolphe Quételet accounted for the great variety of humanity. The archer, he argued, strives to hit the mark but may miss, although even the interference of accidental phenomena creates a result that more or less conforms to an ideal outcome. The accidental deviation in the human world is the result of such approximations to an ideal normalcy of nature. Viewing humanity as a series of "errors" in search of an ideal person, Quételet could apply the "laws of accidental error" developed in contemporary mathematics to the variation in the human population. The result would render variation across the human population to the regularity of probability. Disorder or apparent disorder becomes in this manner a mere epiphenomenon of the underlying symmetry of the superior order of a law-governed activity. Quételet in effect gave rise to a kind of determinism that, once related to a preconstructed grid, rendered a kind of probabilistic chain of being. See Farolfi 1979.

16. The use of statistical information to chart the wealth of the nation had a long tradition in the kingdom of Piedmont as in many European states. The justification for the advance of such inquiries was often an economic one, given that tax registries, tables on commerce, and agricultural data were among the most common sites of information gathering. This is evident early in the French system of information gathering in the very structure of the administrative apparatus designed to conduct investigations (Woolf and Perrot 1984).

17. The anthropological preoccupation that was to influence the collection of data in postrevolutionary France and through much of Europe placed "the people" in the forefront of investigative objects. Stereotypes of the people, however, structured the interpretation of this new font of information: the remodeling of France into new places (departments) and times (calendars), new forms of religion (church), language instead of dialects, and the replacement of customary moral codes with civic codes imposed by overarching powers made the people appear as an "unchanging" mass opposed to the modernizing of society. This is very much the image of the South in Italy and of the peasant world in Italian folk or commonsense ideology (Woolf and Perrot 1984, 90–91).

18. The Italian prefect had a very important political role in the early state, although this influence was soon coined as *prefectocracy*. Prefects were moved frequently so that they were dependent on central authority for their power. The prefect's career often ended in parliament; drawn largely from the same class as the political classes of the central government, the prefect was feared for the close connection with the system of patronage and support of the Italian parliamentary system. Prefects in the young state were sent to the South for punishment. The South was considered a backward and semifeudal wasteland. Ironically, many of the southern prefects (only a few initially came from landholding and lawyer backgrounds) shared this "backward" view of the South with their northern counterparts (Fried 1963).

19. I use *cosmology* here to underscore not only the creation of the social

but the convergence in one site of the state of multiple practices that contained underlying principles capable of constructing a kind of secular cosmos, a law-governed universe—a universe that would expand into the intricate realms of anthropometric comparisons and, eventually, the assurances of scientific affirmation of different orders of persons and things. For a similar gloss of *cosmology*, see Mitchell 1979.

20. Count Cavour (1810–61) was the principal architect of the modern Italian state and served as the first prime minister of the nation. He died shortly after unification.

21. I thank Vanessa Maher for pointing this out.

22. See Kearney 1991 for a discussion of the manner in which the migrant is confronted by the "alien" construct and how this position of ambiguous social, political, and legal status works in a curious dialectic with issues of nationalism, ethnicity, and self. Of course, this process goes both ways, and transnational migrants are less willing to submit to the routine of state. As Kearney notes: "The dialectic of transnational exploitation and resistance takes place on the margins of nations and is both a symptom and cause of the progressive dissolution of the power of these nations to impress themselves as nationalities and as nationalisms on the subaltern peoples within their boundaries. One of the various dimensions of this challenge to the nation-state is the increasing refusal of transnational ethnic minorities to be the objects of study by the disciplines of the nation-state—it might be said that this is but one of a number of ways in which they refuse to be disciplined. . . . One result of this reordering is an increasing refusal of former ethnographic Others to submit to being taken as objects of investigation by the standard disciplines and a corresponding insistence on writing and speaking for themselves" (67).

5. Media Politics and the Migrant

1. Formal education may diminish the religious status of Mourid followers and Marabout. The greater the association with the secular world of the intellectual, the greater the possibility of the loss of faith, according to some religious leaders.

2. Cheikh S had been in Italy many times and traveled widely throughout the country, yet he spoke only a few words of Italian and had no intention of learning more. Like his brother he spoke almost no French. Babacar, drinking tea, said, "I took lessons until my teacher was changed. The other one was no good. The new one was just no good. I couldn't understand anything, so I quit going. I'll go when I get work."

3. There is indeed some overlap of the Catholic and Left lay worlds. This is particularly the case now that the great alignments of Eastern Europe and the West have diminished in the wake of the fall of Soviet Communism. Many of

the former splits between Catholic and Communist in Italy are no longer as sharply drawn. This is clearly seen in the anti-Mafia movement in Sicily, which initially gave birth to the political party La Rete, which includes both former Communists and Catholic Left factions (Kertzer 1977; Schneider and Schneider 1976).

4. These include *Corriere della Sera,* a Milan-based paper, formerly owned by the Crespi industrialist family and *La Stampa,* the Turin-based paper controlled by the Agnelli Group, which owns FIAT. The Rizzoli-Gemina Group, a publishing subsidiary of FIAT, now owns *La Gazzetta dello Sport, La Stampa, Stampa Sera,* and *Il Corriere della Sera.*

5. See the brief discussion of such terms as *nero* and *vu' cumprà* in Maher et al. 1991. Also see the discussion of such distinctions in chapters 2 and 3.

6. Journalism is a profession established in Italian constitutional law as one of the twelve professional orders in Italy. It is thus regulated in a unique manner by the state. This relation stems from a 1928 act of legislation of the Fascist state that established a registry of all journalists. The present order of journalism was established in 1963, however, and its establishment was due largely to the organization of a group of anti-Fascist journalists who hours after the fall of Mussolini began to organize the profession in opposition to its previous Fascist structure (Porter 1983).

7. The journalist-politician is a central figure of the Italian political world. Such important factional and party leaders as Giulio Andreotti (several times premier), the late Ugo La Malfa (historic leader of the Republican Party), Giorgio La Malfa (actual leader of the Republican Party), Arnaldo Fanfani (former secretary of the Christian Democratic Party and president of the republic), and Bettino Craxi (secretary of the Socialist Party) are all practicing journalists. Every president of the republic since 1964 has been a journalist-politician for at least part of his career.

8. Journalists have operated without a contract for some years now. During 1990–1991 journalists went out on strike almost every Tuesday in order to draw attention to the problem of their profession. The labor cost of Italian papers far exceeds that of their American counterparts (Porter 1983). Like many others, contracts must be negotiated at the national level. This involves the government often in negotiations. The government is heavily involved in the Italian newspaper industry controlling prices and, in 1977, linking the cost of newspapers to the cost of living. Some daily Italian papers now cost almost $3 (U.S.) per copy.

9. A series of large theaters based on the American-style multiple theater in one location is planned for construction in Italy in the near future. In Turin within the next few years a fully operating theater on this model should be available in the downtown area. There has been some conflict over this development: some complain that the popular cinema on the American model will

only be a means of debasing and destroying the production of Italian art films that play to much smaller audiences than American and other foreign films or even Italian comedy films, which do much better at the box office.

10. One can join a film club by purchasing a ticket at a local theater that entitles the holder to a discount on the price of film admission for a season of movie going. These tickets run about $15 to $20 (U.S.) a year and entitle the holder to other benefits such as the purchase of tickets to foreign language films.

11. This is particularly true of the themes that I have identified above, such as criminality, work, and health. These issues are part of an ongoing debate within the government. For instance, the sections of the newspaper are marked with notes on the "war against criminality," the "problems of immigration," or well-placed articles on the economy.

12. Until the nineteenth century much of Europe was actually what Benedict Anderson calls polyvernacular: its languages of state and its print languages were often quite different. In Italy, Italian as a national language is a very recent phenomenon: its profusion as a written language has been inhibited for the past forty years by the slowly improving literacy levels of Italy, which have lagged behind other European countries (Anderson 1983).

13. Those opposed to the show maintained that the representation of the Mafia and its many alleged connections to government officials went beyond the world of entertainment and came close to the implication of actual persons. The show had gone too far, in short, and was suppressed. Similarly, the television show *Samarcanda* was threatened with suspension in late 1990 and again in early 1991 for its investigative excursions into Italian political figures. The president of the Republic was involved in the controversy and called for the suspension of the show, and for a period succeeded. *Samarcanda* is one of Italy's most popular shows of its kind.

14. Many aspects of the "criminality against the state" model that I discuss here are examined in the very detailed examination of the anti-Mafia movement in Sicily by Jane Schneider and Peter Schneider (1996). The anti-Mafia movement in Sicily is in many ways a grass-roots social movement that involves the collaboration of former Communist and Catholic organizers. The former mayor of Palermo, Leoluca Orlando, has figured prominently in this movement, initially attempting to enlist the help of the left wing of the Christian Democratic Party to confront this moral issue.

6. Other Crossings: Socialist in Fascist Clothing

1. See fig. 7 for a visual depiction of the title of this chapter.

2. "The fear of black masculinity within white supremacist, patriarchal culture is first and foremost about sexuality—about heterosexuality, about interracial sex—which becomes that taboo yet irresistible space where race, gender

and sexuality collide. The man as opprobrious 'other' is invariably the eroticized other" (Saint-Aubin 1994). I thank Brackette Williams for pointing out this discussion to me. See also the introduction to Williams 1996.

3. In a preliminary report on the history of black soldiers in the Great War, W. E. B. Du Bois notes that the white commanding officers of all black units, concerned over the relations of black officers and other soldiers with "the women of France" as a matter of course, "officially stigmatized the Negroes as rapists; they solemnly warned the troops in speeches and general orders not even to speak to women on the street; ordered the white military police to spy on the blacks and arrest them if they found them talking with French women" (Lester 1971, 155–56). I would like to thank William A. Shack for his many contributions to the research and background for this section.

4. Stephen Kern has spoken of a kind of "simultaneity of multiple distant events," brought on by the conditions of the Great War under which soldiers labored and through which others gained news of such events (Kern 1983, 293). I would argue that this same urgency was given to racist thought drawn together for the civilian populations by countless stories and experiences of battle and accounts circulated to a new world made coherent and real by the Great War. The convergence of colonialist and racist discourses about the "demanding nature of the on-going experience" of the war was utilized in order to confirm visions of different kinds of persons, white and black (Kern 1983, 293). Senegalese soldiers were said to be poor and to lack rigorous training, and black Americans were seen as cowards and rapists. This rhetoric was intended to discredit and deny the role of black soldiers, in effect denying them coeval placement in that "simultaneity" that Kern describes. The culture of time and space was therefore racialized in every dimension in life and even after death. See the discussion of W. E. B. Du Bois of blacks in the Great War in Lester 1971.

5. As Peter Fryer notes, already in the seventeenth and eighteenth centuries "reports of unusual sexual behavior of any kind," and particularly that accorded to the "immemorial view of dark-skinned people as lustful beasts," received an "eager and credulous" audience (Fryer 1984, 139–45).

6. There has also been a discussion of Asian migrants in the research of the Turin group; a substantial portion of the immigrants to Turin in recent years have been Asian. One quarter of the city in particular now has a large Chinese population.

7. "La Capitale, come una gigantesca piovra, inghiotte più facilmente lavoratori stranieri, profughi, rifugiati politici, regolari e clandestini, offre solidarietà di etnie ai nuovi arrivati, facilita contatti, crea occasioni, rende quasi normale, per via del secolare richiamo turistico o religioso, la presenza di migliaia e migliaia di persone diverse per razza, colore della pelle, religione" (*Il Giorno* 1989a).

8. Massimo Pacini, director of the Agnelli Foundation in Turin, Italy has

suggested that the birthrate in Italy has declined in recent years, which would result in a decline in the Italian population (Pacini 1989).

9. The cover term for all of these groups is *North African.* Along with these countries are countries like Senegal, which were among the first to receive restrictions on the manner in which persons from these countries might enter Italy. The first visa regulations were actually imposed on Senegal and Gambia. See Chiaberge 1990.

10. These groups are similar to the Le Pen groups in France. They are separatist, anticentrist and anti-immigrant, including anti-southern-Italian, and they originate in the North of Italy in Lombard and Piedmont. Many political debates have centered on accusations of league philosophy underlying political motivations (*L'Unità* 1990).

11. Giorgio Bassani's *Il Giardino Dei Finzi-Contini* (1962) gives a vivid portrayal of the impact of Fascist legislation on the daily lives and aspirations of an entire community and the climate of these years in Ferrara, Italy.

12. Mia Fuller notes a shift particularly toward the end of 1936 after an "Italian Empire was proclaimed." A racist rhetoric was part of the discourse of the colonies after this, and the issues at stake in Ethiopia began to shift, increasingly becoming those of "control, regulation, planning, and—above all—the direct exercise of power" (Fuller 1992, 214). Fuller moreover points to the importance of the concept of race as being one of the most important in subsequent "spatial organization of bodies and built forms in the new colony."

13. I would like to thank William A. Shack for pointing out the significance of the nature of Ethiopian marriage and other practices.

14. This cartoon is the first in a two-part series: in the following drawing it is Craxi who appears as a black immigrant in a boat while the caricature of Martelli attempts to defend Italy against a clandestine invasion by people of color. The implication is that Craxi only has a suntan from his trips abroad and is not really black.

15. This was clearly not the case in practice, as Italy's treatment of Albanian migrants demonstrates.

16. This is actually a contrast with the Third World often made in literature. The poet Giuseppe Ungaretti, who won the Nobel prize for his poetry in the 1970s, wrote in his notebooks of Egypt that its "deserts held no monument," that the passage of time was not appropriated to the form of the national monument. His work sought actually to give the same power to an Italian landscape, to the many rivers of Italy and the historical events, which were more universal than nationalistic. His poem "The Rivers" is a fine example of this attempt.

17. On threats to male domains, Ong 1990.

18. I would like to thank Heather Merrill-Carter for pointing out the "bounding" aspects of the Third World women in Europe.

7. Desperate Measures: Immigration and the South of the World

1. "Le previsioni per i prossimi anni indicano come le divergenze dei sentieri di crescita tra paesi sottosviluppati e paesi ad alta industrializzazione creerano flussi migratori crescenti in entrata nei vari paesi europei e anche in Italia" (Hornziel 1986, 17).

The report continues: "Eppure nel recente documento del Ministero del lavoro e della prevvidenza sociale 'La politica occupazionale per il prossimo decennio' (Roma, 1985), un capitolo relativo alle previsioni sulle immigrazioni straniere in Italia segnalava come fenomeno nuovo l'arrivo di lavoratori stranieri, per lo più clandestini, impiegati nei settori più dequalificati e abbandonati dalla manodopera locale. Secondo tale rapporto, il Ministero dell'interno indicava in un milione circa il numero degli stranieri a tutt'oggi, mentre alre stime la valutano a più di 700.000 immigrati, in gran parte non ufficiali, occupati nelle zone diverse e dequalificate del mercato di lavoro quali: l'agricoltura, l'edilizia, il settore alberghiero, la pesca, i trasporti, il piccolo commercio ambulante, il lavoro domestico" (Moreover in a recent document of the Minister of Labor, "The Occupational Politics of the Next decade" (Rome, 1985), a chapter revealed projections on the foreign immigration in Italy and signaled as a new phenomenon the arrival of foreign workers, who were also clandestine, employed in unskilled sectors abandoned by the local labor force. According to the report, the Minister of the Interior indicated the number of foreigners to be around one million, while other estimates place the number of immigrants closer to seven hundred thousand, in large part unofficial and employed in such diverse zones of the labor market as agriculture, construction, the hotel sector, transport, fishing, small-scale ambulant commerce, and domestic labor [Hornziel 1986, 17]).

2. "E' a prima vista incredibile che L'Italia, paese di grande e non dimenticata emigrazione, non comprenda che è venuta il tempo di applicare in casa nostra i principi che abbiamo chiesto a gran voce ai paesi che accolsero—a volte in condizioni di clandestinità—gli italiani. Ma la verita è che, al di la delle parole, anche le emigrazione italiana fu il rifiuto egoistico dei poveri, spinti per le vie del mondo per lasciare piu spazio a chi restava. Così, mentre per buoni motivi abbiam ritenuto che le rigide norme di statuti per immigranti in Svizzera fossero forme di discriminazione, noi oggi affermiamo che non siamo un paese di immigrazione, perchè formalmente noi non abbiamo mai chiesto con specifici accordi a nessuno di venire tra noi . . . comunque possono andarsene."

3. "Inoltre, l'immigrazione clandestina, non controllata e regolata, finisce inevitabilmente per rafforzare i mercato nero del lavoro e l'economia sotteranea, perpetuando e moltiplicando il circolo."

4. See Jameson 1990 for the statement derived from Horkheimer and Adorno's *Dialectic of Enlightenment* (1972, 148): "Not Italy is offered, but proof that it exists."

5. Disputes over the legislation—notably, between the bill's author Martelli (a Socialist) and members of the five-party coalition that has ruled Italy through almost all of its fifty postwar governments—nearly ruptured the delicate coalition and caused a government crisis in the debate over immigration. In the political instability in the wake of the bill's passage the government coalition did break up, and the leagues became the heirs to a social and political climate in which opposition to immigration became a major electoral issue. The leagues gained substantially and were elected to local governments across the country.

6. This logic finally worked itself out in a proposal by Martelli, the vice president of the Chamber of Ministers, to use the Italian Naval and Armed Forces in order to stop the influx of immigrants. The proposal was quite serious and involved negotiations at the ministerial level until the intervention of the president of the Republic, Cossiga, halted the notion by pointing out that the function of the National Armed Forces was not that of policing the Italian coastline.

8. Closing the Circle: On Sounding Difference

1. The Italian planned revision of the national health care structure calls for requiring persons making more than approximately $40,000 (U.S.) a year to pay for large portions of health and clinic care. Currently, a large portion of the contributions to this system comes directly from the wages of working-class or dependent workers.

2. Mussolini, who liked to be called the "founder of the Empire," said in one of his most famous policy speeches: "Empires are conquered by arms but kept by prestige" (in Sbacchi 1985, 167). This prestige was perhaps tempered by the fact that Italy had at once gained a colony that had been in the Italian colonizing imagination since the nineteenth century; racial separation and differentiation were reinforced by a militaristic discipline, and offenders were penalized according to racial laws designed to uphold the prestige of Italians (Sbacchi 1985, 167).

3. In the process of state formation in Europe, migrations became increasingly the concern of emergent states and rulers. During the seventeenth and eighteenth centuries demographic shifts in Piedmont were particularly related to the development of a major urban center around the absolutist state with its capital in Turin (Levi 1985). The process of state formation in Italy was a difficult and protracted matter, the many states—French, papal, and Austrian—each leaving its own mark on the landscape, state institutions, and people. The Italian monarchy preferred to speak French and to surround themselves with European and Piedmontese company. It was, rather, the statutes and registers of the Piedmontese constitutional monarchy that provided the foun-

dations of the emergent Italian state and the mechanisms through which an Italian power could be articulated. But it was during the Fascist period that every citizen of the state began to become inculcated into the nation and was for the first time taught a national language.

4. Such statements ring with a continuing violence and xenophobic sentiment in the aftermath of such incidents as that in which Nazi-led youths stormed and firebombed a house for foreigners in the Baltic city of Rostock. See Atkinson 1993.

5. Allan Pred has noted that an increasing portion of local youth in Western European societies find themselves "economically and otherwise marginalized," outside of the larger society. Experiencing a "deep sense of alienation," these youth find themselves involved in various forms of social activities, often against recognized authority figures. This sense of being on the outside may help to align some youth with youth organizations and clubs or in some cases with violence-prone racist groups. See Pred's discussion of Swedish youth groups in his *Recognizing European Modernities: A Montage of the Present* (1995, 236).

Bibliography

Adamson, Walter L. 1980. *Hegemony and Revolution: A Study of Antonio Gramsci's Political and Cultural Theory*. Berkeley and Los Angeles: University of California Press.

Amin, Samir. 1981. "Senegal: The Development of the Senegalese Business Bourgeoisie." In *The Indigenization of African Economies*, ed. Adebayo Adedeji. London: Hutchinson University Library for Africa.

———. 1989. *Eurocentrism*, trans. Russell Moore. New York: Monthly Review Press.

Anderson, Benedict. 1983. *Imagined Communities: Reflections on the Origin and Spread of Nationalism*. London: Verso.

———. 1986. "Narrating the Nation, Race and Nationalism." *Times Literary Supplement*, 13 June.

Appadurai, Arjun. 1990. "Disjuncture and Difference in the Global Cultural Economy." *Public Culture* 2, no. 2 (Spring).

Atkinson, Graeme. 1993. "Germany: Nationalism, Nazism and Violence." In *Racist Violence in Europe*, ed. Tore Björgo and Rob White. London: Macmillan.

Avvenimenti. 1989. "Immigrati di tutto Il Mondo unitevi," Avvenimenti, 11 October.

Bagnasco, Arnaldo. 1990a. *La Città Dopo Ford: Il Caso di Torino*. Turin: Bollati Boringhieri.

———. 1990b. "La Cultura come Risorsa." In *La Città Dopo Ford: Il Caso di Torino*. Turin: Bollati Borghieri.

———. 1977. *Tre Italie: La Problematica Territoriale dello Sviluppo Italiano*. Bologna: Il Mulino.

———. 1988. "Torino: La fabbrica e la città." In *Spazio e Società*. Turin: Dossier.

———. 1986. *Torino: Un Profilo Sociologico*. Turin: Giulio Einaudi.

Bagnasco, Arnaldo, M. L. Biano, A. Michelsons, and N. Negri. 1985. "Rileggere Torino." *Sisifo* 4 (April).

Baker, Kathleen M. 1995. "Drought, Agriculture and Environment: A Case Study from the Gambia, West Africa. *African Affairs* 94:67–68.

Bakhtin, Mikhail M. 1981. "Discourse in the Novel." In *The Dialogic Imagination: Four Essays by M. M. Bakhtin*, ed. Michael Holquist, trans. Caryl Emerson and Michael Holquist. Austin: University of Texas Press.

Balibar, Etienne. 1991. "Es Gibt Keinen Staat in Europa: Racism and Politics in Europe Today." *New Left Review* 186 (March–April).

Balliano, Pierra. 1986. "Crisi e Ristrutturazione del Settore Automobilistico Negli Anni '80." In *Tre Incognite per Lo Sviluppo: Stutture di mercato, scelte technologiche e ruolo delle istituzioni nell'ultimo decennio*, ed. Angelo Michelsons. Milan: Franco Angeli.

Banton, Michael. 1955. *The Coloured Quarter: Negro Immigrants in an English City*. London: Jonathan Cape.

Baránsky, Zygmunt G., and Robert Lumley, eds. 1990. *Culture and Conflict in Postwar Italy: Essays on Mass and Popular Culture*. New York: St. Martin's Press.

Barbagli, Marzio. 1982. *Education for Unemployment: Politics, Labor Markets and the School System—Italy, 1859-1973*, trans. Robert H. Ross. New York: Columbia University Press.

Barbano, Filippo. 1985. "Prima e Nuova Sociologia in Italia." *Quaderni di Sociologia* (sommario del no. 4–5).

———. 1987. *L'Ombra del Lavoro Profili di Operai in Cassa Integrazione*. Milan: Franco Angelli Editori.

Barkan, Joanne. 1984. *Visions of Emancipation: The Italian Workers Movement since 1945*. New York: Praeger.

Barker, J. Ellis. 1921. "The Colored French Troops in Germany." *Current History* 14, no. 4 (July): 594–99.

Barry, Boubacar. 1981. "Economic Anthropology of Precolonial Senegambia from the Fifteenth through Nineteenth Centuries." In *The Uprooted of the Western Sahel: Migrants' Quest for Cash in the Senegambia*, ed. Lucie Gallistel Colvin et al. New York: Praeger.

Barthes, Roland. 1979. *The Eiffel Tower and Other Mythologies*, trans. Richard Howard. New York: Hill and Wang.

Barzini, Luigi. 1964. *The Italians*. New York: Atheneum.

———. 1971. *From Caesar to the Mafia: Sketches of Italian Life*. New York: Library Press.

———. 1983. *The Europeans*. New York: Penguin Books.

Battistini, Giorgio. 1991. "Le Mineranze Linguistiche: Maestri di dialetto ed è subito guerra, Così il Paese torna al passato." *La Repubblica*, 22 November.

Behrman, L. C. 1969. "The Islamization of the Wolof by the End of the Nineteenth Century." In *West African History* (Boston University Papers on Africa, vol. 4), ed. Daniel McCall, Norman R. Bennett, and Jeffrey Butler. New York: Praeger.

———. 1970. *Muslim Brotherhoods and Politics in Senegal.* Cambridge, Mass: Harvard University Press.

Benedict, Ruth. 1947. *Race: Science and Politics.* New York: Viking.

Berreman, Gerald D. 1976. "Race, Caste, and Other Invidious Distinctions in Social Stratification." *Race* 13:385–419.

Bertolotti, Davide. 1840. *Descrizione di Torino,* ed. G. Pomba. Turin: Di Allesandro Fontana.

Bhabha, Homi K. 1994. *The Location of Culture.* London: Routledge.

Bianco, Maria Luisa. 1986. "Quale deindustrializzazione? Alcani mutamenti strutturali nel sistema industriale torinese nel corso dell'ultimo decennio." In *Tre Incognite per Lo Sviluppo: Strutture di mercato, scelte technologiche e ruolo delle istituzioni nell'ultimo decennio,* ed. Angelo Michelsons. Milan: Franco Angeli.

Birnbaum, Lucia Chiavola. 1986. *Liberazione della Donna Feminism in Italy.* Middletown, Conn.: Wesleyan University Press.

Bjorkland, Ulf. 1986. "World-Systems, the Welfare State, and Ethnicity." *Ethos* 5:3–4.

Bocca, Giorgio. 1988. *Gli Italiani sono razzisti? Millioni di immigrati di colore ci mettono alla prova: E i "terroni" sono ancora "terroni."* Milan: Garzanti.

Boilat, Abbé David. 1853 (1984). *Esquisses Sénégalaises.* Paris: Éditions Karthala.

Bonazzi, Giuseppe. 1990. "Lasciare la fabbrica: Casa integrazione e mobilità negli anni ottanta." In *La Città Dopo Ford: Il Caso di Toriono,* ed. Arnaldo Bagnasco. Turin: Bollati Boringhieri.

Boone, Catherine. 1990. "The Making of a Rentier Class: Wealth Accumulation and Political Control in Senegal." *Journal of Development Studies* 22, no. 3.

Bortot, Nero. 1983. "Commenti sulla presenza Straniera in Italia." *Studi Emmigrazione* 71 (September).

Bourdieu, Pierre. 1984. *Distinctions: A Social Critique of the Judgment of Taste,* trans. Richard Nice. Cambridge, Mass.: Harvard University Press.

Bourdieu, Pierre, and Jean-Claude Passerson. 1977. *Reproduction in Education, Society and Culture.* London: Sage.

Braudel, Fernand. 1966. *The Mediterranean and the Mediterranean World in the Age of Philip II.* Vols. 1–2. New York: Harper Torchbooks.

———. 1992. *The Perspective of the World: Civilization and Capitalism, 15th to 18th Century.* Vol. 3, trans. Sian Reynolds. Berkeley and Los Angeles: University of California Press.

Braverman, Harry. 1974. *Labor and Monopoly Capital: The Degradation of Work in the Twentieth Century.* New York: Monthly Review Press.

Brokerhoff, Martin. 1990. "Rural-to-Urban Migration and Child Survival in Senegal." *Demography* 27, no. 4 (November).

Bunce, Michael. 1994. *The Countryside Ideal: Anglo-American Images of Landscape.* London: Routledge.

Burchell, Graham, Colin Gordon, and Peter Miller. 1991. *The Foucault Effect: Studies in Governmentality.* Chicago: Chicago University Press.

Calvino, Italo. 1974. *Invisible Cities.* New York: Harcourt Brace Jovanovich.

Cardoza, Anthony. 1991. "Tra Casta e Classe: Clubs maschili dell'élite torinese, 1840–1914." *Quaderni Storici,* 77 (August).

Carter, Donald Martin. 1991a. "Una confraternità Musilmano in Torino: Il Mourid di Senegal." In *Religioni e Società.* Florence: Rosenberg and Sellier.

———. 1991b. "La Formazione di una Dahira Senegalese a Torino." In *Uguali e Diversi: Il mondo culturale, le rette delle relazione, il lavoro dei Immigrati,* ed. Vanessa Maher et al. Turin: Ires Piemonte.

———. 1992. "Invisible Cities: Touba Turin, Senegalese Transnational Migrants in Northern Italy." Ph.D. diss., University of Chicago.

Castles, Stephen. 1986. "The Guest-Worker in Western Europe: An Obituary." *International Migration Review* 22, no. 4.

Castles, Stephen, and Godula Kosack. 1985. *Immigrant Workers and Class Structure in Western Europe.* 2nd ed. London: Oxford University Press.

Castronovo, Valerio. 1987. *Storia della Città Italiane.* Turin: Editori Laterza.

Cavallari, Alberto. 1992. "Europa L'onda corta Socialista." *La Repubblica,* 25 March.

Ceccarelli, Paolo. 1978. "La Crisi della Città di Sodoma e Il Sindaco Lot: Una storia esemplare usata a guisa di introduzione." In his *La Crisi del Governo Urbano.* Venice: Marsilio Editori.

Chabod, Federico. 1961. *L'Idea di Nazione.* Bari: Laterza.

Cheles, Luciano. 1991. "'Nostaglia dell'avvenire': The New Propaganda of the MSI between Tradition and Innovation." In *Neo-Fascism in Europe,* ed. Luciano Cheles, Ronnie Ferguson, and Michalina Vaughn. London: Longman.

Cheles, Luciano, Ronnie Ferguson, and Michalina Vaughn, eds. 1991. *Neo-Fascism in Europe.* London: Longman.

Chiaberge, Riccardo. 1990. "La lunga marcia degli immigranti: L'Italia del 2000 sarà più 'nera.'" *Il Corriere della Sera,* 2 April.

Chiaramonte, Franca. 1987. "Se la Città diventa Nemica: Come Vivono a Roma I Cittidini Stranieri." *Roma Rinascita* 50 (December).

Chiarello, Franco. 1983. "Economia Informale, Famiglia e Reticoli Sociali." *Rassegna di Sociologia* 2 (April–June).

Chiarini, Roberto. 1991. "The 'Movimento Sociale Italiano': A Historical

Profile." In *Neo-Fascism in Europe*, ed. Luciano Cheles, Ronnie Ferguson, and Michalina Vaughan. London: Longman.

Ciafaloni, Francesco. 1990. "Lo Straniero Fra noi." *Sisifo* 18 (January).

Clark, Martin. 1984. *Modern Italy, 1871–1982*. New York: Longman.

Cohn, Bernard S. 1980. "History and Anthropology: The State of Play," Comparative Studies in History and Society 22, no. 2 (April).

———. 1983. "Representing Authority in Victorian India." In *The Invention of Tradition*, ed. Eric Hobsbawm and Terence Ranger. Cambridge: Cambridge University Press.

———. 1985. "The Command of Language and the Language of Command." *Subaltern Studies* 4: 279–80.

Cohn, Bernard S., and Nicholas B. Dirks. 1988. "Beyond the Fringe: The Nation-State, Colonialism and the Technologies of Power." *Journal of Historical Sociology* 1, no. 2.

Colby, Laura. 1989. "New Pressures: Italians Are Facing Rising Racial Tensions Linked to Immigrants." *Wall Street Journal* (Europe), 4 September.

Colvin, Lucie Gallistel, et al. 1981. *The Uprooted of the Western Sahel: Migrants' Quest for Cash in the Senegambia*. New York: Praeger.

Conti, Angelo. 1990. "Hanno assalito due Senegalese, i carabinieri le arrestano e sospettano un raid." *La Stampa,* 20 March.

Copans, Jean. 1975. "La Sécheresse en Pays Mouride (Sénégal), Explications et Réactions Idéologiques Paysannes." In *Sécheresses et Famines du Sahel. Vol. 2. Paysans et nomades,* ed. Jean Copans. Paris: François Maspero.

———. 1978. "Paysanerie et politique au Sénégal." *Cahiers d'Études Africaines,* 69–70, no. 18:1–2.

———. 1981. "Jean Copans Répond. Les Chercheurs de la confrérie et la confrérie des chercheurs: A chacun son Khalife et Marx Pour Tous?" *Politique Africaine* 1, no. 4 (November).

———. 1988. *Les Marabouts de l'Arachide*. Paris: L'Harmattan.

Copans, Jean, and Jean Jamin, eds. 1978. *Aux origines de l'anthropologie Française: Les Mémoires de La Societe des Observateurs de L'Homme en l'an VIII*. Paris: Le Sycomore.

Corrigan, Philip, and Derek Sayer. 1985. *The Great Arch: English State Formation as Cultural Revolution*. Oxford: Basil Blackwell.

Cowell, Alan. 1992. "Italians Voting, with Focus on Protest Sentiment." *New York Times,* 6 April.

Crapanzano, Vincent. 1973. *The Hamadsha: A Study in Moroccan Ethnopsychiatry.* Berkeley and Los Angeles: University of California Press.

———. 1980. *Tuhami: Portrait of a Moroccan.* Chicago: University of Chicago Press.

Cruise O'Brien, Donal B. 1971. *The Mourid of Senegal: The Political and Economic Organization of an Islamic Brotherhood*. Oxford: Clarendon Press.

———. 1975. *Saints and Politicians: Essays in the Organization of a Senegalese Peasant Society.* London: Cambridge University Press.

———. 1979. "Ruling Class and Peasantry in Senegal, 1960–1976: The Politics of a Monocrop Economy." In *The Political Economy of Underdevelopment: Dependence in Senegal,* ed. Rita Cruise O'Brien. London: Sage Publications.

———. 1981. "La filière musulmane: Confréries soufies et politique en Afrique noire." *Politique Africaine* 1, no. 4 (November).

Cruise O'Brien, Donal B., and Christian Coulon. 1988. *Charisma and Brotherhood in African Islam.* Oxford: Clarendon Press.

———. 1989. "Chapter 9." In *Senegal, in Contemporary West African States,* ed. Donal B. Cruise O'Brien, John Dunn, and Richard Rathbone. Cambridge: Cambridge University Press.

Cruise O'Brien, Rita. 1972. *White Society in Black Africa: The French of Senegal.* London: Faber and Faber.

Curtin, Philip D. 1994. "Why People Move: Migration in African History." Presented at the Charles Edmonson Historical Lectures, Baylor University, Waco, Texas, March 7–8.

Dalle Vacche, Angela. 1992. *The Body in the Mirror: Shapes of History in Italian Cinema.* Princeton, N.J.: Princeton University Press.

Dardano, Maurizio. 1986. *Il linguaggio dei giornali italiani.* Rome and Bari: Laterza.

Dawood, N. J., trans. 1956. *The Koran.* New York: Penguin.

de Grazia, Victoria. 1981. *The Culture of Consent: Mass Organization of Leisure in Fascist Italy.* Cambridge: Cambridge University Press.

Derrida, Jacques. 1985. "Racism's Last Word." In *"Race," Writing, and Difference,* ed. Henry Louis Gates Jr. Chicago and London: University of Chicago Press.

Diarra, Agnes Fatoumata, and Pierre Fougeyrollas. 1974. *Two Studies on Ethnic Group Relations in Africa: Senegal, the Limited Republic of Tanzania.* Paris: Unesco.

Diop, Abdoulaye-Bara. 1981. *La Société Wolof: Le Systemes d'Inegalite et de Domination.* Paris: Karthala.

Diop, Momar Coumba. 1982. "Fonctions et activités des Dahira Mourides Urbains (Sénégal)." *Cahiers d'Études Africaines* 81–83, no. 11: 79–81.

Diop, A. Moustapha. 1985. "Les Associations Murid en France." *Esprit* 102 (June).

———. 1989. "Immigration et Religions: Les Musulmans Négro-Africains en France in Migrations Societe." *Revue de Presse* (Belgique) 1, no. 5–6 (October–December).

———. 1990. "L'Emigration Murid en Europe." *Hommes & Migrations* 1132 (May).

Diouf, Made B. 1981. "Migration artisanale et solidarité villageoise: Le cas de Kanén Njob, au Sénégal." *Cahiers d'Études Africaines* 31, no. 4, 577–82.

Domínguez, Virginia R. 1989. *People as Subject, People as Object: Selfhood and Peoplehood in Contemporary Israel.* Madison: University of Wisconsin Press.

———. 1994. *White by Definition: Social Classification in Creole Louisiana,* 2nd ed. New Brunswick, N.J.: Rutgers University Press.

Doughty, Charles M. 1926. *Travels in Arabia Desert.* London: Jonathon Cape.

Douglas, William A. 1983. "Migration in Italy." In *Urban Life in Mediterranean Europe: Anthropological Perspectives,* ed. Michael Kenny and David I. Kertzer. Urbana and Chicago: University of Illinois Press.

Drake, St. Clair, and Horace R. Cayton. 1962. *Black Metropolis: A Study of Negro Life in a Northern City.* New York: Harper and Row.

Dumont, René. 1974. "Il Senegal dominato dall'arachide." In his *Il Dramma Delle Società Contadine,* trans. Renata Tirelli. Parma: Ugo Guanda Editore.

Dumont, René, and Marie-France Mottin. 1983. *Stranglehold on Africa.* London: André Deutsch.

Eades, J. S. 1993. *Strangers and Traders: Yoruba Migrants, Markets and the State in Northern Ghana.* Edinburgh: Edinburgh University Press.

Ebin, Victoria. 1990. "Commerçants et missionnaires: Une confrérie Musulmane Sénégalaise à New York." *Hommes & Migrations* 1132 (May).

———. 1996. "Making Room versus Creating Space: The Construction of Spatial Categories by Itinerant Mourid Traders." In *Making Muslim Space in North America and Europe,* Barbara Daly Metcalf. Berkeley and Los Angeles: University of California Press.

———. n.d. "Mourides Traders on the Road: The Transition of a Senegalese Brotherhood from Agriculture to International Trade." Social Science Research Council.

Eco, Umberto. 1984. *Semiotics and the Philosophy of Language.* Bloomington: Indiana University Press.

———. 1985. "Innovation and Repetition: Between Modern and Post-Modern Aesthetics." *Daedalus* 114, no. 4 (Fall).

———. 1990. "Quando l'Europa diventerà afro-europea." *L'Espresso,* 1 April.

Efron, David. 1972. *Gesture, Race and Culture.* The Hague: Mouton.

Eickelman, Dale F., and James Piscatori. 1990a. *Muslim Travellers: Pilgrimage, Migration, and the Religious Imagination.* London: Routledge.

———. 1990b. "Preface." In Eickelman and Piscatori 1990a.

———. 1990c. "Social Theory in the Study of Muslim Societies." In Eickelman and Piscatori 1990a.

European Parliament. 1986. La Dichiarazione Contro Il Razzismo. Strasburg, June. SOS Razzismo. Atti del convegno Xenofobia e Razzismo e L'Italia di oggi: L'Italiano tra predgiodizio e solidarieta. Le reccamandazioni della Commissione d'inchiesta del parlamento Europeo sulla recrudescenza del fascismo e razzismo in Europa. Rome, June 30.

Evans-Pritchard, E. E. 1949. *The Sanusi of the Cyrenaica.* Oxford: Clarendon Press.

Fabian, Johannes. 1983. *Time and the Other: How Anthropology Makes Its Object.* New York: Columbia University Press.

Fall, Mar. 1984. "L'Etat Sénégalais et Le Renouveau Récent de L'Islam: Une Introduction." *Mois en Afrique* 19:219–20, 154–59.

Fallers, L. A. 1974. *The Social Anthropology of the Nation-State.* Chicago: Aldine.

Fanon, Frantz. 1963. *The Wretched of the Earth,* trans. Constance Farrington. New York: Grove Press.

———. 1967. *Black Skin, White Masks.* New York: Grove Press.

Farolfi, Bernardino. 1979. "Dall'Antropometrica Militare alla Storia del Corpo." *Quaderni Storici* 42 (September–December).

Federici, Nora. 1983. "Le Caratterisitche della Presenza Straniera in Italia e I Problemi che Ne Derivono." *Studi Emigrazione* 71 (September).

Fernandez, James W. 1986. *Persuasions and Performances: The Play of Tropes in Culture.* Bloomington: Indiana University Press.

———. 1988. "Andulusia on Our Minds: Two Contrasting Places in Spain as Seen in a Vernacular Poetic Duel of the Late 19th Century." *Cultural Anthropology* 3:1.

———. 1991. "Introduction: Confluents of Inquiry." In his *Beyond Metaphor: The Theory of Tropes in Anthropology.* Stanford, Calif.: Stanford University Press.

Findley, Sally E. 1989. "Choosing between African and French Destinations: The Role of the Family and Community Factors in Migration from the Senegal River Valley." *Working Papers in African Studies,* no. 142.

Fofi, Goffredo. 1964. *L'Immigrazione Meridionale a Torino.* Milan: Feltrinelli.

Fortes, Meyer. 1975. "Strangers." In *Studies in African Social Anthropology,* ed. Meyer Fortes and Sheila Patterson. New York: Academic Press.

Foucault, Michel. 1979a. *Discipline and Punish: The Birth of the Prison.* New York: Vintage.

———. 1979b. "Governmentality." In *M/F: A Feminist Journal* 3 (July).

Frappier-Mazur, Lucienne. 1991. "The Social Body: Disorder and Ritual in Sade's Story of Juliette." In *Eroticism and the Body Politic,* ed. Lynn Hunt. Baltimore and London: Johns Hopkins University Press.

Frascani, Paolo. 1980. "Medicina e statistica nella formazione del sistema sanitario italiano: L'inchiesta del 1885." *Quaderni Storici* 45 (December).

Freeman, Gary P. 1986. "Migration and the Political Economy of the Welfare State." *Annals of the AAPSS* 485 (May).

Fried, Robert. 1963. *The Italian Prefects: A Study in Administrative Politics.* New Haven, Conn.: Yale University Press.

Friedman, Alan. 1988. *Agnelli and the Network of Italian Power.* London: Mandarin.

Friedrich, Paul. 1991. "Trope as Cognition and Poetic Discovery." In *Beyond Metaphor: The Theory of Tropes in Anthropology,* ed. James W. Fernandez. Stanford, Calif.: Stanford University Press.

Fryer, Peter. 1984. *Staying Power: The History of Black People in Britain.* London: Pluto Press.

Fuller, Mia. 1992. "Building Power: Italian Architecture and Urbanism in Libya and Ethiopia." In *Forms of Dominance: On the Architecture and Urbanism of the Colonial Enterprise,* Naezar Al Sayyard. Aldershot: Avebury.

Gallino, Luciano. 1982. *Occupati e Bioccupati: Il Doppio lavoro nell'area torinese.* Bologna: Società Editrice Il Mulino.

———. 1985. *Il Lavoro e Il Suo Doppio: Seconda occupazione e politiche del lavoro in Italia.* Bologna: Il Mulino.

Gambi, Lucio. 1980. "Le 'statistiche' di un prefetto del regno." *Quaderni Storici* 45 (December).

Gamble, David P. 1967. *The Wolof of the Senegambia.* London: International African Institute.

Garbesi, Marina. 1990. "Parliamo sempre più Italiano ma il dialetto non tramonta." *La Repubblica,* 9 March.

Gardner, Katy. 1995. *Global Migrants, Local Lives: Travel and Transformation in Rural Bangladesh.* Oxford: Clarendon Press.

Gellner, Ernest. 1981. *Muslim Society.* Cambridge: Cambridge Universtity Press.

Gerth, H. H., and C. Wright Mills. 1977. *From Max Weber: Essays in Sociology.* Oxford: Oxford University Press.

Gibson, Mary. 1986. *Prostitution and the State in Italy, 1860–1915.* New Brunswick, N.J.: Rutgers University Press.

Giddens, Anthony. 1987. *The Nation-State and Violence: Volume Two of a Contemporary Critique of Historical Materialism.* Berkeley and Los Angeles: University of California Press.

Gilbert, Mark. 1995. *The Italian Revolution: The End of Politics Italian Style.* Boulder, Colo.: Westview Press.

Gilman, Sander L. 1986a. "Black Bodies, White Bodies: Toward an Iconography of Female Sexuality in Late Nineteenth Century Art, Medicine, and Literature." In *"Race," Writing and Difference,* ed. Henry Louis Gates Jr. Chicago: University of Chicago Press.

———. 1986b. "Black Sexuality and Modern Consciousness." In *Blacks and German Culture,* ed. Reinhold Grimm and Jost Hermand. Madison: University of Wisconsin Press.

———. 1993. *Freud, Race, and Gender.* Princeton, N.J: Princeton University Press.

Gilsenan, Michael. 1973. *Saints and Sufi in Modern Egypt.* Oxford: Oxford University Press.

————. 1982. *Recognizing Islam: Religion and Society in the Modern Arab World.* New York: Pantheon Books.

Il Giornale. 1989a. "Anche i vu'comprà dicono no, i partiti di governo spiazzati dal blitz del ministro del Lavoro." *Il Giornale,* 16 December.

————. 1989b. "L'Immigrazione è gia una mina vagante e nei prossimi anni andrà anche peggio." *Il Giornale,* 23 November.

Il Giorno. 1989a. "Alla scoperta del Paese che sta cambiando Pelle: L'Esercito degli Scampati all'inferno della povertà." *Il Giorno,* 11 November.

————. 1989b. "Alla scoperta del Paese che sta cambiando Pelle: L'Oceano di clandestini." *Il Giorno,* 3 November.

Gluckman, Max. 1961. *Custom and Conflict in Africa.* Glencoe, Ill.: Free Press.

Goddard, V. A. 1996. *Gender, Family and Work in Naples.* Oxford: Berg.

Goldberg, David Theo. 1992. "'Polluting the Body Politic': Racist Discourse and Urban Location." In *Racism and the City and the State,* ed. Malcom Cross and Michael Keith. London: Routledge.

Gordon, Colin. 1991. "Governmental Rationality: An Introduction." In Burchell, Gordon, and Miller, eds. 1991.

Gramsci, Antonio. 1971. *Selections from the Prison Notebooks of Antonio Gramsci,* ed. Quintin Hoare and Geoffrey Nowell-Smith. New York: International Publishers.

Grillo, R. D. 1980. "Social Workers and Immigrants in Lyon, France." In *"Nation" and "State" in Europe,* ed. R. D. Grillo. London: Academic Press.

————. 1985. *Ideologies and Institutions in Urban France: The Representations of Immigrants.* Cambridge: Cambridge University Press.

Grossi, Paolo. 1981. *An Alternative to Private Property.* Chicago: University of Chicago Press.

Grundle, Stephen. 1990. "From Neo-Realism to Luci Rosse: Cinema, Politics, Society, 1945–85." In Baránski and Lumley 1990.

Haddawy, Husain. 1990. *The Arabian Nights: Based on the Text of the Fourteenth-Century Syrian Manuscript,* ed. Muhsin Mahdi, trans. Husain Haddawy. New York: W. W. Norton.

Hall, Stuart. 1994. "Transnationalism, Globalization and the Dialogues of Cultural Identity." Presented at the Wenner-Gren Foundation Symposium, Spain, June.

Hart, Keith. 1982. *The Political Economy of West African Agriculture.* Cambridge: Cambridge University Press.

Harvey, David. 1990. *The Conditon of Postmodernity.* Cambridge: Basil Blackwell.

Haycraft, John. 1985. *Italian Labyrinth: Italy in the 1980's.* London: Secker and Warburg.

Hellmann, Ellen. 1948. "Rooiyard: A Sociological Survey of an Urban Native Slum Yard." In *The Rhodes-Livingstone Papers, no. 13.* Cape Town: Oxford University Press.

Hermand, Jost. 1986. "Artificial Atavism: German Expressionism and Blacks."
    In *Blacks and German Culture,* ed. Reinhold Grimm and Jost Hermand.
    Madison: University of Wisconsin Press.

Himmelfarb, Gertrude. 1983. *The Idea of Poverty: England in the Early Industrial
    Age.* New York: Knopf.

Hobsbawm, Eric. 1983. "Mass-Producing Traditions: Europe, 1870–1914." In
    The Invention of Tradition, ed. Eric Hobsbawm and Terence Ranger.
    Cambridge: Cambridge University Press.

Horkheimer, Max, and Theodor Adorno. 1972. *Dialectic of Enlightenment,*
    trans. John Cumming. New York: Continuum.

Hornziel, Ijola Maria. 1986. *La Condizione degli Immigrati stranieri in Italia:
    Rapporto al Ministero del Lavoro dell'Istituto per gli studi sui Servizi Sociali.*
    Milan: Franco Angeli.

Hunt, Lynn. 1991. *Eroticism and the Body Politic.* Baltimore: Johns Hopkins
    University Press.

Hunter, Monica (Wilson). 1961. *Reaction to Conquest: Effects of Contact with
    Europeans on the Pondo of South Africa.* London: Oxford University Press.

Ignatieff, Michael. 1985. "Is Nothing Sacred? The Ethics of Television." *Daedalus*
    114, no. 4 (Fall).

The Independent. 1990. "Racism, Immigration and Europe." *The Independent*
    (London) 4 April.

International Herald Tribune. 1990. "Florence Mayor Falls over Racial Attacks."
    International Herald Tribune, 14 March.

James, Henry. 1954. *Daumier, Caricaturist.* Emmaus, Pa.: Rodale Press.

Jameson, Fredric. 1990. *Signatures of the Visible.* New York: Routledge.

———. 1991. *Postmodernism; or, The Cultural Logic of Late Capitalism.* Durham,
    N.C.: Duke University Press.

Jameson, Frederic, and Stuart Hall. 1990. "Clinging to the Wreckage: A Con-
    versation." *Marxism Today* (September), 28–31.

Jelloun, Tahr Ben. 1989. *The Sand Child.* New York: Ballantine.

Jullien, Claude-François. 1992. "1600 Noirs à la recherche d'un toit." *Le Nouvel
    Observateur* 1445: 50–51.

Kearney, Michael. 1991. "Borders and Boundaries of State and Self at the End
    of Empire." *Journal of Historical Sociology* 4, no. 1 (March).

Kern, Stephen. 1983. *The Culture of Time and Space 1880–1918.* Cambridge,
    Mass.: Harvard University Press.

Kertzer, David I. 1977. "Ethnicity and Political Allegiance in an Italian
    Communist Quartiere." In *Ethnic Encounters: Identities and Contexts,* ed.
    George L. Hicks and Philip E. Leis. North Scituate, Mass.: Duxbury
    Press.

———. 1984. *Family Life in Central Italy.* New Brunswick, N. J.: Rutgers Uni-
    versity Press.

Khouma, Pap, and Oreste Pivetta. 1990. *Io venditore di elefanti*. Milan: Garzanti.

Kinzer, Stephen. 1992. "Far Right Gains Sharply in German State Elections." *New York Times*, 6 April.

Klein, Martin A. 1969. "The Moslem Revolution in Nineteenth-Century Senegambia." In *Western African History*, ed. Daniel F. McCall, Norman R. Bennett, and Jeffrey Butler. New York: Praeger.

———. 1979. "Colonial Rule and Structural Change: The Case of Sine-Saloum." In *The Political Economy of Underdevelopment: Dependence in Senegal*, ed. Rita Cruise O'Brien. London: Sage Publications.

Kopkind, Andrew. 1991. "Communism Bolognese: In Italy Red Is Dead," *The Nation*, 21 October.

Kuper, Hilda, ed. 1965. *Urbanization and Migration in West Africa*. Berkeley and Los Angeles: University of California Press.

LaPalombra, Joseph. 1987. *Democracy Italian Style*. New Haven, Conn., and London: Yale University Press.

La Rocca, Orazio. 1992. "Wojtyla. 'Europa razzista': Il Papa condanna le leggi xenofobe." *La Repubblica*, 19–20 January.

Lawrence, Erol. 1982. "Just Plain Common Sense: The Roots of Racism." In *The Empire Strikes Back: Race and Racism in the 70's Britain*. London: Hutchinson.

Layton, Robert. 1995. "Relating to the Country in the Western Desert," in *The Anthropology of the Landscape: Perspectives on Place and Space*, ed. Eric Hirsch and Michael O'Hanlon. Oxford: Clarendon.

Layton-Henry, Zig. 1990. "Citizenship or Denizenship for Migrant Workers?" In *The Political Rights of Migrant Workers in Western Europe*, ed. Zig Layton-Henry. London: Sage.

Lepschy, Giulio. 1990. "How Popular Is Italian?" In Baránsky and Lumley 1990.

Lerner, Gad. 1988. *Operai. Viaggio all'interno della Fiat: La vita, le case, le fabbriche di una classe che non c'è piu*. Milan: Feltrinelli.

———. 1989. "Razzisti si diventa: Gli Italiani e L'immigrazione." *L'Espresso*, 10 December.

———. 1990. "Il Nero in una Stanza: La protesta degli Immigrati: Gli extracomunitati senzatetto occupano a Milano edifici pericolanti. Li sostengono i sindacati e la Curia. Li combattono gli aderenti alla Lega lombarda. E' il primo grave conflitto metropolitano a sfondo etnico." *L'Espresso*, 18 February.

Lester, Julius, ed. 1971. *The Seventh Son: The Thought and Writings of W. E. B. Du Bois*, Vol. 2. New York: Random House.

Lester, Rosemarie K. 1986. "Blacks in Germany and German Blacks: A Little-Known Aspect of Black History." In *Blacks and German Culture*, ed. Reinhold Grimm and Jost Hermand. Madison: University of Wisconsin Press.

Levi, Carlo. 1963 [1947]. *Christ Stopped at Eboli: The Story of a Year,* trans. Frances Frenaye. New York: Farrar, Straus, and Giroux.

Lévi-Strauss, Claude. 1962. *Totemism,* trans. Rodney Needham. Boston: Beacon.

Little, Kenneth. 1965. *West African Urbanization: A Study of Voluntary Associations in Social Change.* Cambridge: Cambridge University Press.

Livi Bacci, Massimo. 1990. "Introduction." In *Le risorse umane nel Mediterraneo,* ed. Massimo Livi Bacci and F. Martuzzi Veronesi. Bologna: Il Mulino.

Lombroso, Cesare. 1871. *L'Uomo Bianco e L'Uomo di Colore.* Padua: Editice F. Sacchetto.

———. 1895. *The Female Offender.* London: T. Fisher Unwin.

———. 1898. *In Calabria (1862–1897).* Catania: Arnaldo Forni Editore.

———. 1968 [1911]. *Crime: Its Causes and Remedies.* Montclair, N.J.: Patterson Smith.

Lonni, Ada. 1990. "Stranieri: Un Osservatorio Torinese." *Sisifo* 20.

Lumley, Robert. 1996a. "Peculiarization of the Italian Newspaper." In *Italian Cultural Studies: An Introduction,* ed. David Forgacs and Robert Lumley. Oxford: Oxford University Press.

———. 1996b. "The Political Cartoon." In *Italian Cultural Studies: An Introduction,* ed. David Forgacs and Robert Lumley. Oxford: Oxford University Press.

Magri, Lucio. 1989. "Nord chiama Sud del Mondo per un lavoro nero e mal pagato." *L'Unità,* 13 November.

Maher, Vanessa. 1986. "Gerarchie del Nazionalismo." *Quaderni Storici* 11, no. 1 (April), 61.

———. 1996. "Immigration and Social Identities." In *Italian Cultural Studies: An Introduction,* ed. David Forgacs and Robert Lumley. Oxford: Oxford University Press.

Maher, Vanessa, et al., eds. 1991. *Uguali e Diversi: Il mondo culturale. Le rette delle relazione Il lavoro dei Immigrati.* Turin: Ires Piemonte.

Manchuelle, François. 1994. "Willing Migrants: Soninke Labor Diasporas, 1848–1960," Ph.D. diss., Bowdoin College, May.

Mancini, Paolo, and Mauro Wolf. 1990. "Mass-Media Research in Italy: Culture and Politics." *European Journal of Communication,* 5:187–205.

Mandel, Ruth. 1990. "Shifting Centres and Emergent Identities: Turkey and Germany in the Lives of Turkish Gastarbeiter." In Eickelman and Piscatori 1990a.

Marcus, George E., and Michael M. J. Fisher. 1986. *Anthropology as Cultural Critique: An Experimental Moment in the Human Sciences.* Chicago: University of Chicago Press.

Martelli, Claudio. 1990. "Presidenza del Consiglio dei Ministri. Claudio Martelli, vice-Presidente del Consiglio dei Ministri, Andreotti, Presidente del Consiglio dei Ministri. Norme Urgenti in Materia di Asilo Politico,

Ingresso e Soggiorno dei Cittadini Extracomunitari e di Regolarizzazione di Cittadini Extracomunitari ed Apolidi già Presenti nel Territorio dello Stato." Legge 28, February, no.39, di conversione del Decreto (legge 30 December 1989, no. 416).

Martinengo, Maria Teressa. 1990. "Auto-censimento dei senegalesi per mettere il Comune di fronte alla realtà Pagano imposte, ma non Esistono: Chiedono la residenza e l'assistenza sanitaria." *La Repubblicà,* 12 November.

Masud, Muhammad Khalid. 1990. "The Obligation to Migrate: The Doctrine of Hijira in Islamic Law." In Eickelman and Piscatori 1990a.

McKay, Claude. 1933. "Once More the German Troops." *Opportunity* 17, no. 11 (November):324–28.

McLellan, David, ed. 1977. *Karl Marx: Selected Writings.* Oxford: Oxford University Press.

Meillassoux, Claude. 1981. *Maidens, Meal and Money: Capitalism and the Domestic Community,* Cambridge: Cambridge University Press.

Michelsons, Angelo. 1986. "La Grande Impresa tra Sviluppo e Crisi." In *Tre Incognite per Lo Sviluppo: Strutture di mercato, scelte technologiche e ruolo delle istituzioni nell'ultimo decennio,* ed. Angelo Michelsons. Milan: Franco Angeli.

Minigione, Enzo. 1986. "Settore Informale e Strategie di Sopravvivenza: Ipotesi per Lo Sviluppo di un Campo di Indagine." In *Strutture e Strategie della Vita Quotidiana,* ed. Franca Bimbi and Vittorio Capecchi. Milan: Franco Angeli.

Mintz, Sidney W. 1995. "The Localization of Anthropological Practice: From Area Studies to Transnationalism." Presented at "Intergenerational Conversations: Anthropology Postwar/Millennial," University of Chicago, 6 November.

Mitchell, Harvey. 1979. "Rationality and Control in French Eighteenth-Century Medical Views of the Peasantry." *Journal of the Comparative Study of Society and History* 21, no. 1 (January).

Mitchell, J. Clyde. 1956. "The Kalela Dance." *Rhodes-Livingstone Papers* 27.

Morgenthau, Ruth Schachter. 1979. "Strangers, Nationals, and Multinationals in Contemporary Africa." In *Strangers in African Societies,* ed. William A. Shack and Eliott P. Skinner. Berkeley: University of California Press.

Morton, Patricia. 1991. *Disfigured Images: The Historical Assault on Afro-American Women.* New York: Greenwood Press.

Nader, Laura. 1988. "Post-Interpretive Anthropology." *Anthropological Quarterly* 61, no. 4.

N'Diaye, El Hadj Fallou. 1990. "La vulgarisation du Mouridisme à l'etranger." *Ndigël,* no. 21, 2ème semestre.

Nead, Lynda. 1988. *Myths of Sexuality: Representations of Women in Victorian Britain.* Oxford and New York: Basil Blackwell.

Negri, Nicola. 1982. "I Nuovi Torinesi: Immigrazione, Mobilita e Struttura Sociale." In *La Citta Difficile: Equilibri e Disequalglianze nel Mercato Urbano,* ed. Guido Martinotti. Milan: Franco Angeli.

Nirenstein, Susanna. 1990. "L'Allarme demografico: Non sara la catastrofe planetaria parola d'esperto." *Mercoledi* 16 May.

Nisbet, Robert. 1966. *The Sociological Tradition.* New York: Basic Books.

Nowell-Smith, Geoffrey. 1990. "Italy: Tradition, Backwardness and Modernity." In Baránsky and Lumley 1990.

Olwig, Karen Fog. 1993. *Global Culture, Island Identity.* Chur, Switzerland: Harwood.

Ondaatje, Michael. 1992. *The English Patient.* New York: Vintage.

Ong, Aihwa. 1990. "State versus Islam: Malay Families, Women's Bodies, and the Body Politic in Malaysia." *American Ethnologist* 17, no. 2 (May).

———. 1993. "On the Edge of Empires: Flexible Citizenship among Chinese in Diaspora." *Positions* 1:3.

Pacini, Massimo. 1989. "Italia ed Europa tra crescita zero e immigrazione." *Il Popolo* 10 November, 19.

Pankhurst, Richard. 1969. "Fascist Racial Policies in Ethiopia, 1922–1941." *Ethiopia Observer* 10, no. 4: 270–86.

Papagaroufali, Eleni, and Eugenia Georges. 1993. "Greek Women in the Europe of 1992: Brokers of European Cargoes and the Logic of the West." In *Perilous States: Conversations on Culture, Politics, and Nation,* ed. George E. Marcus. Chicago: University of Chicago Press.

Parker, David. 1995. *Through Different Eyes: The Cultural Identities of Young Chinese People in Britain.* Aldershot: Avebury.

Passerini, Luisa. 1984. *Torino Operaia e Fascismo.* Rome: Laterza & Figli.

Patruno, Roberto. 1990a. "Dietro il Pestaggio dei tre Lavavetri neri c'e una sordita rivolità tra sbandati." *La Repubblica,* 21 March.

———. 1990b. "Gran Madre, Droga e Neri il borgo diventa razzista, la casa-quartiere dei Nord-Africani, in particolare Marocchini, nella piazza Della Gran Madre." *Stampa Sera,* 20 March.

Pazzagli, Carlo. 1980. "Statistica 'investigatrice' e scienze 'positive' nell'Italia dei primi decenni unitari." *Quaderni Storici* 45 (December).

Pélissier, Paul. 1966. *Les Paysans du Sénégal.* Saint-Yrieix: Fabrègue.

Pellicciari, Giovanni, ed. 1970. *L'Immigrazione Nel Triangolo Industriale.* Milan: Franco Angeli Editore.

Pepe, Guglielmo. 1990. "Basta clandestini Martelli non cede." *La Repubblica* 5 April.

Pick, Daniel. 1986. "The Faces of Anarchy: Lombroso and the Politics of Criminal Science in Post-Unification Italy." *History Workshop Journal* 21 (Spring).

———. 1989. *Faces of Degeneration: A European Disorder, c. 1848–c. 1918.* Cambridge: Cambridge University Press.

Piore, Michael. 1984. *The Second Industrial Divide: Possibilities for Prosperity.*
New York: Basic Books.

Portelli, A. 1989. "Alcune Forme e articulazioni del discorso razzista nella
cultura di massa in Italia." *Critica Sociologia* (April–June):94–97.

Porter, William. 1983. *The Italian Journalist.* Ann Arbor: University of Michigan
Press.

Pred, Allan. 1995. *Recognizing European Modernities: A Montage of the Present.*
London: Routledge.

Pred, Allan, and Michael John Watts. 1992. *Reworking Modernity: Capitalisms
and Symbolic Discontent.* New Brunswick, N.J.: Rutgers University Press.

Press, Charles. 1981. *The Political Cartoon.* London: Associated University
Presses.

Rabinow, Paul. 1989. *French Modern: Norms and Forms of the Social Environment.*
Cambridge, Mass.: MIT Press.

Re, Luciano, and Augusto Sistri. 1988. "L'architettura a Torino." *Spazio e Società.*

Rex, John. 1986. "The Role of Class Analysis in the Study of Race." In *Theories
of Race and Ethnic Relations,* ed. John Rex and David Mason. Cambridge:
Cambridge University Press.

Rinascita. 1986. "Il Terzo Mondo in Europa: Cittadini Senza Diriti." *Rinascita,*
29 March.

Romanelli, Raffaele. 1980. "La nuova Italia e la misurazione dei fatti sociali:
Una premessa." *Quaderni Storici* 45 (December).

Sabel, Charles F. 1985. *Work and Politics: The Division of Labor in Industry.*
Cambridge: Cambridge University Press.

Sahlins, Peter. 1989. *Boundaries: The Making of France and Spain in the Pyrenees.*
Berkeley and Los Angeles: University of California Press.

Saiedi, Nader. 1987. "Simmel's Epistemic Road to Multi-dimensionality."
Social Science Journal 24:181–93.

Saint-Aubin, Arthur Flannigan. 1994. "The Dis-ease of Black Men in White
Supremacist, Patriarchial Culture." *Callaloo* 17, no. 4: 1054–73.

Salem, Gérard. 1981. "De la brousse Sénégalaise au Boul' Mich: Le système
commercial mouride en France." *Cahiers d'Études africaines* 21, nos. 1–3,
81–83.

Sarrocco, Gianni. 1990. "Motovedette contro i 'vu' cumprà, per Senegal e
Gambia reintodotto il visto d'ingresson anche per turismo." *Il Tempo,*
7 April.

Sartre, Jean-Paul. 1963. "Preface." In Fanon 1963.

Sarup, Madan. 1996. *Identity, Culture and the Postmodern World,* ed. Tasneem
Raja. Athens: University of Georgia Press.

Sbacchi, Alberto. 1985. *Ethiopia under Mussolini: Fascism and the Colonial
Experience.* London: Zed Books.

Scamuzzi, Sergio. 1985. "Chi è il Gioccupato." In Gallino 1985.

Schapera, Isaac. 1947. *Migrant Labour and Tribal Life: A Study of Conditions in the Bechuanaland Protectorate*. London: Oxford University Press.

Schlesinger, Philip. 1990. "The Berlusconi Phenomenon." In Baránsky and Lumley 1990.

Schneider, Jane, and Peter Schneider. 1976. *Culture and Political Economy in Western Sicily*. New York: Academic Press.

———. 1996. *Festival of the Poor: Fertility Decline and the Ideology of Class in Sicily, 1860–1980*. Tucson: University of Arizona Press.

Seccombe, Wally. 1985. "Marxism and Demography." *New Left Review* 137 (January–February): 22–47.

Sembene, Ousmane. 1970. *God's Bits of Wood: A Novel of the Independence Struggle in French Africa*. New York: Doubleday.

Shack, William A. 1979. "Open Systems and Closed Boundaries: The Ritual Process of Stranger Relations in New African States." In *Strangers in African Societies*, ed. William A. Shack and Elliot P. Skinner. Berkeley and Los Angeles: University of California Press.

Singer, Daniel. 1991. "The Resistible Rise of Jean-Marie Le Pen." *Ethnic and Racial Studies* 14, no. 3 (July).

Smith, Denis Mack. 1989. *Italy and Its Monarchy*. New Haven, Conn.: Yale University Press.

Smith, Raymond T. 1984. "Anthropology and the Concept of Social Class." *Annual Review of Anthropology* 13: 467–94.

Smith, W. Robertson. 1894. *Religion of the Semites*. London: Adam and Charles Black.

Spotts, Frederic, and Theodor Wieser. 1986. *Italy, a Difficult Democracy*. Cambridge: Cambridge University Press.

Stendhal. [1826] 1959. *Rome, Naples and Florence*, trans. Richard N. Coe. London: John Calder.

Tapper, Nancy. 1990. "Ziyaret: Gender, Movement, and Exchange in a Turkish Community." In Eickelman and Piscatori 1990a.

Tilly, Charles. 1990. *Coercion, Capital and European States, AD 990–1990*. Oxford: Basil Blackwell.

Time. 1990. "A Season of Racial Hatred: Growing Tensions Spark Clashes in Italy and France." *Time* (Amsterdam) 26 March.

Trimingham, John Spencer. 1959. *Islam in West Africa*. Oxford: Clarendon Press.

———. 1980. *The Influence of Islam upon Africa*. London: Librairie du Liban.

Trouillot, Michel-Rolph. 1995. *Silencing the Past: Power and the Production of History*. Boston: Beacon.

L'Unità. 1990. "Saremo Razzisti come Le Pen." *L'Unità*, 6 January.

Viano, Francesco. 1986. "Crisi occupazionale e mercato del Lavoro in Piemonte." In *Tre Incognite per Lo Sviluppo: Strutture di mercato, scelte technologiche e ruolo delle istituzioni nell'ultimo decennio,* ed. Angelo Michelsons. Milan: Franco Angeli.

Vico, Giambattista. 1988 [1744]. *The New Science of Giambattista Vico,* trans. Thomas Goddard Bergin and Max Harold Fisch. Ithaca, N.Y.: Cornell University Press.

Villalón, Leonardo A. 1995. *Islamic Society and State Power in Senegal: Disciples and Citizens in Fatick.* Cambridge: Cambridge University Press.

Vincent, Joan. 1982. *Teso in Transformation: The Political Economy of Peasant and Class in Eastern Africa.* Berkeley and Los Angeles: University of California Press.

Walker, C. H. 1933. *The Abyssinian at Home.* London: Sheldon Press.

Walvin, James. 1972. *The Black Presence: A Documentary History of the Negro in England, 1555–1860.* New York: Schocken Books.

———. 1982. "Black Caricature: The Roots of Racialism." In *"Race" in Britain: Continuity and Change,* ed. Charles Husband. London: Hutchinson.

Webb, James L. A. Jr. 1995. *Desert Frontier: Ecological and Economic Change along the Western Sahel 1600–1850.* Madison: University of Wisconsin Press.

Weber, Max. 1966. *The City,* ed. and trans. Don Martindale and Gertrud Neuwirth. New York. Free Press.

Westermarck, Edward. 1968. *Ritual and Belief in Morrocco.* Vol. 1. New York: University Books.

Wetergaard, Harold. 1932. *Contributions to the History of Statistics.* London: P. S. King & Sons.

White, Hyden. 1978. *Tropics of Discourse.* Baltimore: Johns Hopkins University Press.

Williams, Brackette. 1996. *Women out of Place: The Gender of Agency and the Race of Nationality.* New York: Routledge.

Williams, Raymond. 1976. *Keywords: A Vocabulary of Culture and Society.* New York: Oxford University Press.

Wihol de Wendon, Catherine. 1990a. "Le Cas Français." Presented at the conference Politiche dell'Immigrazione nei Paesi Europei, Turin, 18–19 January.

———. 1990b. "The Absence of Rights: The Position of Illegal Immigrants." In *The Political Rights of Migrant Workers in Western Europe,* ed. Zig Layton-Henry. London: Sage.

———. 1991. "Immigration Policy and the Issue of Nationality." *Ethnic and Racial Studies* 14, no. 3 (July).

Woolf, Stuart. 1979a. *A History of Italy 1700–1860: The Social Constraints of Political Change.* London: Methuen.

———. 1979b. "Statistics and the Modern State." *Journal for the Comparative Study of Society and History* 31, no. 3 (July).

———. 1986. *The Poor of Western Europe: In the Eighteenth and Nineteenth Centuries.* London: Methuen.

Woolf, Stuart J., and Jean-Claude Perrot. 1984. *State and Statistics in France 1789–1815.* New York: Harwood.

Worsley, Peter. 1984. *The Three Worlds: Culture and World Development.* Chicago: University of Chicago Press.

Xadim, Dara Ximatul. 1990. "La vulgarisation de Mouridisme." *Ndigël* 21, 2ème semestre.

Zanchetta, Pier Luigi. 1991. *Essere stranieri in Italia.* Milan: Franco Angeli.

Zempleni, Andreas. 1977. "From Symptom to Sacrifice: The Story of Khady Fall." In *Case Studies in Spirit Possession,* ed. Vincent Crapanzano and Vivian Garrison. New York: Wiley.

Index

Abstractions, 101–27
Abyssinian War, 108
Adorno, Theodor, 199–200, 244n4
Afro-Europe, 205–9
Agnelli Group/Foundation, 145, 167, 168
Agriculture: base of in Italy, 36; base of in Senegal, 17, 58; and migration in Italy, 17; and migration in Senegal, 15–16. *See also* Cereals; Groundnuts; Rural communities
Allen, Henry T., 161
Almirante, Giorgio, 235n2
Amato, Giuliano, 103–4
Americanization, 145
Ames, David, 68
Amulets, 68
Anderson, Benedict, 116, 149, 214; *Imagined Communities,* 218
Andreotti, Giulio, 137, 215
Angels, 93–97, 230n18
Anthropology: and blurring of genres, 206; and imperial frontier, 7; of modern state, 101–4, 206
Anthropometry, 118–19
Antropometrica, 118
Arabian Nights, 231n20
Aristotle, 116
Artisans: Italian, 13; Senegalese, 5, 6, 74, 75–76
Assimilationists, 180–81, 218
Autain, François, 133
Automobile production, 10, 14, 30–33. *See also* FIAT

Ba, Omar: *Ahmadu Bamba in France,* 230n12
Bacci, Massimo Livi, 169–70
Bagnasco, Arnaldo, 26, 30, 41, 42
Baker, Kathleen M., 16
Bakhtin, Mikhail, 129, 149
Balibar, Etienne, 206
Bamba, Amadou/Amadu, Cheikh: and anti-colonialism, 18–19; cultural weeks honoring, 81, 230n12; and Da'ira, 93; exile/ *hijira* of, 56, 63, 82, 84, 228n3, 229n10; later years of, 60–61; and Mouridism, 46, 55–72, 85, 93; as *Serin Touba*/saint, 60, 66, 69; and transnationalism, 48
Baraka, 66, 67, 69
Barthes, Roland: *Eiffel Tower and Other Mythologies,* 41
Barzini, Luigi, 110–11
Bassani, Giorgio, 243n11
Baye Fall, 59–60, 232n28
Benedict, Ruth, 177–78
Berlinguer, Enrico, 137
Berlusconi, Silvio, 144–45, 235n2
Berreman, Gerald, 177–78
Bertolotti, Davide, 116
Bertolucci, Bernardo, 216
Bhabha, Homi K., 219, 221
Bicycle Thief (film), 146
Black caricature, 159–64
Black women, 179, 185–86; primitiveness of, 189; unbridled sexuality of, 188
Bobbio, Norberto, 137
Bocca, Giorgio, 171, 178–83; *Gli Italiani sono razzisti,* 164

Donald Martin Carter is visiting assistant professor of anthropology at Johns Hopkins University. He is currently researching Muslim cultural associations in northern Italy and is working on a book on diaspora.